ORIGINAL INTENTS

Hamilton, Jefferson, Madison, and the American Founding

Andrew Shankman
Rutgers University–Camden

NEW YORK   OXFORD
OXFORD UNIVERSITY PRESS

Oxford University Press is a department of the University of Oxford.
It furthers the University's objective of excellence in research,
scholarship, and education by publishing worldwide.
Oxford is a registered trade mark of Oxford University Press in the UK
and certain other countries.

Published in the United States of America by
Oxford University Press
198 Madison Avenue, New York, NY 10016, United States of America.

Library of Congress Cataloging-in-Publication Data

Names: Shankman, Andrew, 1970- author.
Title: Original intents : Hamilton, Jefferson, Madison and the conflict
    that shaped the American founding / Andrew Shankman (Rutgers
    University-Camden).
Description: New York, NY : Oxford University Press, [2017] |
    Includes bibliographical references and index.
Identifiers: LCCN 2016041477 (print) | LCCN 2016056596 (ebook) |
    ISBN 9780199370139 (paperback : alkaline paper) | ISBN
    9780190673857 (updf)
Subjects: LCSH: Founding Fathers of the United States. | Hamilton,
    Alexander, 1757-1804—Political and social views. | Jefferson,
    Thomas, 1743-1826—Political and social views. | Madison, James,
    1751-1836—Political and social views. | United States. Constitution. |
    Constitutional history—United States. | National banks (United
    States)—History. | Political parties—United States—History. |
    United States—Politics and government—1783-1809. | United
    States—Politics and government—Philosophy.
Classification: LCC E302.5 .S527 2017 (print) | LCC E302.5 (ebook) |
    DDC 973.3092/2—dc23 LC record available at https://lccn.loc.
    gov/2016041477

Table of Contents

Abbreviations

PAH: The Papers of Alexander Hamilton, edited by Harold Syrett et al. (Columbia University Press, 1961–1987).

PJM: The Papers of James Madison, edited by William T. Hutchinson et al. (University of Chicago Press, 1962–1991).

PTJ: The Papers of Thomas Jefferson, edited by Julian P. Boyd et al. (Princeton University Press, 1950–).

Republic of Letters: The Republic of Letters: The Correspondence Between Jefferson and Madison, 1776–1826, edited by James Morton Smith. (W.W. Norton, 1995).

Acknowledgments

We write our books alone, but we live through writing them sustained by friends, colleagues, and family, and it is my pleasure to thank those who helped make *Original Intents* possible. Peter Charles Hoffer first encouraged me to write a book about Hamilton and Jefferson and introduced me to the folks at Oxford University Press. I am thankful to Peter for all of the various ways that he contributed to the forward momentum of the book.

At Oxford I worked with Brian Wheel, who was a thoughtful and encouraging editor. My discussions with Brian shaped and improved the book, and I will always be grateful for his advice and editorial vision. As the book was nearing completion, Brian left Oxford and I had the great good fortune to be assigned to my current editor Charles Cavaliere. I can't imagine the workload Charles inherited, but his warm and welcoming enthusiasm for my book was just what I needed at the end to bring everything to a conclusion. Working with Charles was his always helpful editorial assistant Kate Schnakenberg, who handled all the challenging and troublesome details, and who found the images we decided to use for the book's cover. Charles and Kate have been a pleasure to work with.

Various friends and colleagues read parts of the manuscript. I am enormously grateful to my former graduate student Nicholas Perry Wood, a fantastic scholar and holder of the Cassius Clay Postdoc at Yale for the academic year 2016–2017. Nic arranged for me to give a chunk of the book at the Yale Early American Seminar, and he and his wife Alison Wood were wonderful hosts while I was in New Haven. Zachery Conn, a Yale graduate student, made all the logistical arrangements and provided me a thoughtful reading, as did all the other seminar participants.

Several people read the full manuscript. Thank you to Oxford University Press's reviewers Nicholas Joseph Aieta, Westfield State University; Shelby M. Balik, Metropolitan State University of Denver; Stewart Davenport, Pepperdine University; Gabriel Loiacono, University of Wisconsin at Oshkosh; Karim Tiro, Xavier University; Sean Adams, University of Florida; Len Travers, University of

Massachusetts–Dartmouth; John Craig Hammond, Penn State New Kensington; Jason K. Duncan, Aquinas College; Kevin Adams, Kent State University; Mary Cathryn Cain, Agnes Scott College; Sean R. Busick, Athens State University; Michael A. LaCombe, Adelphi University; and three reviewers who wished to remain anonymous, for their critical and constructive reviews of my manuscript. I benefitted immeasurably from the thoughtful and encouraging reports from the anonymous peer reviewers provided by Oxford. I wish I could thank them all by name, but thanking one, Johann Neem, who made himself known to me after the process was completed, will have to do. To have the endorsement of such a vital, thoughtful, and engaged scholar is truly gratifying.

And how can I ever appropriately thank Nora Slonimsky, a Ph.D. candidate at the CUNY Graduate Center, whose research on Hamilton and intellectual property is going to be very important, and Joanne Freeman of Yale, who is the leading Hamilton scholar of my generation? Nora and Joanne read the full manuscript and provided me detailed, thoughtful, and always constructive suggestions and criticisms. I owe them both a great deal.

Turning closer to home, I must thank my guys at the Rutgers Law School, Adam Scales, Allan Stein, Ray Solomon, and Bob Williams. I thank them for always appreciating a good constitutional argument, for knowing how to make a brilliant one when we needed it badly, and above all for understanding precisely who owns the big red R and for being able to explain why and make it stick to even some of our closest friends.

It is my great good fortune every day to work in a department chaired by my friend, colleague, and comrade Lorrin Thomas. She has shouldered many burdens long before she should have had to, and to the enormous benefit of everybody who works with her. The timely publication of *Original Intents* is only the beginning of the debt I owe to her and shall repay.

Pride of place in any thanks I will ever give belongs to my intelligent, loving, beautiful, life-long friend, my wife Cathy Shankman. I do not have the skill to adequately articulate what our life together means to me, or how it makes possible every single thing I manage to achieve. But I am beyond lucky and grateful for every opportunity to try.

Finally, I dedicate *Original Intents* to my undergraduate mentor Carl P. Parrini and my Ph.D. adviser John M. Murrin, who taught me almost everything.

Introduction

By the summer of 1793 Thomas Jefferson hated Alexander Hamilton. On July 7th of that year Jefferson wrote to his close friend and ally, his fellow Virginian James Madison. Jefferson enclosed the latest of Hamilton's writings, essays titled *Pacificus*, which urged the United States not to join revolutionary and republican France in its war with monarchical Britain. Jefferson believed the United States should join its fellow republic in the fight against Britain, the nation with the most powerful king and aristocracy in Europe. To abandon France, Jefferson felt, was as bad as seeking to install a king in the United States, something he believed Hamilton wanted. To Madison he wrote:

> You will see in these [enclosures] Colo[nel] H[amilton]'s 2nd and 3rd Pacificus. Nobody answers him, and his doctrine will therefore be taken for confirmed. For god's sake, my dear Sir, take up your pen, select the most striking heresies and cut him to pieces in the face of the public. There is nobody else who can and will enter the lists with him.[1]

The hatred was not one sided. A little over a year before, Hamilton wrote to a man named Edward Carrington, like Hamilton a former officer of the Revolutionary Army. Hamilton explained that

> [i]t was not till the last session [of Congress] that I became unequivo-cally convinced of the following truth—that Mr. Madison cooperating with Mr. Jefferson, is at the head of a faction decidedly hostile to me and my admin-istration, and actuated by views in my judgment subversive of the principles of good government and dangerous to the union, peace, and happiness of the country. These are strong expressions. . . . They are the result of a *serious alarm* in

my mind for the public welfare, and a full conviction that which I have alleged is a truth, and a truth which ought to be told and well attended to by all the friends of union and efficient National Government.[2]

The mutual mistrust and loathing is even more remarkable because, at the time Hamilton and Jefferson wrote, both were members of President Washington's cabinet. Hamilton was the Secretary of the Treasury and Jefferson the Secretary of State. By 1793 Hamilton and Jefferson had concluded that they disagreed in every way about what sort of society the United States should be, and about how best to protect the rights to life, liberty, and the pursuit of happiness. But how had the situation come to this, why did it happen?

Hamilton's and Jefferson's arguments were wide-ranging. They began with deep disagreement about how to handle the immense debts the nation had incurred while winning its independence. The conflict over this issue was closely connected to disagreements about how American society should be structured and what sort of economic and foreign policy it should have. Eventually Hamilton and Jefferson focused their argument on whether the United States Congress and the Washington Administration could incorporate a national bank and promote industrial development with the methods Hamilton preferred. Ultimately, their disagreements over these issues could not be separated from their understanding of the United States Constitution. Through their arguments about banks and industrial development, it became clear that Hamilton and Jefferson disagreed profoundly about how to interpret the Constitution. In each of their hands it was simply not the same document; it did not mean the same thing.

Secretary of the Treasury Hamilton interpreted the Constitution as he did, and proposed a national bank, to promote his vision for an industrial future. He believed he could provide a stable and orderly society where the rule of law protected Americans' rights and liberties. Secretary of State Jefferson opposed every aspect of Hamilton's plans. Jefferson believed that opposing Hamilton was the surest way to defend American citizens from a dangerous faction that would use the government for its own purposes and violate the rights and liberties of the people. Without his financial and economic program, Hamilton believed the American Republic would collapse. With them, Jefferson believed the very same thing.

This great conflict can only be understood by exploring Hamilton's and Jefferson's views about banks and things connected to them: taxes, credit and debt, finance, industrial development, and the power to create corporations. To fully understand the argument also requires examining the views of James Madison. He worked closely with Hamilton and Jefferson during the 1780s and early 1790s. Madison could work with both of them because for much of that time there were significant areas of agreement between Hamilton and Madison, between Jefferson and Madison, and even between Hamilton and Jefferson. But by looking carefully at what the three agreed about and why, we can understand why Jefferson and Hamilton came to so mistrust and loathe each other, and why Madison ended up uniting with Jefferson against Hamilton.

When the American Revolution ended in 1783 Hamilton, Jefferson, and Madison all thought the United States was in trouble. They believed the national government was too weak, that the economy was in a shambles, that the people were too divided, and that the newly independent states might go to war with each other. On a personal level the three admired each other a great deal. Jefferson and Madison had long been friends and would grow closer over the next decade. Madison was developing a friendship with Hamilton, and Jefferson and Hamilton certainly thought well of each other. *Original Intents* examines the thirteen years after 1780. It explains why by 1793 Jefferson and Madison hated and feared Hamilton and why he hated and feared them. They all felt as they did by 1793 because for the previous decade they had devoted themselves to solving the nation's problems and preserving its republican institutions. Their argument became so angry, and their passions so powerful, because the job they undertook was so challenging and important.

Like virtually all eighteenth-century political thinkers, Hamilton, Jefferson, and Madison believed that maintaining a republic was perhaps the most difficult task in the history of political societies. American revolutionary leaders read widely in the history of Western political thought. They knew that theirs was only the most recent in a long history of republican experiments. The ancient Greeks had tried to maintain republics, as had the Romans, the Renaissance Italian city-states, and, for a brief period in the seventeenth century, the English. Yet all of these republican projects had failed, or at least that was the lesson eighteenth-century thinkers drew from studying them. The Greek city-states had been overrun, Rome had been seized by emperors, the Italian city-states had produced extensive warfare and violence, and the English had simply given up and brought back the monarchy. It was sad to conclude, but Western history appeared to show that people could not handle self-governance, that they needed the brutal strength of hereditary rulers wielding nearly absolute power. Freedom seemed quickly to produce chaos—what eighteenth-century political thinkers called licentiousness—the condition that in the seventeenth-century the English political philosopher Thomas Hobbes had described as the war of all against all.

What an audacious, even desperate, decision in 1776 to try yet another republican experiment. *Original Intents* explores the first steps that these three immensely influential men took as they began that experiment. They were willing to take those steps because they believed the United States could succeed where so many past societies had failed. Hamilton, Jefferson, and Madison were inspired by their fellow citizens' brave rejection of monarchy, and the immense sacrifices those citizens had made in order to win independence. That Americans accepted such painful ordeals suggested to Hamilton, Jefferson, and Madison that their fellow citizens possessed a great deal of virtue. The three all agreed in 1776 that no republic could succeed without virtue, a term inherited from the ancients of Greece and Rome and re-emphasized during the Renaissance. Citizens with virtue were committed to their society's public good, and were willing to sacrifice their own immediate personal interests and comfort for the sake of the public good if that became necessary. Like so many of their fellow eighteenth-century political thinkers, Hamilton, Jefferson, and Madison believed that the public good was something tangible and knowable—a set of values, ideals, and polices that provided the best possible future course for a nation.

Hamilton, Jefferson, and Madison agreed that monarchy and aristocracy were self-serving institutions that pursued their own interests instead of the public good. Declaring independence in 1776 was a heroic act of virtue. Doing away with monarchy and aristocracy, and creating republican government chosen fully by the virtuous people, gave the new United States the chance to pursue the public good. Yet by the early to mid-1780s Hamilton, Jefferson, and Madison had concluded that far too many of their fellow citizens were no longer behaving virtuously. In the first few years after independence all three became convinced that the new republic was in grave crisis, a crisis serious enough that it could destroy the new republican experiment. Their shared fear drew them together during the 1780s, and allowed them to collaborate to create a new and much stronger national government and constitution.

Yet their collaboration, from the start, masked deep disagreement about why the American people had stopped acting virtuously. The disagreement revealed that Hamilton's conception of the public good was vastly different from Jefferson's and Madison's. Hamilton never lost faith that Americans were right to declare independence. But by the early 1780s he feared that the American Revolution had gone too far. He had come to believe that ordinary laboring Americans had acted so violently during the Revolution that they were destroying the respect these small farmers and craftsmen—the nation's common, ordinary men—had for those Hamilton considered more capable of leading the new Republic: men of education, wealth, and learning. These more accomplished and talented citizens, Hamilton felt, could capably guide their fellow citizens in a dangerous world dominated by hostile monarchies. Hamilton watched with increasing frustration as citizens refused to show respect for and follow the lead of such men.

Hamilton's frustration mounted during the 1780s. He felt that ordinary citizens were preventing the most talented and capable from establishing the conditions that would give the United States political stability and economic strength. Without stability and strength, Hamilton concluded, the new Republic could not end the chaos produced by revolution, and so would never be able to command the respect of foreign nations or back up its declaration of independence. The United States, Hamilton decided, had to be able to beat European monarchies at their own game by creating its own republican versions of those monarchies' financial institutions and industrial enterprises. Securing stability and strength was the public good as far as Hamilton was concerned, and he sought to use the new Constitution to achieve both.

Jefferson and Madison agreed that the United States had to become more stable and much stronger than it was in the 1780s. But they disagreed with Hamilton about what stability and strength looked like and how best to achieve them.

They did not disagree that the United States had to be led by the best educated and most accomplished and so, in general, the wealthiest citizens. But they did disagree with Hamilton about what those men should think and what they should do with the power and authority the people granted them. For Jefferson and Madison, the best possible conditions for a republic—the conditions most likely to encourage virtue in the people—did not imitate or recreate the extensive banking and manufacturing institutions that they associated with European monarchies. Instead, the United States in declaring independence should also declare its independence from things and practices European, especially the financial and industrial enterprises that Hamilton believed the United States had to have.

Jefferson and Madison instead celebrated the unique features of the North American continent. Above all else, they emphasized the vast landmass that could belong to republican citizens if they were willing and able to seize it from the native peoples who already lived on it, and from the European empires that claimed large portions of it. For Jefferson and Madison, land was destiny; the United States would thrive if citizens could escape inequality and dependence. Jefferson and Madison believed that inequality and dependence defined the lives of virtually all Europeans because they could not own their own land, and so depended on resources controlled by others. Monarchy and aristocracy depended on inequality. The United States had the chance to leave behind the conditions of inequality and dependence forever. Clearly, Jefferson and Madison concluded, the public good meant implementing policies most likely to encourage westward expansion. Expansion would lessen or end the nation's economic dependence on Britain, dependence that remained even after winning the Revolutionary War. Jefferson's and Madison's conception of the public good caused them to seek policies that were fundamentally in conflict with Hamilton's understanding of the public good, and with the policies he believed were most likely to achieve it.

Almost immediately, then, after uniting to support the Constitution in 1787, Jefferson and Madison found themselves in complete disagreement with Hamilton about what that constitution meant and what the government it created could and should do. None believed their argument to be a mere difference of opinion about how best to pursue shared goals. By 1793 Jefferson and Madison believed that Hamilton was a monarchist out to destroy the Republic. And Hamilton had concluded that they were doing the work of foreign agents, serving the needs of the violent French Revolution and encouraging anarchy and an assault on natural rights. By 1793 it made sense to each of them to think the worst possible thing about their leading critic.

Original Intents examines why all three supported the Constitution. It discusses the complexities and purpose of the brilliant financial system Hamilton conceived once the Constitution was ratified. Hamilton fit his vision for industrial development into this system, and structured his financial and economic ideas to create a republican society of order, stability, and hierarchy. *Original Intents* also examines the nature of Jefferson's and Madison's opposition to and denunciation of that system, and Hamilton's response to their attack. In denouncing Hamilton's vision, Jefferson and Madison offered an alternative vision for the republican United States. Their vision equated the pursuit of the public good with westward expansion. Jefferson and Madison sought to create a republican nation that would be the "anti-Britain." They hoped the United States would remain almost exclusively agrarian (i.e., agricultural) into the distant future. Instead of Hamilton's European-inspired high finance and industry, Jefferson and Madison hoped to make the United States a nation of independent farming households. *Original Intents* explores and assesses these competing visions and shows how they can best be understood by placing them in the post-revolutionary eighteenth-century context that produced them.

Original Intents ends at the beginning of 1793, the year Jefferson resigned in disgust as Secretary of State from President Washington's cabinet, the year the French Revolution fully entered its most radical phase, and the year that many American citizens answered the plea of Jefferson and Madison that they join them in opposing Hamilton. *Original Intents* cannot tell every story, and it does not explore what resulted after 1793 because Hamilton, Jefferson, and Madison had their bitter conflict. The book explains why they had it, what they thought about it and each other, and why they felt the best public service each could do was to act precisely as he did.

Original Intents is organized into seven chapters. The first three treat the 1780s. Chapters one and two are organized thematically. Chapter one examines Hamilton's, Jefferson's, and Madison's fear of anarchy. It explores why they became convinced during the 1780s that anarchy was engulfing the new United States. Chapter one discusses why Hamilton, Jefferson, and Madison all came to agree during the early 1780s that the United States was in terrible danger, primarily because its citizens were failing to live up to their republican responsibilities. Chapter two discusses the solutions conceived by Hamilton, Jefferson, and Madison, and how their solutions developed over the course of the decade. It explores the origins of the core ideas and fundamental values of each man and shows how different Hamilton's were from Jefferson's and Madison's. Chapter three investigates how the fears and solutions of the three brought them together by 1786–1787 to support a much stronger national government and national constitution. Chapter three explains why during the 1780s the three men remained largely unaware of their very real differences and could thus unite to support the new Constitution, which Hamilton and Madison worked closely together to conceive and promote.

The remaining chapters examine the years from 1789 through 1792. Chapter four explains the foundations of Alexander Hamilton's financial system set out in his first "Report on Public Credit"—the policies of Funding and Assumption of the national and state debts. Chapter five discusses Jefferson's and Madison's response to Hamilton's plan, and explains their complete opposition to the policies of taxation, debt, and finance in the form that Hamilton wanted. The conflict over Hamilton's proposals brought their profound disagreements into the open and made all three men aware that they were engaged in a mighty argument. Chapter six examines the second of Hamilton's three great policy reports, the report to establish a national bank.

The bank plan depended on an understanding and interpretation of the Constitution that was as disgusting to Jefferson and Madison as were the policies Hamilton was promoting. Chapter six shows how the full import of their disagreements became clear to all three. They each concluded that the meaning of the new Constitution was at stake, and that the nation would only be safe if their ideas prevailed. Chapter seven discusses the last of Hamilton's great reports, "The Report on Manufactures." Hamilton's industrial policies relied on the same method of constitutional interpretation as did his national bank. Chapter seven, then, shows this great conflict in full flight, with Jefferson and Madison, and then Hamilton, taking their arguments to the public. By 1792 they were all determined to gain a definitive victory that would destroy the policies they opposed, and forever discredit those who advocated them.

Hamilton, Jefferson, and Madison were greatly respected in their day, and it is no exaggeration that most Americans in the early twenty-first century grant them the status of virtual demigods. We habitually compare our behavior to that of our founders. We ask what they would have thought of the actions we take or choose not to take. We seek to justify what we wish to do by linking it to the approval we insist they would grant us. Throughout our culture and across the political spectrum, we lay claim to our Founding Fathers, and particularly to the three who are the subject of this book. Because we do, we have created multiple Hamiltons, Jeffersons, and Madisons, many of which contradict each other. I make no claim to have the last word about these three men (no one ever will). But I have chosen to shape my story, and to stake my claim, by explaining the conditions Hamilton, Jefferson, and Madison believed they were facing. Their beliefs about these conditions caused them to make the assumptions and draw the conclusions they did about the world around them.

Hamilton's, Jefferson's, and Madison's conceptions and beliefs were not infallible. Like so many of us, most of their actions were perfectly justifiable and defensible, as long as one began by accepting their initial assumptions. Their original intents resulted from those assumptions, assumptions most of us in the twenty-first century are unlikely to accept or to grant. For when discussing the issues that mattered to them most—the meaning of popular sovereignty and the nature of the U.S. Constitution; the relationship between governors and governed; how eighteenth-century governments should tax, borrow, finance debt, charter corporations, and promote economic development—Hamilton, Jefferson, and Madison started from premises that are far from our own. When we come to better understand their original intents, we might not like what we see. At the same time, we might gain a deeper appreciation for the challenges they faced, for complexity, and for the deeply moving and meaningful, but also contingent, confused, and precarious nature of our nation's constitutional, financial, and economic origins.

NOTES

1 *Republic of Letters* 2: 792.
2 *PAH* 11: 428–430, emphasis original.

1

HAMILTON, JEFFERSON, MADISON, AND
THE FEAR OF ANARCHY IN THE 1780s

THE AMERICAN REVOLUTIONARY WAR profoundly affected Alexander Hamilton, Thomas Jefferson, and James Madison. They drew similar conclusions from their experiences of living through it. Their conclusions left them terrified about how the United States government was organized, and about how most Americans had behaved during the struggle for independence. During the early and mid-1780s Hamilton, Jefferson, and Madison each came to fear that the United States was rapidly approaching a state of anarchy that would destroy their republican experiment as it had all previous republican experiments. As the three reached similar conclusions, it seemed likely they would rather easily work together in a shared attempt to solve the nation's problems.

HAMILTON AND THE PROSPECT OF ANARCHY

Alexander Hamilton was the first of the three to conclude that the republican experiment was heading in a tragically wrong direction. He had no doubt the primary reason was the behavior of most of his fellow Americans. Hamilton, who was a lieutenant colonel in the revolutionary army and for most of the war on General Washington's staff, grew bitter because of his wartime experiences. He was furious that the national and state governments failed to adequately supply the army. His anger caused him to conclude that American citizens needed much firmer direction and much stronger government if the republican experiment was to succeed.

In July 1781, after five difficult years of warfare, Hamilton was almost in despair. Considering the actions of the Continental Congress and the citizens it answered to, he declared contemptuously that there had "been many false steps, many chimerical [ridiculous] projects and utopian speculations, in the management of our civil as well as of our military affairs." Much of the mismanagement, the inexcusable and stupid bungling, he blamed on "the natural effect of the spirit of the times dictated by our situation." Americans had rejected monarchy, the most powerful form of government known to the eighteenth century. They had replaced it with a republic, a popular government, chosen by the people. Unfortunately, concluded Hamilton, an "extreme jealousy of power is the attendant on all popular revolutions, and has seldom been without its evils." American citizens had come to so mistrust power that they equated great and concentrated governmental authority with monarchy. In their revolutionary assault on monarchy, they had established a government too weak and pathetic to do anything at all. It was this decision, Hamilton decided, that was the "source ... of the fatal mistakes, which have so deeply endangered the common cause, particularly ... A WANT OF POWER IN CONGRESS."[1]

By 1781 Hamilton hated the Articles of Confederation, the governing agreement that gave much more power to the states than it did to the Confederation Congress. The support the states gave to the national Congress was entirely voluntary. The national government had no power to tax. It could request revenue from the states. But there was no way to punish states that refused to grant the request. Hamilton believed this "extreme jealousy of power" was decimating the army and leading the nation to disaster. Hamilton had no doubt that responsible people would agree with him. In 1780 and 1781, as he watched soldiers go unpaid and sometimes even mutiny, he wrote angrily, "There is hardly at this time a man of information in America, who will not acknowledge, as a general position, that in its present form [Congress] is unequal, either to a vigorous prosecution of the war, or to the preservation of the union in peace." Doing nothing courted disaster. The war might be lost. Even if Americans managed to win it, what condition would the new nation be in after living through such divisive chaos? Hamilton was convinced that a solution had to be found quickly, for soon it would be too late "to rectify our errors. To persist in them becomes disgraceful even criminal."

Yet the young, brash, emotional, and highly intelligent soldier had little confidence that his fellow citizens had the will or ability to correct the situation by themselves. They needed powerful and effective leadership. Hamilton feared that most citizens cared only about "interests of interior moment; and ... we are incapable of those enlightened and liberal views necessary to make us a great and a flourishing people." Hamilton was concerned that the glorious effort to create republican government in America would fail because Americans were making the same mistakes that had destroyed republics in the past. "History is full of examples," he lamented, "where in contests for liberty, a jealousy of power has either defeated the attempts to recover or preserve it in the first instance, or had afterwards subverted it ... by leaving too wide a door for sedition and popular licentiousness." It was essential that Americans maturely set aside their "jealousy of power" for the sake of their republican dreams. For Hamilton concluded, in "a government framed by durable liberty, not less regard must be paid to giving the magistrate a proper degree of authority, to make and execute the laws with rigor . . . [a]s too much power leads to despotism, too little leads to anarchy, and both eventually to the ruin of the people."²

Hamilton's views concerning the relationship between liberty and power were part of an important conversation taking place during the eighteenth century about how governments could rule while also protecting people's rights. In the seventeenth century the Dutch had established a republic (the basic definition of a republic is a government without hereditary rule, without monarchy and aristocracy). The English had experimented with republican government from 1649 to 1660 before restoring monarchy. Republics were at one end of a political spectrum and absolute monarchy, such as that in France under the Bourbon kings, most famously Louis XIV, was at the other. Britain was in the middle. It had a limited, constitutional monarchy. British monarchs were quite powerful, but they were bound by law to share power with Parliament, the British legislature. And the House of Commons, the elected body in that legislature, had the exclusive authority to tax. At the heart of these various political forms were important questions about what sort of government people needed and how best to structure the nations they lived in. Political thinkers agreed that governments should protect people's needs and interests. But governments also needed to command people's obedience. What form of government could best do both?

Hamilton believed doing both depended on the proper balance of power and liberty. In theory absolute monarchs had unlimited power and so obedience was not a problem. But in such governments liberty, the freedom to define your own needs and interests and try to achieve them, was always in danger. What would stop an absolute monarch from taking his subjects' property or suspending the rule of law? Republics solved this problem by getting rid of monarchy. By 1776 most Americans rejected even the British version of monarchy. But Hamilton believed republics could also be dangerous. In a republic, liberty could grow out of control. Phrases Hamilton used, such as "popular licentiousness" showed how concerned he was about the proper use of liberty. Good governments protected the peoples' liberty and natural rights. Yet governments had to keep enough power to be able to punish those who violated the rights and liberties of others.

Hamilton thought that liberty and power were friends, not enemies. Liberty needed power to make sure that the orderly and stable conditions necessary to enjoy liberty were available to all. Hamilton proclaimed himself a "friend to order, to rational liberty."³ Terms such as "durable liberty" and "rational liberty" showed that Hamilton understood the lessons eighteenth-century thinkers drew about the republics of the past. Hamilton thought liberty was essential, but people who came into sudden possession of it by, say, overthrowing a monarchy and winning a revolution, had little experience with using it responsibly. Hamilton believed such people often made mistakes due to their rage about the tyranny they had suffered. This rage caused the "jealousy of power" and the weakening of government to the point where there were no responsible checks on liberty. Inevitably, Hamilton concluded, a tragic pattern emerged, which had destroyed the republics of the past. Liberty gave way to licentiousness. Once liberty degenerated into licentiousness, a disastrous process began that could not be stopped. Licentiousness gave way to anarchy, a condition in which people did whatever was right in their own eyes. Anarchy was so terrifying that people looked to any powerful figure that could save them from it. To escape anarchy, people became willing to accept tyranny and despotism, which could at least allow them the relative safety that came with fearful obedience.

Hamilton was convinced the United States faced this danger in 1781 under the Articles of Confederation. Power was so hobbled that liberty was dangerously close to tipping into licentiousness. That was why the people had to grow out of their "jealousy of power." They had to commit to "durable liberty," and close the "too wide door for sedition and popular licentiousness." Only then could the people create a stronger national government that would command their loyalty and govern them firmly and well. The problem was that under the Articles of Confederation the state governments were too powerful. Hamilton had no doubt that, due to "human nature," each state would "advance its own authority upon the ruins of the confederacy." He was also convinced that important men in each state would be jealous to keep their authority. These men would "be more devoted in their attachments and obedience to their own particular governments, than to the union." This "selfishness" would "promote a disposition for abridging the authority of the federal government; and the ambition of men in office in each state, will make them glad to encourage it."[4]

Hamilton concluded that the United States needed a fundamental restructuring. For the new republic to succeed, the peoples' first loyalties, especially the loyalties of prominent citizens, had to be to the national government, not the states. As things stood in the early 1780s, everything about the political, social, economic, and cultural arrangements of the United States favored the state governments. Hamilton was highly concerned that the state governments possessed "more empire of the minds of their subjects than the general one." They dominated the thinking of American citizens because they had so much more power and did most of the actual governing. Quite simply, the states mattered and the Confederation Congress did not. The dangerous result was that the citizens viewed the states, not the national government, "as the arbiters and guardians of their personal concerns by which the passions of the vulgar, if not of all men, are most strongly affected." If the states sought to subvert or disregard the national government, under current conditions it was clear to Hamilton the people "in every difference . . . will side with them against the common sovereign."[5] Nothing would change as long as the states did most of the things people associated with being governed. As long as the states and not the national government taxed, regulated trade, and were far more visible in people's lives, "durable liberty" would be precarious. The relationship between the states and the national government had to change. Hamilton complained to his own Governor, New York's George Clinton, that "[e]veryday proves more and more the insufficiency of the confederation."[6]

When describing the inadequacies of the Articles of Confederation, Hamilton drew heavily on his personal experience, particularly his fury over the treatment of the revolutionary army. By the early 1780s the paper money printed by the Confederation Congress was worthless because it was not backed by the power to tax. Soldiers and officers often went unpaid, or were given promises of future payment in the form of debt certificates. Yet without the power to tax, it seemed unlikely that the Confederation Congress could ever pay. In 1782 Hamilton wrote to his friend and mentor, the merchant and financier Robert Morris, that denying the national government the power to tax was the most dangerous example of the "jealousy of power" that often resulted from republican revolution. The far too weak national government, Hamilton informed Morris, was a raging symptom of "the general disease which infects all our constitutions, an excess of popularity." The people seemed to think that the only alternative to monarchical despotism was the absence of any meaningful authority. "There is no *order* that has a will of its own," Hamilton lamented. Those who were expected to govern were far too dependent on the ever shifting whims of those they were supposed to be governing. As a result, the "inquiry constantly is what will *please* not what will *benefit* the people. In such a government there can be nothing but temporary expedient, fickleness, and folly."[7]

Hamilton also expressed his outrage in a letter to George Washington. To Washington Hamilton opened his heart, telling his commanding officer, "I write as a citizen zealous for the true happiness of this country, as a soldier who feels what is due to an army which has suffered everything and done much for the safety of America." He was furious, he told Washington, about the treatment of the soldiers. Hamilton was so angry he worried that he might have gone too far in his zealous honesty. He closed his letter with an apology for his harshness, telling Washington "I sincerely wish *ingratitude* was not so natural to the human heart as it is . . . I often feel a mortification which it would be impolitic to express that sets my passions at variance with my reason."[8]

But as furious as Hamilton was, Washington agreed with him and reinforced Hamilton's belief that the Articles of Confederation was too weak to effectively govern the new United States. In spring 1783, Washington wrote to Hamilton that no "man can be more opposed to state fund[ing] and local prejudices than myself. . . . No man perhaps has had better opportunities to *see* and to *feel* the pernicious tendency of the latter than I have." To Washington's deep sorrow, the greatest impact fell on his soldiers. Though he could not condone it, Washington could understand why the soldiers' anger was producing an "unhappy spirit of licentiousness." Washington was terrified that it could lead to "civil commotions and end in blood." Conditions were as grave as Hamilton believed. "Unhappy situation this!" wrote Washington sorrowfully. Indeed, he was not sure he could manage the crisis. "The predicament in which I stand as a citizen and soldier is as critical and delicate as can well be conceived," he admitted to Hamilton. His position was impossible, the "suffering of a complaining army on one hand, and the inability of Congress and tardiness of the states on the other, are the forebodings of evil; and may be productive of events which are more to be depreciated than prevented."[9]

THE RISING CONCERNS OF JEFFERSON AND MADISON

Between 1776 and the mid-1780s, Jefferson and Madison came essentially to agree with Hamilton. In the final years of the war they both experienced the fear and frustration of the invasion of their home state Virginia by the British. Jefferson and Madison concluded that it was reckless to declare independence without also creating a government that could defend the Republic. Like Hamilton, Madison was frustrated that the national government did not have the power to tax. Denied taxing power, the national government could not lead the nation in war. By 1780 Madison feared the result would likely be disaster. Deeply angry, he wrote to Jefferson describing "the shameful deficiency of some of the states which are most capable of yielding their apportioned supplies." The states' refusal to tax and provide revenue meant that the "troops are in consequence exposed."[10] Since the Articles of Confederation required unanimous consent to alter its structure, just one state could deny the national government taxing power.

Madison also agreed with Hamilton that the treatment of the army was disgraceful, and was the fault of the state governments having too much power and the national government too little. In spring 1780, in a desperate letter to Jefferson, Madison predicted disaster. The nation's future was bleak with the

army threatened with an immediate alternative of disbanding or living on free quarter; the public treasury empty; public credit exhausted . . . Congress complaining of the extortion of the people; the people of the improvidence of Congress, and the army both; our affairs requiring the most mature and systematic measures; and the urgency of occasions admitting only of temporizing expedients . . . Congress . . . recommending plans to the several states for execution and the states separately rejudging the expediency of such plans.

If the states would not grant the Confederation Congress the taxation it requested, the only solution was a stronger national government that could tax. "Believe me Sir," Madison implored Jefferson, "as things now stand, if the States do not vigorously proceed in collecting the old money and establishing funds for the credit of the new that we are undone. . . ."[11]

By 1781, the same year that Hamilton was spelling out his concerns, Madison wrote to Jefferson that if the revolution was to survive, Americans had to commit to "arming Congress with coercive powers." Madison was deeply frustrated as he unburdened himself to Jefferson, writing "the whole confederacy may be insulted and the most salutary [useful] measures frustrated by the most inconsiderable state of the union." He could point to a recent enraging example. Madison reminded Jefferson that when the other states had agreed to stop exporting to try to keep needed supplies at home for the war, "Delaware absolutely declined coming into the measure, and not only defeated the general object of it, but enriched herself at the expense of those who did their duty."[12] And like all states in the Confederation, Delaware could not be prevented from doing as it pleased. Jefferson was slow to answer this letter, which was dealing with matters that Madison considered gravely important. Madison was so concerned about the weakness of the national government, and the prospect that effective republican government could collapse, that in mid-January 1782, nine months after sending it, Madison asked after his letter, writing to Jefferson, "Pray did you receive a letter from me enclosing a proposition declaratory of the coercive power of Congress over the states? It went by an Express...."[13]

Jefferson had not answered as quickly as Madison wanted. But he certainly shared his concerns. In 1784, during his six-month stint as a member of the Confederation Congress, Jefferson wrote to Madison describing his disgust over the weakness of the national government. It would have been a comedy if it were not such

JAMES MADISON,
FOURTH PRESIDENT OF THE UNITED STATES.

This image depicts a somewhat more youthful James Madison than the old founding father we normally see. He looked much more like this during the 1780s as he began to fear for the republican future of the United States.

a dangerous tragedy, Jefferson decided. Frustrated, he admitted to Madison that representatives of only eight states had bothered to show up to sit in the Confederation Congress, though nine states were required for a quorum. Of the eight that had come, "6 ... are represented by two members only." That raised the likelihood of deadlocked state delegations without a tie-breaking vote. As a result, reported Jefferson, we "have not [sat] above 3 days I believe in as many weeks." Jefferson and his colleagues had begged for enough congressmen to actually have a congress. "Admonition after admonition has been sent to the states," he told Madison, "to no effect. We have sent one today. If it fails, it seems as well we should all retire. There have never been 9 states on the floor ... but for a day or two." Jefferson, quite simply, was embarrassed at the truly pathetic situation he felt he had been reduced to. He admitted to Madison, the "smile is barely covered now when the federal towns are spoken of. I fear that our chance at this time is desperate."[14]

By the end of the American Revolution Jefferson and Madison were fully in agreement with Hamilton that the national government had to gain the power to tax, regulate trade, and enact laws that the states would have to obey. The two Virginians had no doubt the United States had barely managed to win the Revolutionary War in spite of its government, not because of it. After the war Jefferson grew even more frustrated with the weakness, and often the absence, of national authority. The many letters from Madison also helped convince him to support a stronger national government with the power to tax. In early summer 1783 he wrote to Madison after Congress had yet again asked the states to change the Articles of Confederation and to grant it taxing power. Worried, Jefferson informed Madison that the discussion in the Virginia legislature about strengthening the national government was not going well. In fact, he admitted that his "hopes of the success of the congressional propositions ha[d] lessened exceedingly." And Jefferson knew just who to blame: "Mr. [Patrick] Henry had declared in favor of the impost [a tax on imported goods]: but when the question came on he was utterly silent. I understand it will certainly be lost if it is not already."[15]

Patrick Henry (who had famously proclaimed in 1775, "Give me liberty or give me death") was one of the most famous Virginians and opposed his state giving up any power. Hamilton could easily have cited him as the prime exhibit of the state-oriented grandees who sought to keep the national government incapacitated. Feeling as he did, Jefferson came to hate Henry. In 1784 Jefferson hoped in vain for a convention to improve Virginia's government. Yet the famous, and famously eloquent, Henry thwarted him at every turn. And so, Jefferson wrote to Madison, in the end "the proposition for a convention has had the result I expected." Patrick Henry seemed prominent and talented enough to defeat those who sought dramatic changes in government. "While Mr. Henry lives," Jefferson wrote bitterly, "another bad constitution would be formed, and saddled forever on us. What we have to do I think is devoutly to pray for his death. . . ."[16]

Yet Patrick Henry was merely a powerful symptom, not the source of the problem. Certainly in Jefferson's view, people such as Henry clung to their power at the state level. By doing so they caused the national government to remain so weak that it could not defend the Republic. But the far greater problem was that the United States desperately needed defending. Jefferson had no doubt that monarchies were the inevitable and implacable enemies of republics. Republican societies showed that people did not need monarchs, and monarchs were terrified that their own subjects might come to that conclusion. Britain was already seeking to destroy the U.S. economy by denying Americans access to the markets of its West Indian colonies. Jefferson believed it could do so because men such as Patrick Henry prevented the national government from becoming strong enough to stand up to Britain. Yet if the national government could simply gain the power to tax, it could build a navy and defend the nation's interests. By the mid-1780s Jefferson felt any reasonable person should be able to see that the national government needed to be made much stronger.

Updating Madison on the doings of the Confederation Congress in spring 1784, Jefferson explained that many people "think that our commerce is going and getting into vital agonies by our exclusion from the West Indies." But despite the collapse of trade there was reason to hope. In response to Madison's question "Is the impost gaining or losing ground?" Jefferson answered excitedly, "Gaining most certainly." He was relieved to report that Georgia, North Carolina, and New York were all likely to grant the national government the power to tax. He was also hearing that Connecticut would follow the others. Tiny Rhode Island seemed the most opposed. But Jefferson was confident that "when every other shall have adopted it she will." The new taxing power was coming in the nick of time, Jefferson admitted, and would relieve him of a deep humiliation. The conduct of their own state, led by the likes of Patrick Henry, was beyond embarrassing, and "Virginia must do something more than she has done to maintain any degree of respect in the union and to make it bearable to any man of feeling to represent her in Congress." Thank goodness reform was finally coming, for the "public necessities call distressingly for aid, and very ruinous circumstances proceed from the inattention of the states to furnishing supplies and money."[17]

By that summer Jefferson was growing in confidence, convinced that what he, Madison, and Hamilton viewed as dangerous disorder would soon end. In Boston, he wrote to Madison, it was now all but certain that Massachusetts would join the reform movement and grant the national government the power to regulate trade and to tax it. From many places he was hearing "the conviction growing strongly that nothing can preserve our confederacy unless the band of union, their common council, be strengthened."[18] Yet Jefferson was wrong to hope. Again, not all of the thirteen states agreed to grant the national government the power to tax, and Virginia did not change its attitude about paying the taxes the Confederation Congress requested.

By 1785 Jefferson and Madison were panicking. Madison wrote to Jefferson in late summer of that year that the lack of national authority allowed Britain to violate citizens' commercial rights, seriously threatening the nation's economy. People were growing fearful and restless, demanding action, even if it was rash and thoughtless. Madison confided to Jefferson that he feared the worst possible outcome if the hard times of economic depression continued, perhaps civil war between states and the general collapse of law into anarchy. In the republics of the past, similar conditions had caused people to follow irresponsible and dangerous leaders who promised something better. Times like these were the crucial tipping point, when liberty degenerated into licentiousness and then anarchy. "I tremble for the event," Madison confessed, when so many felt "the strongest motives to . . . irregular experiments. The danger of such a crisis makes me surmise that the policy of Great Britain results as much from the hopes of affecting a breach in our confederacy as of monopolizing our trade."[19]

NEW YORK FOCUSES HAMILTON'S FEARS

In 1785 Hamilton was in complete agreement with Madison. In fact, he was willing to describe the specifics of the "irregular experiments" that had Madison so worried. In spring 1785 Hamilton wrote to fellow New Yorker Robert Livingston, the Chancellor of New York State, (the state's highest ranking judicial officer) that the situation in New York had become critical for "those who are concerned for the security of property or the prosperity of government. . . ." New York's lawmakers were rushing from "durable liberty" to anarchy. It was vital "to put men in the Legislature whose principles are not of the leveling kind." New Yorkers had elected the wildest

and most irresponsible people, and the "spirit of the present legislature is truly alarming, and appears evidently directed to the confusion of all property and principle."[20]

Hamilton believed he understood why New York faced such a crisis. In a brief
pamphlet written the year before, he had acknowledged that the citizens of the young
United States suffered from terrifying economic conditions. Facing such circumstances, nothing was "more common than for a free people, in times of heat and violence, to gratify momentary passions, by letting into the government principles and
precedents which afterwards prove fatal to themselves."[21] Hamilton blamed most of
this bad behavior on the Governor of New York, George Clinton. Clinton, it seemed
to Hamilton, governed in ways that propelled liberty into licentiousness. Clinton
became Governor during the revolution as the war brought chaos to New York.
British soldiers captured New York City in late summer 1776. For the remainder of
the war there was little central authority in the state. Ordinary people had filled the
vacuum and had pushed the revolution in the direction they wanted based on their
own understanding of their needs, ideals, values, and interests.

In the midst of these turbulent events, Clinton proved a very popular governor by
responding to what many ordinary New Yorkers wanted. In the northeast corner of
New York, Clinton agreed to let the small farmers living there seize land often owned
by wealthier men, and to gain independence from New York State by forming a new
state, Vermont. In the Hudson River Valley north of New York City, during the most
difficult years of the war revolutionaries in towns such as Poughkeepsie and Albany
had governed themselves almost as independent city republics. For years they made
their own laws, set wages and prices, and even printed their own money. New Yorkers
like these elected and then reelected Clinton during and after the revolution into
the 1790s. Clinton promised that he would protect their interests if they rebuilt and
respected state government once the war ended. He kept his word. Many who had
been tenants before the revolution were allowed to keep land they had taken. Under
Clinton New York printed a large amount of paper money, causing serious inflation
and a decline in the value of the currency. That was good for those in debt, usually
poorer people, since they could pay off their debts with money worth much less than
the value of what they had originally borrowed. In effect, printing massive amounts of
paper money redistributed property from the wealthy to the poor.[22]

Clinton had been a solid but not a leading New Yorker before the revolution. The
turbulent revolutionary situation allowed men like Clinton to rise in importance and
gain positions of greater authority than they ever could have achieved had there been
no revolution. Hamilton did not object to people rising higher than the station in life
into which they were born. Rather, he objected to the way in which men like Clinton
rose. In fact, Hamilton had also risen very high because of the revolution, and from
a much lower place than where George Clinton had started. Hamilton was born on
the tiny West Indian island of Nevis into such obscurity that we are not sure whether
in the year 1755 or 1757. His parents were not legally married and so he was, literally,
a bastard. Because he displayed exceptional talent from a young age, the principal
men of the island sent him to the mainland colonies where he graduated from Kings

As this modern photograph of Hamilton's birthplace shows, he was born into abject poverty and obscurity. Yet his rise was a fairly common story of the eighteenth-century British Empire, which depended on established and powerful men noticing talent in younger men and assisting them to find places where they could be useful. Hamilton's rise was not the modern story of the self-made immigrant; rather, it was a story of the late British Empire. When established older men assisted talented younger men, their efforts were intended to validate and preserve a reasonably flexible social order that remained hierarchical. Hamilton sought to preserve these values and ideals after the Revolution.

College (later renamed Columbia University) in New York City. He was an impressive young man and caught the attention of wealthy and powerful New Yorkers such as Philip Schuyler. The Schuylers were one of New York colony's leading families and moved in a social orbit far above Hamilton, and far above Clinton. Hamilton so impressed Schuyler that he consented to Hamilton courting his daughter Elizabeth, and the two married in late 1780.

Like Clinton, Hamilton had risen very far very fast. But he rose in a way that, in his view, respected both liberty and order. A society without liberty denied people of talent the opportunity to better themselves simply because of the station into which they were born. But a society that responsibly made use of liberty allowed for the measured, controlled, and sober rise of those with great ability. A well-ordered society encouraged the talented to rise, but did so in ways that did not rip apart the social fabric or threaten fundamental values and institutions. Rising in the way he had, Hamilton felt, reinforced the social order. A just and proper society provided measured and responsible pathways to self-improvement. Such a society struck an essential balance between the corrosive inflexibility that kept people imprisoned in their place of birth, and the wild overthrow of all structure and constraint that brought chaos. Hamilton was convinced that Clinton's rise resulted from forces that threatened the social order. A proper social order preserved the authority of respectable men like Schuyler, allowing them to make reasoned decisions about talented young men like Hamilton. Clinton was rising, Hamilton decided, because of the revolutionary turbulence that was removing constraints from the people and allowing them to act licentiously. Rather than rise because he earned the respect of the most respectable, Clinton rose because he was pandering to the most dangerous whims of an increasingly rash and violent majority.

Hamilton believed New Yorkers would be far better off if they looked to very different sorts of men to lead them. When describing how ordinary New Yorkers ought to act, Hamilton focused on the relations between the sorts of laboring people, especially urban craftsmen, who in New York usually voted for Clinton, and the great merchants, the men of wealth and standing who were often connected to people like Hamilton's father-in-law. Hamilton argued that small craftsmen made a mistake by electing people like themselves, or people like Clinton. Clinton and his supporters, Hamilton maintained, did whatever the people wanted in order to remain in power. They were concerned only with "what will *please* not what will *benefit* the people." Yet citizens needed to understand that they should want something very different from their statesmen and leaders, something more high-minded and impressive than mere pandering.

Rather than voting for irresponsible upstarts like Clinton and his followers, craftsmen were better off electing "merchants in preference to persons of their own professions or trades." Hamilton argued that if the laboring men thought about it, they would realize "the merchant is their natural patron and friend," and could better protect their needs and interests than they could themselves. Merchants were more qualified to speak in public and better equipped to understand confusing matters of legislation, and so were the best representatives for the laboring men below them in social and economic status. If they judged sensibly, concluded Hamilton, "artisans and manufacturers will commonly be disposed to bestow their votes upon merchants and those whom they recommend. We must therefore consider merchants as the natural representatives of all these classes of the community."[23]

Merchants, along with large landowners and the best educated and most learned, were best qualified to preserve liberty, and republican institutions, and to protect the interests of all citizens. When free republican citizens voted thoughtfully and judiciously, insisted Hamilton, "the representative body . . . will be composed of landholders, merchants, and men of the learned professions." There was no need for an elected assembly to include any others, for where was "the danger that the interests and feelings of the different classes of citizens will not be understood or attended to by these three descriptions of men?" The most responsible members of the community were deeply committed to protecting the property rights of all, and devoted to the order and stability that allowed for "durable liberty." After all, Hamilton asked rhetorically,

[w]ill not the landholder know and feel whatever will promote or injure the interests of landed property? . . . Will not the merchant understand and be disposed to cultivate, as far as may be proper, the interests of the mechanic and manufacturing arts to which his commerce is so nearly allied? Will not the man of the learned profession . . . promote . . . the general interests of society?[24]

Yet Clinton and his followers disagreed! One of the most vocal dissenters among Clinton's supporters was Melancton Smith of Poughkeepsie. Smith, like Clinton, was a middling property owner who had seized his opportunities and risen to much greater prominence during the revolution. New Yorkers elected him to various state-level political offices. In speeches and pamphlets Smith argued that representatives to elected assemblies should not be drawn only from the wealthy merchants, land-owners, and the most highly educated. Instead, said Smith, "representatives [should] resemble those they represent." Smith's legislature would look very different from Hamilton's. It would "be a true picture of the people, possess a knowledge of their circumstances and their wants, sympathize in all their distresses, and be disposed to seek their true interests." To be effective, a legislature elected by and for the people also needed to have a deep understanding of "the common concerns and occupations of the people, which men of the middling class of life are, in general, more competent to than those of a superior class."[25]

Without such diverse representation, Smith insisted, "the government will fall into the hands of the few and the great. This will be a government of oppression." Smith accepted that the wealthy and highly educated belonged in the legislature. But they must not sit there alone, for it was often the case that they were far from the ideal representatives of most people. In fact, when compared to the wealthy, Smith argued, those "in the middling circumstances have less temptation; they are inclined by habit, and the company with whom they associate, to set bounds to their passions and ap-petites." Merchants, great landowners, and learned men, concluded Smith, were often less desirable representatives than the "yeomanry of the country [who] are more tem-perate, of better morals, and less ambition, than the great." The wealthy did "not feel for the poor and middling class; the reasons are obvious—they are not obliged to use the same pains and labor to procure property as the other. They feel not the inconve-niences arising from the payment of small sums."[26]

Smith provided a powerful example of the language and tone Clinton and his supporters used throughout the 1780s. They believed they were creating a more equal society where the wealthy and powerful would not be able to exploit their fellow citizens. But Hamilton believed Clinton's popularity came from indulging the worst impulses of his fellow New Yorkers. Hamilton believed that Clinton showed con-tempt for the rights of property. For Hamilton, New York provided a clear example that focused his concerns. In order to preserve his power and place, Clinton violated natural rights and so moved liberty to licentiousness. Clinton and those like him, Hamilton insisted, encouraged people's most dangerous impulses, and they did so for the most selfish reasons.

Just as Jefferson had concluded about Patrick Henry in Virginia, Clinton, Hamilton was convinced, would never provide New York with "durable liberty." He had chosen popularity and his own self-promotion over the rule of law and the repub-lican lawmaker's duty to protect the natural rights of all. After the revolution, accused Hamilton, "he had formed a close connection with a particular set of characters, in whose public and private views he was continually embarked." His alliance was solely to benefit himself and not the people. Hamilton insisted that all Clinton wanted was "to keep himself in place—to perpetuate himself in the enjoyment of the power and profit of the office he holds." In a monarchy someone looking to get ahead would pander to the King and his courtiers. But in a republic Clinton knew better than to seek the judicious guidance of "the wealthy and the great. . . ." In the new Republic "the jealousy of power" meant that those most concerned for natural rights, the rule of law, and the stability of "durable liberty" were shunned in the name of popularity and pandering. "It is well known," complained Hamilton, "that large property is an object of jealousy in republics, and that those who possess it seldom enjoy extensive popularity." Of course the "Governor was aware that he would have risked the loss, rather than have promoted the continuance of what he possessed, by connecting himself with men of that class; and that his purpose could be better answered by an opposite course."

For Hamilton, Clinton was the most recent example of what had destroyed republics going back to ancient Greece. "The history of republics," Hamilton warned, "affords more examples of individuals arriving at dangerous pre-eminence, by a policy similar to that which seems to have been pursued by the Governor, than in any other mode." It was the policy of telling the great mass of people what they wanted to hear, of violating the rights of property and law to gain a temporary advantage at the expense of the long-term protection of every citizen's rights and interests. Clinton had clearly committed that crime, charged Hamilton, for the "cry against men of property has been carried to an extreme by the friends of the Governor, which ought to alarm the considerate of every class." That was how republics died, for there was "no stronger sign of combinations unfriendly to the general good, than when the partisans of those in power raise an indiscriminate cry against men of property. . . . Such a cry is neither just nor wise. . . ." "By destroying the confidence of the body of the people in men of property," declared Hamilton, Clinton made it "easy for aspiring men, in possession of power, to prosecute schemes of personal aggrandizement and usurpation."[27] Clinton's New York showed "that despotism may debase the government of the many as well as the few." Despotism of the many was the licentiousness that led to anarchy, and all knew or should have known "that licentiousness is the fore-runner to slavery."[28]

* * *

During the 1780s Jefferson, Madison, and especially Hamilton each concluded that anarchy threatened to destroy the United States. And, as it always had in the past, anarchy would lead to tyranny and the return of monarchy. It was clear to each of them that the new nation and its citizens needed a much stronger national government. Only then could the people preserve the Republic from its enemies, and from themselves.

NOTES

1 *PAH* 2: 650, emphasis original.
2 *PAH* 2: 650–651.
3 *PAH* 2: 651.
4 *PAH* 2: 655–656.
5 *PAH* 2: 655–656.
6 *PAH* 3: 240.
7 *PAH* 3: 135, emphasis original.
8 *PAH* 3: 305–306, emphasis original.
9 *PAH* 3: 277–278, 330, emphasis original.
10 *Republic of Letters* 1: 186–187.
11 *Republic of Letters* 1: 136.
12 *Republic of Letters* 1: 186–187.
13 *Republic of Letters* 1: 211.
14 *Republic of Letters* 1: 294.
15 *Republic of Letters* 1: 251–252.
16 *Republic of Letters* 1: 353–354.
17 *Republic of Letters* 1: 314–315.
18 *Republic of Letters* 1: 321.
19 *Republic of Letters* 1: 373.
20 *PAH* 3: 609
21 *PAH* 3: 485–486.
22 On New York in the revolution, see Alfred F. Young, *The Democratic Republicans of New York; The Origins: 1763–1797* (Chapel Hill, NC: University of North Carolina Press, 1967); Edward Countryman, *A People in Revolution: The American Revolution and Political Society in New York, 1760–1790* (Baltimore, MD: Johns Hopkins University Press, 1981); Thomas Humphrey, *Land and Liberty: Hudson Valley Riots in the Age of Revolution* (DeKalb, IL: Northern Illinois University Press, 2004).
23 *The Federalist Papers,* edited by Clinton Rossiter (Mentor Books, New York: 1916), 214–215.
24 *The Federalist Papers,* 216.
25 Alfred F. Young, ed., *The Debate Over the Constitution, 1787–1789* (Chicago: Rand McNally and Company, 1965), 27.
26 Young, ed., *The Debate Over the Constitution*, 27–28.
27 *PAH* 5: 320–322.
28 *PAH* 3: 495.

2

SEEDS OF DISAGREEMENT IN THE 1780s

～ ────────────────────────────────────

HAMILTON, JEFFERSON, AND MADISON agreed on a great deal during the 1780s. Yet when we look closely at how they thought "durable liberty" could best be protected, there were stark differences between Hamilton and Jefferson. It is also clear that, fundamentally, Madison's thinking was much closer to Jefferson's than to Hamilton's. During the early 1780s Hamilton conceived the ideas of his financial system, which laid the foundation for his program of industrial development. During these same years, Jefferson and Madison developed their view that the Republic should remain a nation mostly of farmers. This primarily agricultural nation should be supported by a national government that enabled westward expansion and secured worldwide free trade and global markets in which to sell agricultural surpluses. Yet during these years the three, if anything, believed they were allies, possibly even friends, as each of them grew more contemptuous of the government they were living under and more concerned about the nation's future.

HAMILTON'S SOLUTIONS TO THE PROBLEM OF ANARCHY

As his denunciation of George Clinton made clear, when Hamilton considered how to prevent licentiousness he relied heavily on wealthy men who owned large amounts of property. Hamilton sought a much stronger national government, and looked to the wealthiest citizens to lead the nation. Yet he could also write to his close friend John Laurens, "in perfect confidence I whisper in your ear, I hate money-making men."[1] Hamilton did not seek great personal wealth. It is essential to understand that, because he is easily misunderstood. For Hamilton did plan to strengthen and further enrich men of great wealth and property. He welcomed a large national debt, a stock market, a powerful national bank, and industrial development.

It is easy to see Hamilton, and many quite wrongly have, fitting comfortably into a modern Wall Street firm, and getting along well with corporate CEOs and hedge fund managers. Superficially, Hamilton might at first glance look at home in the twenty-first century. But what mattered to him most were the classical ideals of glory, honor, and virtue—the willingness to place a greater public good ahead of personal interest.[2] What truly motivated Hamilton was the challenge of balancing liberty and power to prevent both the licentiousness of the people from below, and the tyranny of the few imposed from above. In seeking this balance, Hamilton was influenced by the world he knew best and by his assessment of the strength of European monarchies. Republics had to prevent internal chaos and rot—liberty giving way to licentiousness. They also had to guard against external weakness, the danger that powerful European monarchies would use large armies and navies to destroy them. The Dutch Republic had entered a long decline in the eighteenth century after Louis XIV of France had subjected it to punishing warfare at the end of the seventeenth century. Hamilton was determined to make sure that the American Republic would not suffer a similar fate and would be able to defend itself.

Hamilton grew up in the fast-paced commercial world of the British West Indies. While still a young teenager he had helped to run a prosperous mercantile firm. He understood the wealth and power that commerce brought. And through his experiences in the army, he understood that monarchies raised vast sums of money and used them in very destructive ways. To survive, Hamilton believed, a republic needed to use many of the same tactics and methods that monarchies had created or refined: taxing, borrowing and deficit spending, and building state institutions such as large and well-equipped armies and navies. To do those things, a republic needed to draw on the wealth and talents of those citizens who understood how commerce, debt, and credit worked, and who could conceive workable plans of taxation. Hamilton believed the best way to establish "durable liberty" was to empower men of property who had the most to lose from licentiousness.

Empowering and enriching such men was not an end in itself. Hamilton hoped to make men of property more wealthy and powerful. But he planned to do so within a structure that attached them to the national government, not the states. The national government could then provide wealthy citizens with the incentives to cherish and protect the natural rights of life, liberty, property, and the pursuit of happiness for all. The United States would establish internal order by restoring the most responsible to places of power and authority. It could then develop the external strength it needed to protect itself from European monarchies. What drove Hamilton was the honor and glory of creating "durable liberty" and a long-lived republic, particularly when so many in the past had failed to do so.

Toward the end of the Revolutionary War, Hamilton almost ended his friendship with George Washington by demanding the honor of a military command rather than remaining in the relative safety of the general staff. Hamilton insisted that he be reassigned to the southern theater, the most dangerous fighting of the war. He had to go "southward," he insisted, to Washington. With deep frustration he reminded his mentor that he had already "explained to you candidly my feelings with respect to military reputation, and how much it was my object to act a conspicuous part in some enterprise that might perhaps raise my character as a soldier above mediocrity." Hamilton cared so much for honor he was furious that French soldiers would earn more glory than he and other Americans. He poured out his anguish to his friend Laurens:

> Our countrymen have the folly of the ass and all the passiveness of the sheep in their compositions. They are determined not to be free and they can neither be frightened, discouraged, nor persuaded to change their resolution. If we are saved France and Spain must save us. I have the most pigmy feelings at that idea, and I almost wish to hide my disgrace in universal ruin. Don't think I rave.[3]

We must always remember these fundamental motivations as we seek to understand why Hamilton set out on the course that he did.

For Hamilton "durable liberty" began with a strong national government. Republican government needed to do many of the things European monarchies did, especially tax and borrow. Hamilton believed taxing and borrowing were the foundation for everything. Hamilton concluded that over a decade before he became Secretary of the Treasury in 1789 and was able to put his ideas into effect. In 1779 and 1780, during a very difficult time of the war, he sketched his ideas for how best to preserve "durable liberty" and the revolution. The revolution was dying, Hamilton insisted, because Americans could not pay for it. The need was clear and "[t]here was but one remedy, a foreign loan." The new republican government had to be able to borrow. And that meant it also had to be able to tax. All governments with sound credit, Hamilton proclaimed, had shown that borrowing only worked when "assisted by a vigorous system of taxation."

Only with the power to tax and borrow would the Articles of Confederation government "have complete sovereignty in all that relates to war, peace, trade, finance, and the management of foreign affairs." A government with that "complete sovereignty" would also be able to issue sound money, establish reliable banks, and do "whatever else relates to the operations of finance." Still a young and relatively obscure man writing alone in an army camp in the midst of an increasingly desperate war, Hamilton imagined a powerful government with extensive taxing power. He hoped for "perpetual revenues . . . a land tax, poll tax or the like which together with the duties on trade . . . would give Congress a substantial existence and a stable foundation for their schemes of finance." Hamilton believed all of his hopes were interrelated and reinforcing. As he imagined a brighter future, he concluded that there were "four ways all of which must be united—a foreign loan, heavy pecuniary taxes, a tax in kind, a bank founded on public and private credit." "The only plan," Hamilton concluded, was "one that will make it the immediate interest of the monied men to cooperate with government in its support."

A foreign loan was essential, and could never succeed without the support of "monied men." But Hamilton believed a national bank, which united the national government and the wealthiest private citizens, was equally crucial. "[M]onied men" were just as important to the bank's success. If he could only somehow make the government strong and respectable, Hamilton thought, his first act would be to create "an American bank, instituted by authority of Congress for ten years under the denomination The Bank of the United States." The bank would connect the stronger national government to the "monied men," which was "the principle with the Bank of England." To defeat England, the United States had to beat its former master at its own game. It had to raise vast revenue, for "something of a similar principle in America will alone accomplish the restoration of paper credit and establish a permanent fund for the future exigencies [needs] of government." The Bank of England, Hamilton was convinced, was the heart of powerful Britain. "The Bank of England," he wrote enviously, "unites public authority and faith with private credit." This connection between a powerful government and the confidence and support of the wealthiest Britons willing to lend their money, produced "a vast fabric of paper credit. . . ." Without that credit, "England would never have found sufficient funds to carry on her wars; but with the help of this she has done and is doing wonders."

Hamilton admitted to himself that "the examples cited are from nations under despotic governments." But did that have to be the case? Why, wondered Hamilton, "can we not have an American bank?" Credit and such a bank depended on a close relationship between the wealthiest citizens and a much stronger national government. But, he asked himself, were "our monied men less enlightened to their own interest or less enterprising in the pursuit" than the British? The problem was a national government too weak to defend the Declaration of Independence or fight the revolution. The Articles of Confederation government did nothing to reach out to or rely on the Republic's virtuous and public-spirited "monied men." As a result, they did not have "sufficient confidence in the government and in the issue of the cause . . ." If only the government could "inspire that confidence by adopting the measures I have recommended . . . it would give a new spring to our affairs."

The partnership between the national government and the "monied men" lay at the heart of Hamilton's ambitions plans to humble Britain, win the revolution, and build a strong and glorious republican nation. Again and again, he returned to the need for this partnership, and its central importance for the bank he wanted. The "first step to establishing the bank," he kept reminding himself, would be "to engage a number of monied men of influence to relish the project and make it a business." A strong government able to tax, and that established a bank supported by "monied men," would solve the nation's financial problems and the embarrassment of its paper money. If only his plans could be implemented, "the bank notes [would] bear interest to obtain a ready currency and . . . induce the holders to prefer them to specie [gold and silver] to prevent too great a run upon the bank at any time beyond its ability to pay." Once the bank issued sound and reliable paper bank notes, they

This portrait of Alexander Hamilton was drawn in 1773, the year he arrived in North America, at the age of around 16 or 17. He first conceived the main features of his financial system only six years after this portrait was drawn. We always view the founders as old men, yet Hamilton looked far closer to the teenager in this portrait when he first began to spell out his plans for the nation's future.

could safely be used as paper money, which would "promote commerce by furnishing a more extensive medium which we greatly want in our circumstances[;] I mean a more extensive valuable medium. We have an enormous nominal one at this time; but it is only in name."[4]

Clearly Hamilton's financial and economic ideas were sophisticated and complex. But in these early statements of them he hoped to accomplish three straightforward things. First, create a government that could tax and borrow. Second, create a national bank that would be a partnership between this stronger national government and the wealthiest citizens of the republic. Third, provide the nation with what he called an "extensive valuable medium," which he believed would be possible if the first two goals were accomplished.

Hamilton's thinking shows that he understood a development that began in the seventeenth century called the financial revolution.[5] Beginning with the English and the Dutch, governments began to tax more efficiently, which allowed them to borrow extensively. European governments borrowed from wealthy subjects or citizens and used the taxes they collected to pay interest on their debts. By the mid-eighteenth century a government that people trusted to pay the interest, such as Britain, borrowed at a low rate of around three percent. Britain did not have to pay off its debt as long as it paid the interest it owed. By 1750 the British government was in debt about £70 million, which would have the impact of about $1.5 trillion in the twenty-first century. The British owed a lot, but they did not have to tax at a level to pay off £70 million. Instead, they had to tax enough each year to pay about three percent of £70 million, a little over £2 million. With the rapid growth of the British economy, taxing that amount was possible.

Governments able to tax gained access to far larger amounts of money through borrowing. But the ability to borrow, especially at reasonable costs, depended on keeping the promise to pay the interest. The government that paid the interest on its debt every year before it spent on anything else was said to be funding its debt. Hamilton felt it essential that the United States fund its debt.

Hamilton's second goal was to create a national bank. The government should support the bank and attract the moneyed men to invest in it—to buy the stock the bank issued. Investment by the government and the moneyed men, and deposits of tax revenue, would make the bank a powerful engine of financial and economic growth, making the investment profitable. This partnership would lead the moneyed men to connect their interests and first loyalties to the national government, not to their state governments. As the bank grew profitable, it could lend to the government. The bank would get an additional source of income from the interest it collected on these loans from the government. The bank could use this income to help pay the interest on its own bank stock, which would make the bank stock a reliable source of income, boosting the incentive to purchase it.

Hamilton's third goal was to create an "extensive valuable medium." Another term he often used was "circulating medium." A circulating medium is a convenient instrument of value, usually paper money, used to purchase goods and services. Hamilton had said the national government and the state governments had "an enormous nominal [medium] but it is only in name." He meant that the governments had printed vast amounts of paper money during the war. Today our paper money is backed by the full faith and credit of the United States government. In the eighteenth century, especially in the new United States, people had little reason to have much faith in the government. Paper money could hold its face value (the term is *remain at par*) as long as people believed they could exchange the paper for its par value in specie (gold or silver). If people were confident they could do so, they would usually choose not to since paper was so much easier to use than specie. Once they lost confidence, people might decide paper money had no value and refuse to use it. By the early 1780s the Confederation Congress had issued so much paper money that not even the most foolish believed it was backed by specie. By 1781, right around the time that Hamilton was turning his thoughts to financial solutions, Continental dollars were no longer being accepted as payment for goods and services. They had only a "nominal" value.[6]

Hamilton believed his third objective depended on the first two. If the government funded its debt and the bank issued stock, the funded debt and the bank stock would be represented by paper stock certificates that had a face value. Though not backed by specie, they would bear interest. As the government and the bank showed they were trustworthy by paying the interest, the debt certificates and banks stocks would become valuable and desirable since they were interest-bearing and therefore income-generating. As Hamilton explained, bank stock and funded government debt certificates could be used as paper "money and of a more advantageous kind." Because the stock bore interest, unlike money it continued to generate greater value.

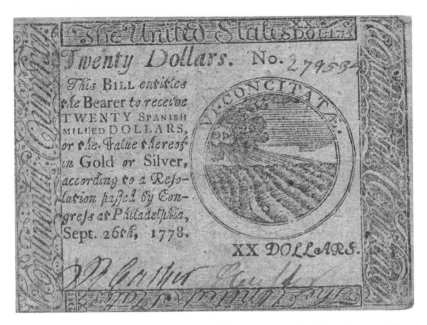

During the Revolutionary War the Continental Congress issued millions of paper dollars such as this twenty-dollar bill. By 1781 the paper money was worthless.

Hamilton felt that this form of currency was actually superior to paper money, for "every man will prefer a species of money which answers all the purposes of a currency and even when lying idle brings in a profit to the possessor."[7] This medium could circulate at par as long as the interest was paid, even though it was not backed by gold and silver.

Hamilton had no doubt the American Revolution and "durable liberty" depended on achieving his three objectives. And those three objectives depended entirely on linking "the interest of the state in an intimate connection with those of the rich individuals belonging to it . . . ." If he could somehow establish that relationship, it would turn "the wealth and influence of both into a commercial channel for mutual benefit, which must afford advantages not to be estimated . . . ."[8]

Hamilton's plan made perfect sense to him. Yet how could the weak national government hope to do any of it? In autumn 1780 Hamilton had an idea that would later become a central source of conflict with Jefferson and Madison. The Confederation Congress, Hamilton insisted, had much more power than people realized. He reasoned that when they declared independence and established a republican government with the Articles of Confederation, the American people had intended that this government protect them from Britain. It was clear, Hamilton told himself, that "the manner in which Congress was appointed would warrant, and the public good required, that they should have considered themselves as vested with full power to preserve the republic from harm." This "full power," to Hamilton, meant that the

Articles of Confederation government was sovereign. And as the political theory of the seventeenth and eighteenth centuries had taught him, to be sovereign meant having complete authority to carry out what it was your responsibility to do. The Articles of Confederation government had already "done many of the highest acts of sovereignty . . . the declaration of independence, the declaration of war, the levying of an army, creating a navy, emitting money—all these implications of complete sovereignty were never disputed . . . " It did not matter that the powers the Articles of Confederation listed as belonging to the Confederation Congress appeared limited. It had the full authority to do what was necessary to make use of the powers it did have, for "[u]ndefined powers are discretionary powers, limited only by the object for which they were given—in the present case, the independence and freedom of America."[9]

The Confederation Congress had a clearly stated responsibility to lead the revolution and to "preserve the republic from harm," while securing "the independence and freedom of America." Hamilton was arguing that this responsibility carried with it the implied power to do the things necessary to fulfill it. It would make no sense, Hamilton concluded, to charge a government with a responsibility but then deny it the power to fulfill it. Clearly, raising an army was necessary. But that meant Congress could also do what was necessary to pay for the army. This logic made sense, but it could also lead to a vast expansion of the government's power. Who would decide what was necessary? And were there any limits to what a government could define as necessary? Hamilton's notion that "undefined powers are discretionary powers" begged these questions.

JEFFERSON'S AND MADISON'S SOLUTIONS TO THE PROBLEM OF ANARCHY

During the first half of the 1780s Jefferson and Madison had grown just as worried as Hamilton. They also began to consider solutions to anarchy. Yet their values and worldview were starkly different from Hamilton's. Throughout the 1780s these differences remained hidden as all three agreed that the national government had to be made much stronger. But the origins of their momentous conflict with Hamilton in the early 1790s can be found by looking at what Jefferson and Madison were saying in the 1780s, well before the three realized that they disagreed about so much.

By 1785 Jefferson was in France, serving as Minister Plenipotentiary (similar to an ambassador). Writing to Madison from Paris, Jefferson could view the British enemy up close. His solutions for how to deal with Britain showed a way of thinking about the world that would have made no sense to Hamilton, and that was incompatible with his three objectives. In 1785 Britain was giving the United States only very limited access to its West Indian colonies, which prior to 1776 had been the most important markets for the thirteen colonies. Yet Jefferson thought that Britain's assault on American commerce might be a blessing in disguise. Jefferson had an unshakeable faith that the independent United States was actually stronger than Britain. He thought a republic of independent farmers living on their own land was better able to act collectively than a monarchy in which many subjects were dependent and divided by great inequality of wealth and power. Jefferson was confident the United States could coerce Britain because it grew agricultural necessities and primarily imported from Britain "gew-gaws" (cheap trinkets). Jefferson believed that reducing the trade between the United States and Britain, for the time being, would wean Americans from an unhealthy desire for British "luxuries," while showing Britain how dependent its empire truly was on American agriculture.[10] In the meantime, a nation producing agricultural necessities could always find alternative markets for its exports.

While Hamilton was conceiving his three objectives, Jefferson was drawing very different conclusions about the world and the place of the new republican United States within it. Despite the British achievements that had so impressed Hamilton, Jefferson did not believe Britain was stronger than the United States. Britain could service a huge debt; it had a far bigger army and navy, and its economic output was significantly larger. Yet Jefferson believed that the way Britain produced wealth made it weaker than the United States, and less prepared to win in the sort of conflict he wanted the two nations to have.

Jefferson viewed Britain as a typical European monarchy. Monarchies were less able than well-governed republics to call upon their subjects to act with virtue, to accept demanding and painful sacrifices for the sake of the public good. Jefferson's time in France reinforced his beliefs about the inherent weakness of monarchies. In France he lived in a monarchy that he felt had far more in common with Britain than either nation had with the United States. In October 1785 he wrote to Madison describing an experience that had a dramatic effect on him. He had gone for a walk in the countryside about 40 miles from Paris. On his ramble he had encountered a French peasant woman. Curious about "the conditions of the laboring poor" Jefferson struck up a conversation. He was shocked to learn that she lived as a day laborer making 8 sous a day (the smallest coin in France). The woman had two children and had to work 75 days to pay her rent, though often she could get no work at all.

Jefferson was powerfully affected by the woman's story and on their parting gave her 24 sous. He remarked to Madison that the poor woman "burst into tears of gratitude ... [s]he had probably never before received so great an aid." Jefferson related to Madison that the encounter had stayed with him and led "into a train of reflections on that unequal division of property which occasions the numberless instances of wretchedness which I have observed in this country as it is to be observed all over Europe." Jefferson was disgusted by the extremes of wealth and poverty he was witnessing in France, and he associated gross inequality with monarchy itself. A powerful and wealthy few controlled far more property than they needed, while the great majority suffered like his walking companion. It was the fault of monarchy because the wealthy used the power of the government to create and preserve these inexcusable conditions. The remedy, Jefferson was certain, was republican government.

Jefferson acknowledged to Madison "that an equal division of property is impracticable." But monarchy depended on a grossly unequal distribution of wealth and power. Jefferson was certain those conditions would destroy republican values and institutions. In a republic, he informed Madison, due to "the consequences of this enormous inequality producing so much misery to the bulk of mankind, legislators cannot invent too many devices for subdividing property." Fortunately, in the United States there was a great deal of land and far less concentration of wealth and power. Republican statesmen did not have to undo terrible conditions. Instead they had to make sure they never arose. Republican statesmen and citizens had to understand that the "earth is given as a common stock for man to labor and live on." The independent United States would preserve its republican values and institutions, Jefferson was confident, as long as it rejected the practices of Europe. It must never seek to recreate the financial institutions that supported monarchy, or the policies that produced "a great number of manufacturers and tradesmen" making "gew-gaws." Rather, the United States should remain a nation of independent farmers. Statesmen had to ensure "that as few as possible shall be without a little portion of land." In a republic, Jefferson informed Madison, the "small holders are the most precious part of the state."[11]

Clearly, Jefferson felt great sympathy for the poor Frenchwoman he had met. But he did not believe that people in her condition could be republican citizens. Poverty reduced people to dependence. Dependent people could not challenge the views of those with the power to starve their families. With such economic and social inequality, the right to vote could never be freely exercised, which made political equality impossible as well. Jefferson provided a clue to what he thought a republic should look like when he insisted that "as few as possible sh[ould] be without a little portion of land," and proclaimed that "small holders are the most precious part of the state." Jefferson explained this thinking more clearly in the longest piece of writing he ever undertook, his *Notes on the State of Virginia*, written during the war and published in the mid-1780s.

Jefferson was quite proud of his book. When Madison did not give his views quickly enough, he wrote, prompting, "I am anxious to hear from you on the subject of my *Notes on Virginia*."[12] In *Notes* Jefferson explained that republican America should be fundamentally different from monarchical Europe. The "political economists of Europe," he wrote, believed "that every state should endeavor to manufacture for itself; and this principle, like many others, we transfer to America, without calculating the difference of circumstance which should often produce a different result." Such thinking made sense in Europe, where the wealthy and powerful controlled far more land than they needed. As a result, in "Europe the lands are either cultivated or locked up against the cultivator." Because of the power and privilege that came with monarchy, Europeans had to develop manufacturing "of necessity not of choice, to support the surplus of their people." Thankfully that was not true in the republican United States. Given "the immensity of land," the citizens of the Republic were free to consider a question impossible to ask in monarchical Europe: "Was it best . . . that all our citizens should be employed in its improvement, or that one half shall be called off from that to exercise manufactures and handicraft arts for the other?"

For Jefferson the answer was obvious: "Those who labor in the earth are the chosen people of God, if ever He had a chosen people, whose breasts He made His peculiar deposit for substantial and genuine virtue." Independent farmers were uniquely qualified to fulfill the challenging duties of republican citizenship, for "[c]orruption of morals in the mass of cultivators is a phenomenon of which no age nor nation has furnished an example." Farmers who owned their land were independent in a way that the makers of "gew-gaws" never could be. They produced a surplus that never went out of style. Makers of "gew-gaws" relied on the patronage and largesse of the wealthy and powerful. Like the poor Frenchwoman, they were dependent, and "[d]ependence begets subservience and venality, [it] suffocates the germ of virtue." The social conditions of Europe guaranteed monarchy. It was highly unlikely, unless there was a profound and revolutionary intervention, that republican institutions could ever exist there. "The mobs of great cities," Jefferson proclaimed, "add just so much to the support of pure government, as sores do to the strength of the human body." In order to preserve republican institutions, American independence, and liberty and freedom, Jefferson concluded, "[w]hile we have land to labor . . . let us never wish to see our citizens occupied at a work bench. . . . [L]et our workshops remain in Europe."[13]

Jefferson glorified agriculture and expressed contempt for large-scale manufacturing and the world of banking and finance connected to it. By holding such views, Jefferson entered into an important conversation taking place during the eighteenth century.[14] Since at least the middle of the seventeenth century, led by the English, Dutch, and French, Europe had grown much wealthier. The size of many European empires had grown, and European nations controlled a growing number of profitable colonies. Rising wealth allowed governments to tax and borrow at higher levels, leading to more government spending on the military and projects to increase economic growth. All of these developments produced larger markets for manufactured goods and greater demand for the labor of those who made them. By the 1780s only one-third of the English population worked on the land. Though the percentage was much higher in France, the most powerful Western European countries were creating more diverse economies of agriculture, commerce and finance, and manufacturing.

European "political economists" were well aware of these developments. They knew that quite rapidly their modern world was creating much more wealth than had existed in the past. It was also creating cities of unprecedented size, and vast and growing populations who did not work at traditional jobs directly connected to agriculture. Many, including Jefferson, pointed out that creating new vast amounts of wealth also produced much greater economic and social inequality. Much of the wealth went to the masters of this new world, those who understood complicated matters of finance and credit, and who had access to valuable government contracts and special privileges. During the eighteenth century many writers debated what to think about this strange new world that so many in Europe and its colonies had entered.

These rapid changes led many to consider what caused human societies to transform and develop over time. European political economists such as Adam Smith, David Hume, Voltaire, Jean Jacques Rousseau, and Bernard Mandeville all wrote about these issues, as did many others. In general, eighteenth-century political economists (Hamilton, Jefferson, and Madison among them) believed that human societies developed through four stages. The four stages generally recognized by eighteenth-century political economists were: hunting and gathering, pasturage (the domestication of animals), agriculture, and advanced commerce and manufacturing. Eighteenth-century thinkers concluded that societies were like people; they were born, grew up, matured, and finally decayed and died. As a society went through the stages of its life cycle, each of these stages produced the conditions that led to the next stage. Progression to the fourth stage, followed by decline, decay, and death, was inevitable.

Eighteenth-century political economists identified the third stage with the origins of the most impressive of humanity's achievements. With agriculture, people remained in place with a more varied diet and reliable food supply. Bare survival became much easier and larger concentrations of people allowed for a division of labor. More wealth allowed for commerce. Larger towns created markets where those with craft skills specialized in woodworking, pottery, cloth-making, and fine arts, which they sold or exchanged for agricultural goods. Gradually over the centuries, towns swelled in size as did nations. The processes of manufacturing grew larger and more complex. Wealthier and more sophisticated rulers began to tax and borrow, and the modern world of the eighteenth century emerged.

The fourth stage produced great wealth, complexity, and sophistication. But with great wealth came excessive luxury, the lust for "gew-gaws," and great inequality and poverty. Critics of eighteenth-century developments, such as Jefferson, argued that societies in the fourth stage produced millions like the poor Frenchwoman who were desperate, dependent, and so easily controlled and dominated. Jefferson believed the third stage was far more desirable than the fourth. But even more important, Jefferson also believed that, at least for a very long time, the United States could escape from the inevitable progression through the stages and the decay, decline, and death that followed. The new Republic could long postpone this fate because of its "immensity of land."

The United States could move across space and so postpone development through time into the fourth stage.[15] By remaining a nation of farmers, the United States would over the decades and centuries continually recreate the ideal conditions for a republican society. The agricultural third stage did not produce the great wealth of the fourth stage, but societies of small independent farmers distributed much more equally the wealth they did create, Jefferson reasoned. At the same time, men who lived on their own land were independent in a way that wage laborers never could be. Jefferson believed that small farmers were uniquely capable of virtue—the willingness to consider the broader public good and work to achieve it. They would not necessarily do so, but they would be free to do so if they chose, unlike those who depended on the wealth of the powerful. The simpler, more equal third agricultural stage produced the ideal social, economic, political, and cultural conditions for a republic of "durable liberty."

Madison agreed with Jefferson about what sort of society and economy was best for a republic. Like Jefferson and unlike Hamilton, Madison wanted a much faster process of westward expansion. He also considered control of the Mississippi River vital. In a letter to Jefferson from August 1784, Madison wrote that the future of the republican United States depended on "the settlement of the western country." That settlement, in turn, depended on the Republic gaining "the free use of the Mississippi."

Spain controlled New Orleans and the mouth of the Mississippi River in 1784, and was highly concerned about U.S. westward expansion. Madison believed the United States would have to force Spain to allow free use, which was a primary reason why he thought a stronger national government was essential. Without westward expansion and access to the Mississippi, Madison did not think republican institutions or social relations could survive in the United States. With "a free expansion of our people," he told Jefferson, "the establishment of internal manufactures will not only be long delayed: but the consumption of foreign manufactures long continued increasing." Madison believed that those conditions were crucial. If an expanding nation of farmers continued to purchase desirable, but not essential, manufactures from Europe, "all the productions of American soil required by Europe in return for her manufactures, will proportionally increase."

Yet if the United States could not get access to the Mississippi, that would stymie westward expansion since people would have no access to market as they moved farther from the Atlantic coast. Madison contemplated that situation with horror. It would bring European conditions to the United States, for instead of being farmers "on the waters of the Mississippi," republican citizens would be forced to become "manufacturers on those of the Atlantic. . . . "[16]

Madison was convinced that the United States had to seize control of the interior of the North American Continent from the European powers and the native Indians who claimed it. If the nation failed to do so, its rapidly growing population would remain bottled up along the Atlantic coast. Growing and confined populations bred the conditions that produced the fourth stage, which alarmed Madison just as much as it did Jefferson. In a letter of June 1786, Madison praised Jefferson's "reflections on the idle poor of Europe, [which] form a valuable lesson to the legislators of every country, and particularly a new one." Though it was true that a freer government could prevent many of the injustices Jefferson had witnessed in Europe, Madison feared that republican government alone could not solve the problems Jefferson had described. Even the best republican government needed the proper material conditions for independence, equality, and citizenship. The key to those conditions was enough land to sustain a society of independent farming families. The citizens of the United States were immeasurably better off than the subjects of European monarchies, Madison agreed with Jefferson. But he informed his dear friend, "Our limited population has probably as large a share in producing this effect as the political advantages which distinguishes us." No matter how good the government, Madison feared, a "certain degree of misery seems inseparable from a high degree of populousness."

The most pressing issue of political economy, Madison concluded, was "that which relates to the most proper distribution of the inhabitants of a country fully peopled." Madison thought that a republican government was far more likely to care about this issue than a monarchy. But any solution required enough land to prevent people from becoming dependent on resources controlled by others. When there were far too many people for the available land, the surplus population became "manufacture[r]s of superfluities, idle proprietors of productive funds, domestics, soldiers, merchants, mariners," all the occupations that fueled the financial revolution and the monarchical wars for empire. Republican government had to break this vicious cycle. And a republican government with vast lands available for the seizing had the chance to do it. It was Madison's fervent hope that from "a more equal partition of property must result a greater simplicity of manners, and a less proportion of idle proprietors and domestics." The combination of those economic and social conditions and "a juster government" would mean "less need of soldiers either for defense against dangers from without, or disturbance from within."[17] A republic, "a juster government," with enough land to move across space and recreate the third stage could avoid all of the unfortunate conditions of modern monarchies.

Jefferson and Madison agreed with each other because they were shaped by their early experiences of being born and raised in Virginia. Virginia was remarkably close to the ideal republic both of them imagined and hoped the United States would become. Orange County, Virginia, where Madison grew up, had a population of 1,100 adult white men, nearly all of whom owned more than 50 acres of land, usually viewed as the minimum necessary to be an independent farmer.[18] Jefferson grew up witnessing similar conditions. Both also saw conflict among white Virginians as the revolution neared, and they blamed it on rising difficulty in gaining access to land.

Like Hamilton, Jefferson and Madison wanted a much stronger national government. But they wanted such a government so that it could vigorously pursue policies very different from Hamilton's three objectives. It would not be easy to conquer the North American continent. Indians claimed the land because their ancestors had lived on it for thousands of years, and Spain and Britain, and eventually France too, had real interest in preventing the United States from expanding west. Jefferson and Madison believed that the national government would need to mobilize its resources. It would even need at times to raise revenue by taxing and borrowing. But it would do so not to build powerful, centralizing financial institutions, or to forge connections between the government and moneyed men. It would instead spread the population much more widely. By doing so, it would prevent the concentration of both people and wealth. It would make sure for a very long time that citizens remained farmers with easy access to land, so that the banks and workshops, and all that went with them, remained in Europe.

There were two indefensible ironies in this vision for the Republic. The first was that a set of beliefs intended to create greater equality and independence among citizens required that the United States violently seize land that had long belonged to Indians. The republic of Jefferson's and Madison's imagination could succeed only by violating the rights and claims of native peoples. Historians have called the second irony the American paradox. Throughout Virginia, while most adult white men were independent, hundreds of thousands of blacks were enslaved. The American paradox was that in Virginia, unlike Europe, wealthy white men did not need to control the labor of poorer white men and their families because they claimed ownership of so many black men and women. Plantation owners such as Jefferson and Madison could imagine poorer white men as useful, productive independent farmers and citizens, as "the chosen people of God," because they did not need their labor to maintain their plantations. Paradoxically, and in ways neither of them faced, Jefferson's and Madison's inspiring endorsements of freedom and equality were powerfully connected to and depended on their significant participation in slavery.[19]

Jefferson and Madison took ideas of freedom and equality very seriously. They believed there could be no republican citizenship, no republic at all, without them. They confined who they thought could function as citizens to adult white men. Their decision to do so was profoundly self-serving and allowed them to ignore monumental injustices that they and their fellow Americans were committing. Yet their commitment to providing those they believed could be citizens with the proper conditions for citizenship produced ideas that were very different from Hamilton's.

***

In the mid-1780s these seeds of disagreement between Hamilton and the two Virginians were buried. The differences Jefferson and Madison had with Hamilton, and that he had with them, were barely noticeable. They went unnoticed by all three because each of them was so desperate to create a much stronger national government that could resolve the problems of the 1780s as they understood them. With such complete agreement that the United States needed a new national government, the first order of business was to make one. If they managed it, and it seemed doubtful in 1785 that they would succeed, it was highly likely their significant differences would become obvious to all. Only by uniting and gaining a momentous constitutional victory, could the later bitter conflict become possible.

NOTES

1 *PAH* 2: 53.
2 Joanne Freeman, "Dueling as Politics: Reinterpreting the Burr-Hamilton Duel," *William and Mary Quarterly* 53 (1996): 289–318.
3 *PAH* 2: 347, 509.
4 *PAH* 2: 239, 244–246, 408, 411, 413–416.
5 On the financial revolution, see P. G. M Dickson, *The Financial Revolution in England: A Study in the Development of Public Credit, 1688–1756* (London: Macmillan, 1967); John Brewer, *The Sinews of Power: War, Money, and the English State, 1688–1783* (London: Unwin Hyman, 1989); Carl Wennerlind, *Casualties of Credit: The English Financial Revolution, 1620–1720* (Cambridge, MA: Harvard University Press, 2011); Donald Swanson, *The Origins of Hamilton's Fiscal Policies* (Gainesville, FL: University of Florida Press, 1963).
6 Allan Kulikoff, "'Such Things Ought Not to Be': The American Revolution and the First National Great Depression," in Andrew Shankman, ed., *The World of the Revolutionary American Republic: Land, Labor, and the Conflict for a Continent* (London: Routledge, 2014), 134–164, 139.
7 *PAH* 2: 247.
8 *PAH* 2: 249.
9 *PAH* 2: 401.
10 *Republic of Letters* 1: 366.
11 *Republic of Letters* 1: 390–391.
12 *Republic of Letters* 1: 381.

13 Thomas Jefferson, *Notes on the State of Virginia* (Harper and Row, 1964), 157–158.
14 Drew R. McCoy, *The Elusive Republic: Political Economy in Jeffersonian America* (Chapel Hill, NC: University of North Carolina Press, 1980).
15 The phrase is Drew McCoy's, *The Elusive Republic,* 186.
16 *Republic of Letters* 1: 341.
17 *Republic of Letters* 1: 423–424.
18 Lance Banning, *The Sacred Fire of Liberty: James Madison and the Founding of the Federal Republic* (Ithaca, NY: Cornell University Press, 1995), 83.
19 Edmund S. Morgan, "Slavery and Freedom: The American Paradox," *Journal of American History* 59 (1972): 5–29.

3

A FRAGILE UNITY: SUPPORTING THE CONSTITUTION

 ───

DURING THE STRUGGLE TO draft and ratify the Constitution, Hamilton on the one hand, and Jefferson and Madison on the other, were unaware just how profound their disagreements were about critical issues that mattered for the future of the United States. Despite their many potential sources of disagreement, Hamilton, Jefferson, and Madison all agreed that the Articles of Confederation had to be improved or replaced. In the mid-1780s the goal of improving the Articles of Confederation overshadowed their disagreements. Their very different goals all depended on creating a national government strong enough to assert the nation's interests and to mobilize resources to secure and protect them. From 1786 through 1788, that shared commitment to a much stronger national government brought Hamilton closer to the two Virginians than he had ever been before, or would ever be again.

SEEKING A STRONGER GOVERNMENT

Jefferson understood that future control of the West required force. His ideal republic needed a much stronger national government able to act forcefully. Writing from Paris in 1786, he informed Madison that it was "indispensably necessary that with every respect to everything external we be one nation only, firmly hooped together. Interior government is what each state should keep to itself."[1] In general, Jefferson thought the states should govern affairs within their borders, but the national government should decide all matters that affected more than a single state.

Jefferson, therefore, was highly supportive of Madison's efforts to replace the Articles of Confederation with a constitution that created a much stronger national government. Madison and Hamilton made the first serious effort to strengthen the

This group portrait of Hamilton and Jefferson, along with John Adams and Robert Morris, depicts the two men in happier times when they joined together to lead the nation in revolution. During their service together during the Continental Congress, Hamilton (*third from left*) and Jefferson (*standing*) could not have imaged the hatred they would feel for each other just a few years afterward.

national government by calling for a national convention in Annapolis, Maryland, in 1786. Too few states showed up to accomplish anything, but those attending agreed to meet the next May in Philadelphia. That was the meeting that produced the United States Constitution. Jefferson was troubled that nothing had been accomplished in Annapolis. He wrote to Madison in December 1786 expressing his sorrow that the Annapolis convention had failed. But he urged Madison to remain hopeful. The failed convention could end up mattering a great deal, for if "it should produce a full meeting in May, and a broader reformation, it will still be well." But the May meeting had to succeed, for Spain and Britain were taking advantage of the nation's weak government, and "the disposition to shut up the Mississippi [River] give[s] me serious apprehensions of the severance of the Eastern and Western parts of our confederacy."[2]

Without westward expansion and use of the Mississippi River, all the conditions that made a republic possible would disappear, of that Jefferson had no doubt. The difficulty of getting land and independence was leading to the terrible behavior of many people and all the problems of the 1780s. But Jefferson believed the source of those problems was that citizens could not get the land they needed. People's desperation and poverty produced their licentious behavior. The weak national government was at fault, not the people.

Jefferson blamed the weak national government because it could not improve the conditions that caused the people's bad behavior. Therefore, he was very sympathetic to a group of poor farmers from Massachusetts who rose up in 1786 to shut down the state courts. They were threatened with foreclosure and the loss of their land and so, as far as they and Jefferson were concerned, with the loss of their freedom and independence too. Jefferson heard about what is known as Shays's Rebellion just a few months before the Constitutional Convention. Soon after learning of it, he wrote from Paris to Madison that he hoped people would sympathize with the terrible conditions that had caused the Westerners to act rashly. It was not their fault, for they had "suffered from the stoppage of the channels of commerce, which . . . must render money scarce, and make the people uneasy."

Rebelling against a government of the people was of course "absolutely unjustifiable," but Jefferson urged compassion and understanding. Indeed, the engaged frustration of the followers of Daniel Shays spoke well for the future prospects of the United States. Citizens were not sitting idly by and accepting conditions that everybody knew threatened to undermine the hard-won victory of the revolution. Jefferson could not condemn their spirit, which he hoped would prevent "the degeneracy of government and nourish a general attention to public affairs." Indeed, the people owed a great deal to Shays, for, Jefferson informed Madison, "I hold it that a little rebellion now and then is a good thing, and as necessary in the political world as storms in the physical." "Honest republican governors," Jefferson explained, should be "mild in their punishment of rebellions, as not to discourage them too much. It is a medicine necessary for the sound health of government."[3]

Hamilton had a very different reaction to Shays's Rebellion. It reinforced his views that the republic needed a stronger national government to handle external affairs, and to forcibly police and discipline citizens and govern internal affairs as well. Daniel Shays deserved no sympathy. He was "a desperate debtor [who had] plunged [Massachusetts] into a civil war." The dangerous 1780s had been filled with "menacing disturbances," but Shays and his followers were responsible for "actual insurrection and rebellions in Massachusetts." The actions of Shays and his followers proved, as far as Hamilton was concerned, that leaving internal affairs solely to each state government, as Jefferson wished, would never work. If the states continued to have full authority over all matters within their state borders, Hamilton had no doubt there would only be more events like Shays's Rebellion. "The tempestuous situation, from which Massachusetts has scarcely emerged," Hamilton warned, "evinces that dangers of this kind are not merely speculative."

Armed assault on law and property, argued Hamilton, hurt the entire nation. The response could not be limited to the state where the violent outburst happened to occur. In this case, the United States had been fortunate that Shays was an unimpressive nobody with few followers. But, Hamilton worried, what "if the malcontents had been headed by a Caesar or a Cromwell? Who can predict what effect a despotism established in Massachusetts would have upon the liberties of New Hampshire or Rhode Island; of Connecticut or New York?"[4] The matter affected many states, and the national government had to have the authority to intervene before a dangerous situation spread beyond a single state.

Fortunately, the "desperate debtor" was no Julius Caesar or Oliver Cromwell. But to Hamilton he showed how ordinary people acted licentiously when they did not have the benefit of strong government supported by the better sort—the wealthy and well educated. The rebellion convinced Hamilton that the state governments and their popular branches, the legislatures, could not be trusted to sit in judgment of people like Shays, who threatened "durable liberty" and "order and law." When punishing treason, Hamilton argued that "a single man of prudence and good sense, is better fitted . . . to balance the motives, which may plead for and against the remission of the punishment, than any numerous body whatever." After all, the people engaged in treason also elected the legislature, and "we might expect to see the representation of the people tainted with the same spirit, which has given birth to the offense."[5]

Shays's Rebellion had a dramatic effect on Madison as well, and his reaction to it was closer to Hamilton's than to Jefferson's. A few weeks before the start of the Constitutional Convention he wrote to Jefferson about what he hoped to accomplish there. He considered the licentiousness of the 1780s "truly alarming." He was terrified that the events of the troubled post-revolutionary period had "tainted the faith of the most orthodox republicans," and might even discredit the idea of republican government. Any changes "in favor of stable government not infringing fundamental principles" were desirable if they could transform "our present situation." Like Hamilton, Madison had concluded that it would not change the present situation enough merely to increase the national government's power over issues outside of each state's borders. Shays's Rebellion was proof that the national government had to be "clearly paramount to [the] state Legislative authorities." It could not simply assume new powers to tax and regulate trade. Madison felt it also was essential "to arm the federal head with a negative in all cases whatsoever on the local legislatures." Only when the national government had the power to veto any law passed at the state level could it prevent a majority within a state "from oppressing the minority within themselves by paper money and other unrighteous measures which favor the interests of the majority."[6]

Madison had long feared that majorities would abuse their liberty by behaving in licentious ways that violated the rights of minorities. Shays's Rebellion focused and intensified his fear. Though he was deeply relieved that the rebellion had been put down, he did not think the danger had ended. Like Hamilton, he worried that the sentiment that produced the rebellion had filtered deeply into the people of Massachusetts, and would affect local politics into the future. In such a case, elections and other republican institutions were part of the problem, for the "insolence is in many instances countenanced by no less decisive marks of popular favor than elections to local offices of trust and authority."[7] Like Hamilton, Madison had serious doubts that state legislatures would punish licentious acts if they were popular with the majority. Less than a month before the Constitutional Convention began, Madison wrote to Jefferson that, if anything, the state legislatures were likely to aid, not prevent, licentiousness. The followers of Shays had been dispersed, but Madison was hearing "that they mean to try their strength in another way; that is, by endeavoring to give the elections such a turn as may promote their views under the auspices of constitutional forms."[8]

Madison feared that Shays and his supporters might accomplish their goals by being the majority, in his view a riot by election. That possibility suggested to him the gravest danger the republican United States faced. In a republic, where the right to vote was so extensive, Madison reasoned that popular branches of government would do what majorities wanted. They would obey the majority even when it supported people like Daniel Shays. In a republic, Madison concluded, liberty was threatened far more by the majority than by the minority. In a monarchy clearly the wealthy and powerful minority was the source of tyranny. But it was a mistake, Madison believed, to conclude that the minority was the only potential source of tyranny. If the majority was angry, discontented, and desperate, and if it was not limited in what it could do by effective government, it could easily abuse the rights of the minority. Violation of natural rights was tyranny whether committed by a king upon the many or by a republican majority upon the few. But the tyranny of the majority was the problem faced uniquely by republics.

The ultimate solution, Madison believed, was to recreate the conditions of the third stage for as long as possible. Citizens living in near social and economic equality and independence would have no reason to look for people to oppress. But there was never an excuse to allow tyranny in any form. Madison shared Jefferson's vision for the United States. But with the immediate problem, his belief that majorities right now were acting tyrannically, a government had to be created to deal with them. As he explained to Jefferson, the constitutions of both the nation and the states needed to create branches of government that were more insulated from the people, and less likely to act on the whims of majorities. The state legislatures were far too easily manipulated.

In addition to a veto of all state laws, Madison believed a stronger national government needed a two-house legislature with a Senate elected for six years. This lengthy term would insulate the national senators from a temporary and rash majority far more than state legislatures ever could be. Greater insulation, Madison insisted to Jefferson, "would not be dangerous to liberty." In fact the Senate would better protect liberty by "correcting the infirmities of popular government." Committed republicans, whose faith had been "tainted" by episodes like Shays's Rebellion, would see it restored by such a Senate, which could "prevent the disgust against the form which may otherwise produce a sudden transition to some very different one." That was the true danger, that the licentiousness majority would create anarchy followed by the longing for a restoration of order, even if it meant the return of monarchy. "It is no secret to any attentive and dispassionate observer of the political situation in the

U.S.," Madison insisted to Jefferson, "that the real danger to republican liberty has lurked in that cause."[9]

HAMILTON AND MADISON AT THE CONVENTION

At the Constitutional Convention Hamilton and Madison focused on the business at hand (Jefferson was still in Paris). In the summer of 1787, whatever Madison might hope to accomplish later, westward expansion had stalled and a future in the third stage was uncertain. But these difficulties did not give anxious majorities an excuse to violate the natural rights of minorities. The nation needed a government that could respond to the immediate problem of the tyranny of the majority. Hence Madison defended a powerful Senate—an upper house that would serve for six years. He initially supported that Senate being chosen by the lower house of the national legislature. Ultimately he settled for it being chosen by the state legislatures, rather than being directly elected by the voters. Longer terms and indirect elections would protect the Senate from needing to frequently seek majority approval. Finally, as he had suggested in his letter to Jefferson, at the Convention Madison argued for the national legislature receiving the power to veto all acts by the state legislatures.

Madison had no doubt the danger of majority tyranny was real, and would only grow greater over time. In a speech of June 26th at the Convention, Madison argued that the United States at present had far more social, economic, and political equality than European monarchies. It had no hereditary titles "nor those extremes of wealth and poverty" typical in Europe. But that would change over time. From the start, the Republic had to establish a government that could protect individual rights into the future. It could not wait to do so until a distant time when an angry and poor majority had little interest in doing so. The Constitutional Convention, Madison proclaimed, was "framing a system which we wish to last for the ages," and so must "not lose sight of the changes which ages will produce."

In the future the United States would face the same problem of too many people for too little land that already plagued the monarchies of Europe. There would be a growing number of citizens "who will labor under all the hardships of life, and secretly sigh for a more equal distribution of its blessings." As this population became the majority, the temptation to have a grand riot by election would grow very great. Already the 1780s had produced "symptoms of a leveling spirit." The fundamental question facing the Constitutional Convention was how "is this danger to be guarded against on republican principles?" "Among other means," said Madison, "by the establishment of a body in the Government sufficiently respectable for its wisdom and virtue, to aid on such emergencies."[10] In the distant future the United States would have the inequality that came with extensive population and the fourth stage. But the critical question was: How far away was that future? What many might have missed in Madison's speech was his use of the phrase "[a]mong other means." The "other means" could prevent that future for a very long time if virtuous statesmen ensured westward expansion and worldwide free trade to sell agricultural surpluses. If they did, they would postpone "those extremes of wealth and poverty" and the disruptions they brought.

There is no evidence that Hamilton and Madison talked about the third and fourth stages at the Convention. They did focus on the business at hand, building the stronger national government that could limit the power of the state legislatures and prevent the tyranny of the majority. To the limited extent that he could know Madison, Hamilton grew to like and respect him. He rose quickly when Madison finished speaking on June 26th to endorse his views. According to Madison's notes, in his speech Hamilton explained that he "concurred with Mr. Madison in thinking we are now to decide forever the future of republican government; . . . if we did not give to that form due stability and wisdom, it would be disgraced and lost . . . forever." Hamilton, virtually always honest, perhaps to a fault, stated boldly that he did not "think favorably of republican government." But he was committed to it, and so "addressed his remarks to those who did think favorably of it, in order to prevail on them to tone their government as high as possible." Hamilton proclaimed himself a "zealous . . . advocate for liberty," which required supporting the liberty of unpopular and weak minorities from a potentially dangerous majority. Madison was right "that nothing like an equality of property existed" in the United States, even in 1787. But his fellow delegates had to understand, Hamilton insisted, that economic inequality resulted from citizens freely using their talents, which were also not equally distributed. Economic inequality "would unavoidably result from the very liberty itself." And it was the duty of republican government to protect all the results produced when citizens made use of their liberty, even though the "inequality of property constituted the great and fundamental distinction in society."[11]

Hamilton and Madison agreed on the business at hand of forming a much stronger national government. But Hamilton was content to accept that "durable liberty," given people's unequal talents, guaranteed social and economic inequality. Madison did not disagree (neither did Jefferson). But Hamilton was comfortable accepting that inequality was simply the price of "durable liberty." The primary responsibility of a government was to prevent those angered by inequality from threatening what "durable liberty" produced. Hamilton could conclude that "providence has distributed its bounties in the manner best adapted to the general order and happiness."[12] Madison believed that a virtuous government should recreate the conditions of the third stage across space. If it did so, it could for a very long time reduce and even resolve the conflict between individual liberty and the unequal outcomes it produced. Eventually the government would have to make sure that the poor did not violate the rights of the rich. But accepting the fact of inequality and protecting the wealthy was only the very last resort. For as long as possible, Madison believed, the government should use every means at its disposal to both protect natural rights and prevent large concentrations of wealth and social and economic inequality.

There were major differences between Hamilton and Madison, but in the short term they agreed on a great deal. They supported each other at the Convention, and they wrote dozens of letters to each other over the months afterward strategizing about how to get their states, New York and Virginia, to ratify the Constitution. Most importantly, they wrote almost all of the essays of the *Federalist Papers*, the most thorough analysis and defense of the Constitution ever produced.

MADISON'S FEAR OF THE MAJORITY AND FEDERALIST 10

In early September 1787, as the Convention was winding down, Madison wrote to Jefferson describing what the new plan for government looked like. He had not gotten everything he wanted. The national government would not be able to veto state laws. But it had a powerful president, a strong senate elected for six years, and an independent judiciary. Most important, the national government could tax, and the Constitution forbade the state governments from printing paper money. The new government was truly federal, power was divided between the national government and the states, and the states still wielded a great deal of authority. But the new proposal was a sweeping transformation. Outlining the changes for Jefferson, Madison allowed that the "extent of them may surprise you."[13]

Madison wrote a series of letters to Jefferson after the Convention. In them, and in his contributions to the *Federalist Papers*, he explained where he thought the threat to liberty came from in the United States, and how the new constitutional government needed to be understood so that the threat could be dealt with. Madison told Jefferson that it was almost impossible to imagine in the United States the traditional threat to liberty found in European monarchies: a great despotic consolidation of power at the top that allowed rulers to oppress the people. The real threat was not the concentration of power in the hands of a small group. Instead, it was that a majority could not be stopped if it was determined to violate the law and natural rights. In all republics the majority was the real power, and "wherever the real power in a government lies, there is the danger of oppression." The gravest threat to liberty the United States faced, Madison sought to convince Jefferson, was "not from the acts of government contrary to the sense of its constituents, but from acts in which the government is the mere instrument of the major number of constituents." The majority acting tyrannically would most likely destroy republican government, for "[w]herever there is interest and power to do wrong, wrong will generally be done. . . ." In a republican government "the political and physical power" was held by the "majority of the people, and consequently the tyrannical will of the sovereign is not to be controlled by the dread of an appeal to any other force in the community."[14]

Madison understood that he offered an unorthodox understanding of the source of tyranny. But much of the theorizing about tyranny had come from examining monarchies, not republics. That was why political thinkers emphasized the "tendency in all governments to an augmentation of power at the expense of liberty." But, Madison explained to Jefferson, tyrannical power in the hands of a few was a threat only if power was sufficiently concentrated so that a few could seize it. That was not the case in the United States. There were no powerful financial institutions, or a small group with vast property holdings who could control the fortunes of others.

Power was so attenuated, in fact, that there was no counterweight to the majority, which could act however it pleased. It was true that power "when it has attained a certain degree of energy and independence goes on generally to further degrees." But in the United States power was not sufficiently concentrated to achieve the energy that would enable further dangerous concentration.

Jefferson needed to understand that when power was spread as thinly and widely as it was in the United States, a very different sort of danger threatened. In a republic the "tendency is to further degrees of relaxation, until the abuses of liberty beget a sudden transition to an undue degree of power." The United States faced the problem of all past republics. Without a degree of power and authority, liberty would lead ultimately to anarchy and the need for order that only a tyrant could provide. "It is a melancholy reflection," Madison lamented to Jefferson, "that liberty should be equally exposed to danger whether the government have too much or too little power."[15]

In the republican United States could liberty ever be in danger from a small, powerful minority at the top, the traditional source of tyranny in monarchies? It was unlikely, Madison explained to Jefferson. There were, of course, in every society small groups wealthier than the rest who longed for more wealth and power. Perhaps they might trick the people into electing them, and through "a succession of artful and ambitious rulers, may by gradual and well-timed advances, finally erect an independent government on the subversion of liberty." But that prospect was so far-fetched that it could hardly be taken seriously, especially when compared to the very real threat of the tyranny of the majority that was at that very moment threatening liberty. Considering the possibility of a small group of tyrants somehow seizing control of government, Madison confessed to Jefferson, "I must own that I see no tendency in our governments to danger on that side."[16]

For Madison, the real, really the only, threat to liberty in the United States was the majority acting licentiously. An obvious way to control the majority was to create a government independent of majority will, but that would invite the traditional threat to liberty found in monarchies. Republics needed to come up with republican solutions to the unique republican problem of the tyranny of the majority. To provide that solution, and to explain it to Jefferson in ways that could reassure him to support the Constitution, Madison praised the federal structure of government the Constitution provided. But just as important, he merged that praise with a celebration of the third stage and a large society of independent farmers moving across space. His point to Jefferson was that the new Constitution provided the best chance for recreating the third stage across the North American continent.

Madison discussed how to manage the majority and preserve the third stage in his most important contribution to the *Federalist Papers*, "Federalist 10." Madison explained that the Constitution could "break and control the violence of faction." Building on themes he had explained to Jefferson, Madison wrote in "Federalist 10" that those who cared for "public and personal liberty" worried that the current national government did not have enough authority to protect liberty and enforce law. Without a sufficient concentration of power, "our governments are too unstable."

As a result, "public good is disregarded in the conflicts of rival parties, and . . . measures are too often decided, not according to the rules of justice and the rights of the minor party, but by a superior force of an interested and overbearing majority." People were forming factions to pursue their own interests at the expense of others and the public good. Faction, insisted Madison, was poison to a republic. And what was a faction? A faction, Madison explained, was "a number of citizens, whether amounting to a majority or a minority of the whole, who are united and actuated by some common impulse of position, or of interest, adverse to the rights of other citizens, or to the permanent and aggregate interests of the community."[17]

In defining faction this way, Madison showed that we cannot apply to him our modern notions of democracy. In the twenty-first century we believe that all adult citizens are equal and equally capable of participating in the decisions that determine the course our nation takes. That a majority supports an idea makes it credible. Madison, Jefferson, and of course Hamilton, did not believe that majority support for something automatically made it credible. Madison was confident that there were "permanent and aggregate interests of the community," a tangible and knowable bundle of ideas and policies that were better than any alternatives, and that should be protected, supported, and enacted. Promoting the "permanent and aggregate interests" was the public good, which did not change whether or not the majority accepted it.

For Madison, the public good was clear: Support the new constitution, create a national government strong enough to protect each citizen's natural rights, and enact the laws that gave each citizen the best chance to enjoy life, liberty, the pursuit of happiness, independence, and equality. The government should use its power to ensure westward expansion to recreate the third stage across space, and to enforce worldwide free trade for the nation's independent citizen-farmers. Madison believed he knew the public good because of his deep learning, his careful thought about the needs of republics, and due to the wealth that brought him the independence and leisure to devote himself to public affairs. He did not believe that most of his fellow citizens had the learning or leisure to understand the public good. And it was from that vast group that majorities formed. Madison concluded that the ideas of that majority deserved no particular respect merely because a large group, less able to understand the public good, wished to do something that a small group better able to comprehend it knew violated the public good. The notion that a majority's support conferred legitimacy invited the tyranny of the majority.

Factions, whether minority or majority, were clearly very dangerous, Madison believed. But there was no choice except to live with them. A society that forbade factions was worse than one that allowed them. Factions resulted when free citizens judged for themselves and acted on those judgments. Yet though that made things messy and dangerous, "[l]iberty is to faction what air is to fire, an ailment without which it instantly expires." Factions were terribly regrettable. But, wrote Madison, "it could not be a less folly to abolish liberty, which is essential to political life, because it nourishes faction than it would be to wish the annihilation of air, which is essential to

animal life, because it imparts to fire its destructive agency." To survive, to be worthy
of survival, republics had to allow their citizens the freedom to think and act independently. And since citizens were imperfect and fallible, concluded Madison, "different
opinions will be formed. . . . The latent causes of faction are thus sown in the nature
of man." Where there was liberty there would always be faction. Echoing Hamilton's
remarks at the Convention, Madison wrote that over time the unequal distribution
of talent inevitably produced economic inequality, and "the most common and durable source of factions has been the various and unequal distribution of property."
Inequality resulted from liberty, and "[t]hose who hold and those who are without
property have ever formed distinct interests in society."[18]

Factions were highly dangerous. But since "the causes of faction cannot be removed . . . relief is only to be sought in the means of controlling its effects." In a republic the dangers of a minority faction were easily dealt with. No matter how selfish
a minority was, the majority possessed the power and could prevent minorities from
violating the public good. The real danger, as Madison had warned Jefferson, was the
tyranny of a majority faction. Republican government, the cure for a minority faction, was uniquely vulnerable to a majority faction. In a republic, if a majority formed
determined to trample natural rights and oppress minorities or individuals, warned
Madison, "the form of popular government . . . enables it to sacrifice to its ruling passion or interests both the public good and the rights of other citizens." The central
dilemma of all republics was how to "secure the public good and private rights against
the danger of such a faction, and at the same time to preserve the spirit and the form
of popular government. . . ."[19]

A just republic had to prevent majorities from behaving badly while preserving
government chosen by the majority. The solution to the republican dilemma, Madison
argued, had two parts. Together they could preserve a republican government chosen
by the majority, but one that could prevent the majority from forcing its government
to act unjustly. The first part was the structure the Constitution provided: a republican government that was a federal system, with power divided between a now much
stronger national government and the states. If citizens ratified the Constitution, the
national government would have a great deal more authority. The national government would be further removed than the state governments, from the passions of
temporary, rash, and local majorities. As a result, the national government could consider all suggestions carefully. It could decide to act only on ideas that survived longer
scrutiny, and were reasonable enough to spread widely to the larger population now
required to form a majority at the national level.

But the constitutional federal structure could only work if it was connected
to sustained movement across space. Westward expansion was the second part of
Madison's solution. As population grew, it also had to spread. A large population
living in a vast space was far less likely to form a majority united around a single view.
And in a republic such a majority was the principal—really, Madison believed, the
only—source of tyranny. The stronger national government the Constitution provided had the power to forcibly accomplish westward expansion. "Extend the sphere"

of settlement, wrote Madison, "and you take in a greater variety of parties and interests; you make it less probable that a majority of the whole will have a common motive to invade the rights of other citizens; or if such a common motive exists, it will be more difficult for all who feel it to discover their own strength and act in unison." A much larger nation would have a much larger electorate. In a larger republic it was more likely that men of national reputation, the truly enlightened, those with the resources and capacity to understand the public good, would manage to gain election to national office. With the new constitutional order, citizens would be much more likely to elect "representatives whose enlightened views and virtuous sentiments render them superior to local prejudices and to schemes of injustice." Such a government would be chosen by a majority of the voters, but would have sufficient authority and distance from them to guide them wisely. That would make it much harder for a majority to form and act in the licentious ways that led to anarchy, and ultimately the restoration of monarchy. Thus, concluded Madison in "Federalist 10," in "the extent and proper structure of the Union . . . we behold a republican remedy for the diseases most incident to republican government."[20]

Madison's vision for the new constitutional republic depended on expansion across space. In a letter to Jefferson he rehearsed the themes of "Federalist 10" to make sure his friend understood this. In the weeks after the Constitutional Convention, Madison wrote to Jefferson that our "form of government in order to effect its purposes must operate not within a small but an extensive sphere." In the letter Madison explained to Jefferson that factions were inevitable. He gave the same reasons he had in "Federalist 10," because "[h]owever erroneous or ridiculous these grounds of dissension and faction may appear to the enlightened statesman or the benevolent philosopher, the bulk of mankind who are neither statesmen nor philosophers, will continue to view them in a different light."

But Jefferson needed to know that Madison understood that the new Constitutional order could work only if the nation accomplished rapid westward expansion. Jefferson should join him in supporting the Constitution because ratifying it was the best way to ensure that movement across space became the top priority. Westward expansion would be first on the agenda after ratification, promised Madison, precisely because factions were inevitable, "and a majority when united by a common interest or passion cannot be restrained from oppressing the minority." Only a large republic could limit the power of a majority for "what remedy can be found in a republican government, where the majority must ultimately decide, but that of giving such an extent to its sphere, that no common interest or passion will be likely to unite a majority of the whole number in an unjust pursuit." The new constitutional order provided the national government sufficient authority to enforce the rule of law and protect minority rights. But that authority would never become a dangerous concentration of power because in "the extended Republic of the United States, the General Government would hold a pretty even balance between the parties of the particular states, and be at the same time sufficiently restrained by its dependence on the community, from betraying its general interests."[21]

Madison also emphasized that the Constitution was already attracting statesmen and philosophers. After Massachusetts (home to Daniel Shays) ratified the Constitution, a relieved Madison wrote to Jefferson, "The prevailing party comprised . . . all the men of abilities, of property, and of influence. In the opposite multitude there was not a single character capable of uniting their wills or directing their measures." Those who opposed the Constitution were primarily "ignorant and jealous men, who had been taught or had fancied that the convention at Philadelphia had entered into a conspiracy against the liberties of the people at large, in order to erect an aristocracy for the rich and well-born, and the men of education. They had no plan whatever. . . ."[22] Madison insisted to Jefferson that those sorts of citizens were safest when men of greater vision governed them, and made sure they could live as independent farmers in the third stage. The people's "durable liberty" was too precious and fragile to be left to the people to protect without firm guidance.

CONVINCING JEFFERSON

In seeking Jefferson's endorsement, Madison connected supporting the Constitution to several ideas that Jefferson cherished. Jefferson agreed with Madison about the extensive sphere, and that "durable liberty" was safest in the third stage. And he also agreed just as strongly that virtuous statesmen, and not the people themselves, were most likely to seek the public good. Like Madison, Jefferson's republic depended on the statesmen and philosophers to govern. As he explained to John Adams, the nation's first vice president and its second president, "[T]here is a natural aristocracy among men. The grounds of this are virtue and talents." In the letter to Adams, Jefferson distinguished between this natural aristocracy and "an artificial aristocracy founded on wealth and birth." But Jefferson agreed with Hamilton and Madison that the great majority of citizens were likely to misuse power and misunderstand the best course for realizing the public good. Especially in a republic, where those holding office changed frequently, Jefferson told Adams the "natural aristocracy I consider as the most precious gift of nature for the instruction, the trusts, and government of society." Government chosen by the majority was likely to succeed only if the majority wisely elected natural aristocrats, for "that form of government is the best which provides the most effectually for a pure selection of these natural aristoi into the offices of government."[23]

Jefferson thought citizens would always need to remain keenly observant of their governors. Only careful scrutiny by citizens would keep rulers from becoming unaccountable and tyrannical. Yet Madison's arguments had convinced him. After hearing that nine states had ratified the Constitution, the number needed for it to replace the Articles of Confederation, Jefferson wrote to Madison, "I sincerely rejoice at the acceptance of our new constitution." He had decided that the Constitution was "a good canvass on which some strokes only want retouching."

Madison had persuaded Jefferson. In deciding to support the Constitution, in particular Jefferson had found convincing Madison's arguments about the source of republican tyranny. As he praised the new Constitution, he told Madison, "I like very much the general idea of framing a government which should go on of itself peacefully, without needing continual recurrence to the state legislatures." Madison was so persuasive that Jefferson was more worried that the national legislature was too accountable to the majority than that the new government was a dangerous concentration of power. The new government had to have the power to tax, and that power belonged to the House of Representatives. Jefferson agreed, therefore, that, unlike the Senate, the people should elect its members directly. But a legislature chosen directly by the people was clearly less reliable than the Senate, which was not. Jefferson feared that "a house chosen by them will be very illy qualified to legislate for the union, for foreign [policy] etc."

Since the people would elect the House of Representatives directly, that house would likely have fewer natural aristocrats than the Senate or the Executive and Judicial branches. But in the end all would be well, Jefferson concluded. Madison had convinced him that the new constitutional order provided the best chance for a government powerful enough to expand west and recreate the third stage across space. Relieved, Jefferson explained to Madison, "I think our governments will remain virtuous for many centuries; as long as they are chiefly agricultural and this will be as long as there shall be vacant lands in any part of America." Of course, the future would bring great challenges. Jefferson did not doubt that when Americans grew "piled up on one another in large cities, as in Europe, they will become corrupt as in Europe." But now that sad fate could be postponed into the distant future. There was enough time to consider solutions, and a sound governing structure to enact them. Proper citizens could be taught to cherish liberty and discern the true natural aristocrats among them. "Above all things," Jefferson informed Madison, "I hope the education of the common people will be attended to; convinced that on their good sense we may rely with the most security for the preservation of a due degree of liberty."[24]

Jefferson did not think the Constitution was perfect, but what plan of government was? The national government was now much stronger and natural aristocrats would likely rule. But they would not rule unaccountably. Jefferson placed great confidence in the federal structure Madison had praised to him. Though it was much stronger than it had been, the national government was still limited in its power, and "the limited powers of the federal government and the jealousy of the subordinate [state] governments afford a security which exists in no other instance. . . . The jealousy of those subordinate governments is a precious reliance."[25]

HAMILTON'S GLASS, LESS THAN HALF FULL

As the new constitutional Republic began in 1788, Jefferson and Madison were reasonably happy. Was Hamilton? At the Convention he pleaded with his fellow delegates to make a national government that was sufficiently "high toned." He had to conclude that in the end they had not done so. The news, though, was not all gloomy. In the final days of September 1787, just two weeks after the Constitutional

Convention ended, Hamilton wrote out his thoughts on the strengths and weaknesses of the new government. There was certainly reason to be pleased, for "the new constitution has in favor of it a very great weight of influence of the persons who framed it, particularly the universal popularity of General Washington." Beyond that, Hamilton was confident it would receive the support of the moneyed men he considered so important for a well-ordered republic. The Constitution would enjoy "the good will of the commercial interests . . . the good will of most men of property . . . who wish a government of the union able to protect them against domestic violence . . . which the democratic spirit is apt to make on property." Indeed, the new constitutional order would be supported by any who were "anxious for the respectability of the nation."

All that was well and good, but it was outweighed by the horrible dangers the Constitution had not been able to address. Hamilton began to list all the things that could go wrong. To his alarm, his list quickly grew long. He worried about George Clinton and all those like him, the "*inconsiderable* men in possession of considerable offices under the state governments who will fear the diminution of their consequence, power and emolument [payment] by the establishment of the general government and who can hope for nothing there." These ambitious "men of office possessed of talents and popularity . . . for their own aggrandizement will oppose the quiet adoption of the new government." Hamilton also anticipated "the opposition of all men much in debt who will not wish to see a government established one object of which is to restrain the means of cheating creditors." But above all, he expected and feared "the democratic jealousies of the people which may be alarmed at the appearance of institutions that may seem calculated to place the power of the community in a few hands and to raise a few individuals to stations of great preeminence."

The next several months seemed to Hamilton to confirm his fears. Both he and Madison faced enormous challenges in their states ratifying conventions. Virginia (despite Patrick Henry leading the opposition) finally voted to ratify, but only by the narrow margin of 89 to 79. The vote of the smaller New York convention was even closer, 30 to 27. Many changed positions at the end when New York learned that Virginia had become the tenth state to ratify, and so had joined the new constitutional union. New York would be left out with only North Carolina and Rhode Island. Under these conditions even Melancton Smith had switched his vote.

Despite these narrow victories, Hamilton could easily imagine a nightmare scenario given the forces he thought were hostile to the Constitution. As he considered all the awful possibilities, he decided it was likely the new government would "beget such struggle and animosities and heats in the community that the circumstances conspiring with the real necessity of an essential change in our present situation will produce civil war." It was a deeply pessimistic prediction, and Hamilton hoped that a "good administration [could] conciliate the confidence and affection of the people and perhaps enable the government to acquire more consistency than the proposed constitution seems to promise for so great a country." If right from the start the best and wisest governed the nation, perhaps the stronger national government could "triumph altogether over the state governments and reduce them to an entire subordination dividing the larger states into smaller districts." He could also hope that with sensible policies the "organs of the general government may also acquire additional strength." But if neither of those things happened, Hamilton concluded, "in the course of a few years, it is probable that the contests about the boundaries of power between the particular [state] governments will produce a dissolution of the union. This after all seems to be the most likely result."[26]

The only outcome that did not end in violence, bloodshed, and civil war was the complete dominance of the national government over the states, the very governments that Jefferson viewed as "afford[ing] a security which exists in no other instance" against too great a concentration of power at the national level. But for Hamilton, the Constitution did not create anything close to enough concentration of power or centralized authority in the national government. The evidence for that was the continued importance of the state governments and the "inconsiderable men" who ran them.

* * *

But by 1788 the Constitution had been ratified and Washington elected President. Jefferson and Madison were confident that their work was mostly finished. They looked forward happily to a new era of peace and stable liberty. Hamilton was far less confident. But quickly President Washington appointed him Secretary of the Treasury. At long last Hamilton held a position where he could do something about his profound concerns. Thomas Jefferson would not remain happy for very long. And neither would James Madison.

NOTES

1 *Republic of Letters* 1: 410.
2 *Republic of Letters* 1: 458.
3 *Republic of Letters* 1: 461.
4 *PAH* 4: 312, 317, 397–398.
5 *PAH* 4: 626–627.
6 *Republic of Letters* 1: 470.
7 *Republic of Letters* 1: 473.
8 *Republic of Letters* 1: 474.
9 *Republic of Letters* 1: 555–556.
10 Winton U. Solberg, *The Constitutional Convention and the Formation of the Union* (Champaign, IL: University of Illinois Press, 1990), 176–177.
11 *PAH* 4: 218.
12 *PAH* 5: 321.
13 *Republic of Letters* 1: 490–491.
14 *Republic of Letters* 1: 564–565.
15 *Republic of Letters* 1: 564–565.
16 *Republic of Letters* 1: 564–565.
17 Clinton Rossiter ed., *The Federalist Papers* (New York: Mentor, 1961), 77.
18 *Federalist Papers* 78–79.

19 *Federalist Papers* 80.
20 *Federalist Papers* 82–84.
21 *Republic of Letters* 1: 500–502.
22 *Republic of Letters* 1: 531.
23 Lester J. Cappon ed., *The Adams–Jefferson Letters: The Complete Correspondence Between Thomas Jefferson and Abigail and John Adams* (New York: Simon and Schuster, 1959), 388–389.
24 *Republic of Letters* 1: 512–514, 545.
25 *Republic of Letters* 1: 587.
26 *PAH* 4: 275–277, emphasis original.

4

DISAGREEMENT: REVENUE, COMMERCE, DEBT, AND THE REPORT ON PUBLIC CREDIT

〰 ───

In 1789 George Washington was unanimously elected President of the United States, and he appointed Hamilton Secretary of the Treasury and Jefferson Secretary of State. Virginians elected Madison to the first House of Representatives. All three would now serve in the national government (temporarily located in New York City), whose creation they had so strongly supported. Hamilton, Jefferson, and Madison all hoped the new Constitution would allow them to accomplish their goals. Hamilton's goals depended on maximizing revenue for the new national government. Very quickly disagreement developed between him and Jefferson and Madison over whether maximizing revenue should matter more than other concerns. In 1790 Hamilton also produced his complex and brilliant "Report on Public Credit," which laid the foundation for the three objectives he had set out for Robert Morris a decade earlier. In this report he called for the national government to fund the considerable debt it had incurred from fighting the American Revolution. The "Report" also recommended that the national government take over responsibility for all of the Revolutionary War debts of the state governments. With the "Report on Public Credit," Hamilton staked out a very clear and powerful position that shocked and infuriated Jefferson and Madison.

PUBLIC CREDIT AND MADISON'S COMMERCIAL DISCRIMINATION

Hamilton moved quickly to connect the national government with leading moneyed men. In September 1789 he wrote to the wealthy Philadelphia merchant and financier Thomas Willing, President of the Bank of North America, the bank which had been founded by Robert Morris, "You will probably have learned ere this reaches you my appointment to the office of Secretary of the Treasury." Hamilton told Willing he knew how difficult his task would be and that he was counting on the support of wealthy and substantial citizens like him. Hamilton knew that Willing and those equal to him in standing understood "my inviolable attachment to the principles which form the basis of public credit." He hoped this knowledge would "insure the confidence of those who have it most in their power to afford me support."[1]

Hamilton's top priority was to secure public credit so that the nation could borrow cheaply and easily. But public credit was equally important to Jefferson and Madison. Their conflict with Hamilton began over how best to achieve credit worthiness, and over what policies a financially sound nation should pursue. Over a year before Hamilton wrote to Willing, Jefferson wrote to Madison celebrating the effect ratification of the Constitution would have on the nation's public credit. Jefferson argued that extensive borrowing and a vast public debt were outrages committed by monarchies in the fourth stage. But he explained to Madison, "[T]ho' I am the enemy to the using our credit but under absolute necessity, yet the possessing a good credit I consider as indispensible in the present system of carrying on war." Stationed in Europe, Jefferson understood the profound importance of public credit. It was obviously the source of Britain's great strength, the foundation that made it the most powerful nation in the world. The ability to tax and generate substantial revenue reliably meant that British officials "never borrow without establishing taxes for the payment of the interest, and they never yet failed one day in that payment."[2]

It was dangerous that the bitterest enemy of the United States could borrow so cheaply and easily from its own people, and especially in the money markets of Amsterdam. Jefferson sadly related to Madison that the United States could barely borrow there at all. The Dutch bankers knew that the United States was borrowing from banks to pay the interest on loans it owed to other banks. American debt sold for up to eight percent below its face value, while British debt never failed to trade at par. Yet Jefferson was hopeful about reversing this dismal situation. News of better days for the United States had already spread to Europe and "the whole body of money dealers . . . look forward to our new government with a great degree of partiality and interest." Jefferson had been able to explain the new power to tax, and brighter future prospects "enabled us to set the loan of last year into motion. . . ."[3] Indeed, so excited was Jefferson about the future possibilities for the Constitution and public credit, that in 1788 he sent Madison a lengthy set of tables and calculations about how to restore credit and pay off the debt. He sent his calculations, he informed Madison, because he believed that "funding their foreign debt will be among the first operations of the new government." If any doubted that funding the debt should be the first priority, Jefferson could assure them that the Dutch expected "a very satisfactory provision for the payment of their debt from the first session of the new Congress."[4]

Establishing public credit was also a top priority for Madison. Like Jefferson, he fit public credit into his vision of a republican society in the agricultural third stage. Madison linked the Constitution with public credit in one of his earliest speeches in

Congress, which he gave in April 1789. The Constitution, Madison explained, had rescued the nation and its government "from the state of imbecility." The government now had to keep its past promises. The United States had "to revive those principles of honor and honesty that have too long lain dormant. The deficiency in our treasury has been too notorious. . . . Let us content ourselves with endeavoring to remedy the evil." Yet already Madison was growing concerned about how the debt would be handled. He worried that the new government was so concerned about establishing public credit that it might ignore the painful conditions many citizens had experienced during the 1780s. Public credit had to be established, and "a national revenue must be obtained." But Madison knew that the public debt was a very complicated matter. Whatever system he and his fellow statesmen devised for dealing with it, "the system must . . . not be oppressive to our constituents."

The least oppressive method for raising revenue, Madison told his fellow Representatives, was an impost, a tariff. Light tariffs on imported good would raise substantial revenue to pay interest on the debt and establish public credit, because American citizens purchased so many imported manufactured goods. But light imposts would not discourage foreign imports and so would also not threaten Madison's other crucial goal, free trade, and "the general regulation of commerce, which in my opinion, ought to be as free as the policy of nations will admit."[5]

Jefferson and Madison wanted public credit. But they also believed that an international system of free trade, which allowed farmers to sell their agricultural surpluses, was equally important. Madison knew it would be difficult to achieve both. He believed that the new national government would need to fight for free trade with aggressive policies aimed at Britain. Madison called these aggressive policies commercial discrimination. In seeking confrontation with Britain, Madison created conflict with Hamilton, who believed that Madison's policy proposals would diminish revenue and so endanger his plans before he could even get started on them.

Madison's commercial discrimination responded to the commercial policies of Britain. Since the end of the Revolutionary War, Britain had sharply restricted the access of American ships to the West Indies, the United States' largest export market. British shipping dominated the carrying trade, the transport of American exports. Britain undercut American vessels and made it risky to invest in shipbuilding for fear that American-built ships would not be able to compete with British ships. British dominance of the oceans and of international commerce, Madison believed, was a mortal threat to the United States.

Madison argued that to get free trade in the long run, for now the United States had to reject free trade. On April 9, 1789, the day after he gave his speech calling for the impost, Madison explained why for now the United States needed to impose far more than light imposts on Britain. Madison believed in free trade. But the United States had to respond to the hostile actions of Britain that were harming "the great staple of America . . . agriculture." It was natural for the vast majority of U.S. citizens to be farmers, and so into the distant future there would be little domestic demand for the agricultural surpluses they produced. That made foreign markets—and the free trade that would allow universal access to them—essential. Yet, how could the Republic secure free trade as quickly and fairly as possible? Certainly the United States could simply throw open its ports to all comers, and hope other nations did the same. But clearly Britain had no intention of offering the United States the same access. If the Republic was going to secure free trade, it would have to do so with force. To begin with, it would need to punish nations that prevented the unrestricted flow of international commerce.[6]

In this effort to punish Britain, Jefferson was Madison's staunch ally. In response to a letter from the South Carolinian Edward Rutledge, who was furious about British commercial policy, Jefferson assured him that "I participate fully in your in-dignation." He then mentioned the efforts in Congress to respond to the restrictions. Jefferson held out hope to Rutledge that efforts of those like Madison would soon secure the free trade that was so vital to an agricultural republic.[7]

Since a republic of farmers in the third stage would do best in a system of global free trade, why did Jefferson and Madison demand government intervention and constraint of trade? And how did they think such government action would support their goal of promoting free trade? Madison explained in his April speech that the forceful policies would be limited to Britain, the nation that prevented free trade. Madison argued that real free trade supporters understood free trade could only exist in a global system that was fair and equitable. It was precisely this fairness and equity that Britain prevented. Britain had not come to dominate global commerce by earn-ing its premier position through fair competition, Madison insisted. Rather, Britain controlled the international commerce of the United States because for a century at least it had forcibly organized international commerce to suit its interests. It did so primarily by artificially controlling the trade of the colonies. After independence it continued to do so because of the tremendous naval advantages it had gained through its artificial control during the colonial period. The United States had won its inde-pendence, yet "almost all of [our] commerce is transacted thro' the medium of British ships and British merchants. . . ."[8] Under these conditions, a U.S. commitment to free trade right away would perpetuate the situation and allow Britain to dominate global commerce on the unfair playing field it had created. Discrimination would meet force with force. But U.S. force would not distort free trade. It would challenge and undo the British distortions that made free trade impossible. In defending his proposal, Madison explained that he wished "to give such political advantages to those nations as might enable them to gain their proportion of our direct trade from the nation who has acquired more than is naturally her due."[9]

Many of Madison's fellow Congressmen opposed his policy of commercial dis-crimination. The first objection to Madison's proposal was doubt that the United States could force Britain to change. The second was that commercial discrimination would drastically reduce government revenue since, for a time, discrimination would sharply limit trade with Britain. Fewer British imports would mean fewer goods to tax, resulting in less revenue. With less revenue, the interest on the public debt might go unpaid, placing public credit in jeopardy. Hadn't Madison himself already agreed that public credit was essential to the nation's safety?

Madison did his best to address both challenges. In a series of speeches he gave in the House of Representatives in April and May 1789, he insisted that the United States could force Britain to accept free trade and to respect its rights as an independent nation. Furthermore, the United States had to use force because force was what Britain respected. If the United States remained passive, Britain's actions made it clear "that until we are able and willing to do justice to ourselves, she will shut us out from her ports and make us tributary to her." It was obvious that until the United States "restore[d] the stream of commerce to its natural channel, we shall find no relaxation on the part of Britain, the same obnoxious policy will be pursued while we submissively bear the oppression."[10]

Madison argued that the United States could coerce Britain because it was an agricultural republic in the third stage. The United States exported foodstuffs, agricultural necessities. Britain exported manufactured luxuries. Madison was confident that a republic of farmers could manage to live without British imports, and could coerce Britain by strategically withholding its agricultural surpluses. A relatively short confrontation would expose British dependence and force global free trade. Now was the time, Madison informed the House of Representatives, to demonstrate the power of an agricultural republic. Citizens and statesmen simply had to realize the nation's unique qualities and therefore its true power. The Republic was in an excellent position to "wage a commercial warfare with that nation [Britain]." The "produce of this country is more necessary to the rest of the world than that of other counties is to America," Madison insisted. And the situation was especially stacked in favor of the United States when it came to the British West Indies. It was obvious, Madison told his fellow representatives, "that they could neither prosper nor subsist without the market of the United States; they were fed from our granaries. Without our lumber . . . they could not carry on their trade or support their establishments."[11]

Madison explained his position quite clearly in a letter he wrote to Jefferson during the time he was thinking carefully about commercial discrimination. He informed Jefferson that commercial discrimination would succeed because the United States "had no reason to apprehend a disposition to G.B. to resort to a commercial contest." The British would not survive the denial of American agriculture due to Britain's "dependence on us being greater than ours on her." Again referring especially to the West Indies, Madison gloated to Jefferson that the "supplies of the United States are necessary to the existence, and their markets to the value, of her islands. The returns are either superfluities or poisons." The key word was "superfluities." Agriculture was necessary; manufactures imported from Britain were enjoyable, even highly desirable, but not essential. If it came to a trade war, Americans "could do almost wholly without such supplies, and better without than with many of them."[12]

Forbidding commerce with Britain for a time would also lead to an expansion of American shipping and naval strength, Madison argued. He knew the fear that the United States could not build enough ships to carry the bulk of its agricultural exports. Many worried that if the Republic, all of a sudden, denied entry to British ships, the price of carrying freight would rise disastrously high. But to make the American Revolution matter, to defend the claim of independence, Madison told the House, the United States had to increase its "maritime strength." If the United States imposed commercial discrimination, claimed Madison, Britain would be forced to accept free trade. In addition, the sudden absence of British shipping would vastly increase investment in American shipping. This second benefit would give a firm backing to the claims of independence. Madison urged his fellow Representatives to realize that "we have maritime dangers to guard against, and we can be secured from them no other way, than by having a navy and seamen of our own." Investment in American shipping would come once the United States began to coerce Britain. There could be no half measures, and no passive acquiescence to a world made by the colonial experience. Congress had to understand that the British "Parliament has been on the watch to seize every advantage which our weak and unguarded situation exposed; she has bound us in commercial manacles, and very nearly defeated the object of our independence."[13]

There was one major objection to commercial discrimination left: that it would greatly reduce the volume of commerce and therefore the amount of government revenue. Madison could not counter this charge. For the foreseeable future commercial discrimination would mean less revenue for the government. Madison repeated that he valued public credit. Nevertheless, in May 1789 as debate about commercial discrimination was winding down, he could only respond to concerns about lost revenue by stating that the benefits of discrimination far outweighed the drawbacks. The policy was crucial, and so if discrimination "reduces the revenue, it is a good object so far as the reduction goes. . . ."[14]

Madison failed. He explained bitterly to his father on July 5, 1789, that the House of Representatives had voted down discrimination. Angrily he informed his father that "G. Britain is in fact put on the same footing with the most favored nation, altho' she has shown no disposition to treat with the U. States, and will probably be confirmed by such a measure in the belief, that America, even if under a united government, would be unable to unite her counsels on this subject." Yet Madison could not have been too surprised. A great many in Congress worried about the loss of revenue that commercial discrimination would bring. Opponents of the policy, such as the highly influential Philadelphia merchant, financier, and future U.S. Senator William Bingham, a close friend of Hamilton's, had written directly to Madison informing him of their opposition. Bingham had argued that the United States would have to submit to a great many things "in order to regain the credit we have lost." For Bingham (and for Hamilton) nothing mattered more than the ability to borrow. Public credit was the foundation for everything else, for independence, for republican institutions, for "durable liberty." Thus Bingham was explicit regarding his opposition to commercial discrimination, explaining to Madison that his "principal objection arises from the injurious tendency it will have on public credit, whose support claim so devoted an attachment, on the part of the United States."[15]

HAMILTON LOOKS TO BRITAIN

Hamilton had said almost nothing publicly during the discrimination debate. But privately he had already begun his series of lengthy and thoughtful conversations with George Beckwith, a major in the British army and an aide to the Governor-General of Canada. Beckwith had come directly from London to New York City, the temporary national capital, to warn against the commercial retaliation Madison called for.[16] Madison was profoundly frustrated by the "deep hold the British monopoly had taken on our country" and by the "difficulty experienced by France and Holland in entering into competition." The Dutch had long been a republic. With the storming of the Bastille in July 1789, the French appeared poised to build a much freer political society. Madison believed that given this exciting prospect, "the market of France was particularly desirable to us." But in his talks with Beckwith, Hamilton rejected this position. In a conversation of October 1789, he stated that he wanted close and peaceful cooperation between Britain and the United States. He told Beckwith that the prospects for such cooperation had improved now that the people had ratified the Constitution. Unlike the Articles of Confederation, the Constitution had "established a government upon principles that in my opinion render it safe for any nation to enter into treaties with us, either commercial or political."

As usual, Hamilton was quite open and honest about what he wanted and hoped to accomplish. He informed the British agent, "I have always preferred a connection with you, to that of any other country. *We think in English*, and have a similarity of prejudices, and of predilections." Hamilton knew as well as anybody how valuable French assistance had been during the American Revolution. He also understood that many were growing excited about the possibilities of a revolutionary transformation of French government and society. But Hamilton had no doubt that Britain had far more to offer as a commercial partner, and thus was a far greater potential source of revenue. To Hamilton the choice was obvious, and he told Beckwith, "[A]lthough France has been indulgent to us in certain points, yet what she can furnish, is by no means so essential or so suited to us as your productions, nor do our raw materials suit her so well as they do you."

In their conversation, Hamilton admitted that his hope for a much closer relationship with Britain was unpopular. The hostility of much of the public mattered, for even the wisest and best ordered "government of a country cannot altogether change either the taste or the disposition of a people." Yet he was confident the Washington Administration's policy was "to form a commercial treaty with you to every extent, to which you may think it for your interest to go." All future prospects, Hamilton believed, demanded such a treaty. He admitted to Beckwith that when he considered "the rapid increase of this country, its extent, taste, and disposition, I do think a treaty of commerce might be formed upon terms advantageous to both countries; for unless this can be done, I know very well nothing of this nature can be affected." Therefore, Hamilton suggested that Britain moderate the commercial policies that had so angered Madison. He advised that Britain allow U.S. access to the West Indies "under certain limitations of size of vessels, so as merely to enable us to carry our produce there, and to bring from thence the productions of those Islands to our own ports."[17]

A treaty allowing limited access to the British West Indies would not challenge British commercial or naval supremacy. It would keep American commerce oriented toward Britain and away from France. Maintaining a close connection with Britain while keeping a peaceful but distant connection to France was necessary, for Hamilton feared that licentiousness could return to the United States. He worried that France could become a major source of instability if the challenge to royal authority, begun that summer, flared out of control.

In the same month that he conversed with Beckwith, Hamilton wrote to his old comrade in arms, the Marquis de Lafayette. The most radical phase of the French Revolution was still a few years away, but Hamilton had grave concerns about the effect the French could have on world politics. Hamilton explained to Lafayette that he welcomed resistance to tyrannical governments. He considered himself "a friend to mankind and to liberty." As a friend of liberty, Hamilton told Lafayette, "I rejoice in the efforts which you are making to establish it. . . ." Yet only three months after the storming of the Bastille, Hamilton had begun to doubt that the changes the French were seeking would lead to "durable liberty." He regretfully explained to Lafayette, "I fear much for the final success of the attempts, for the fate of those I esteem who are engaged in it, and for the danger in case of success of innovations greater than will consist with the real felicity of your nation." Already, Hamilton believed he could detect a growing licentiousness among the French, a portent of likely future violence and anarchy. To Lafayette he admitted, "I dread disagreements among those who are now united . . . about the nature of your constitution; I dread the vehement character of your people, whom I fear . . . [you] may find it more easy to bring on than to keep within proper bounds, after you have put them in motion."[18]

France reminded Hamilton far too much of George Clinton's New York. Britain, not France, was the safer partner. Hamilton assured Beckwith that in his view the United States was "connected with you, by strong ties of commercial, perhaps of political friendships." Hamilton even imagined a future military alliance suggesting that "our naval exertions in future wars, may in your scale be greatly important." Yet he had honestly admitted his sense of how most of his fellow citizens felt. He hastened to add that these views were "my opinions, they are the sentiments, which I have long entertained, on which I have acted, and I think them suited to the future welfare of both countries."

Despite Hamilton's assurances, Beckwith was quite concerned about the sentiments of the nation, particularly Madison's proposals. In responding, Beckwith was just as candid as Hamilton. He reminded Hamilton that the British government would have been furious about "the effect of your revenue bill, had it passed in the form in which it appeared in your prints, with those discriminating clauses, which undoubtedly were leveled at us." Beckwith was confused by the source of the proposal, admitting to Hamilton "that I was much surprised to find amongst the gentlemen who were so decidedly hostile to us in their public conduct the name of a man, from whose character for good sense, and other qualifications I should have been led to expect a very different conduct." Hamilton did all he could to reassure Beckwith, and in doing so revealed some of his views of his friend Madison. He did not pretend to misunderstand Beckwith and admitted readily, "you mean Mr. Madison from Virginia." Hamilton confessed that he had been "likewise rather surprised at it." But he advised Beckwith not to take Madison's enthusiasm too seriously. He greatly valued and respected Madison, Hamilton told the British agent, but the "truth is, that although this gentleman is a clever man, he is very little acquainted with the world. That he is uncorrupted and incorruptible I have not a doubt; he has the same end in view that I have . . . but [his] mode of attaining it is very different."

Hamilton was supremely confident that, as Secretary of the Treasury, President Washington would rely on him to shape commercial policy. And so Beckwith could take comfort, for Hamilton "was decidedly opposed to those discriminating clauses, that were so warmly advocated by some gentlemen." And Hamilton was not alone. Though a majority of the nation might very well have favored commercial discrimination, those whose views mattered most did not. Hamilton assured Beckwith that he had gone to a great deal of trouble "to obtain information from our mercantile [i.e., American merchants] here upon this subject, who with a few exceptions were against every species of distinction, upon the principle that it would be productive of a war of commerce."[19]

For Hamilton revenue and peaceful relations with Britain would bring order and "durable liberty." Hamilton was both excited and concerned about "the rapid increase of this country, its extent, taste, and disposition. . . ." Most citizens were anti-British and the United States was large and growing larger. A smaller republic had already been ungovernable during the 1780s, Hamilton believed. Citizens were not governed well because they were not connected to good government. A closer relationship with Britain would maximize revenue, and revenue would pay for a series of ambitious plans to finally bring good government and "durable liberty" to the nation and its unruly citizens.

WHAT TO DO ABOUT ALL THAT DEBT?

Hamilton could begin none of these plans unless he had the revenue to fund them, and so the time it had taken to prevent commercial discrimination had set him back some months. Having defeated commercial discrimination, and so having secured extensive revenue, Hamilton could now make the public debt the foundation of a sophisticated and complex financial system and program of economic development. He hoped this program would connect the nation's wealthy citizens to the national government, create powerful national institutions, and build a social order that would forever prevent the licentiousness of the 1780s.

In 1790 the debt of the United States and of the state governments, incurred by massive borrowing to fund the Revolutionary War, was $79 million. It is impossible to be precise in tracking the value of money over time, but that amount would be roughly equivalent to the impact of $7 trillion in the U.S. economy of the twenty-first century. The state governments owed $25 million and the national government owed the remaining $54 million. Of that $54 million the nation owed $13 million to foreign, mostly Dutch, creditors. Hamilton's plans depended on how ownership of the debt had changed since the Revolutionary War. When they went into debt, the states and the national government had borrowed from hundreds of thousands of citizens to purchase the goods and services necessary to fight the revolution. About $17 million was owed to soldiers who were given debt certificates as promises of future payment. Debt certificates had also been given to farmers, tailors, cobblers, blacksmiths, and other laborers, who helped feed, clothe, shoe, and arm the revolution. During the 1780s economic depression, the collapse of the value of paper currency, and declining revenue prevented citizens from being paid back, or even from receiving the interest they were owed. Yet they still had to pay their private debts and taxes during very difficult economic times.

Over the course of the 1780s, convinced they would never be paid back, many debt holders sold their debt certificates for gold and silver. Buyers, pointing to the risk they were taking that the debts might never be paid, purchased debt at far below the original value.[20] By 1790 a few thousand people owned most of the $66 million of domestic debt. In Pennsylvania in 1790 a mere 434 people owned debt certificates with a face value of $4.6 million, which would have the impact of around $423 billion in the U.S. economy of the twenty-first century.[21] The debt had become a difficult issue. Who should be reimbursed? And should any attention be paid to original holders who sold under duress? If Congress honored only its obligations to current holders, the government would be transferring a massive amount of public revenue to a small group of the wealthiest citizens.

Congress charged Secretary of the Treasury Hamilton to write a report proposing what to do about the debt. Hamilton had been surprised by commercial discrimination, so he reached out to Madison as he began to write what he would title his "Report Relative to a Provision for the Support of Public Credit." It is likely that Hamilton viewed the disagreement over commercial discrimination as a temporary strain on a valued friendship. Certainly almost everything Madison had said over the previous decade suggested that he understood the extreme urgency of establishing public credit, and so would be eager to help think through how to deal with the vast public debt. In his letter to Madison, Hamilton stressed that it was vitally "important that a plan as complete and as unexceptionable as possible should be matured by the next meeting of Congress." Conveying his warm feelings and high regard for Madison, Hamilton requested, "May I ask of your friendship to put to paper and send me your thoughts on such objects as may have occurred to you for an addition to our revenue, and also as to any modifications of the public debt which could be made consistent with good faith [for] the interests of the Public and its Creditors?"[22]

Madison's answer gave Hamilton little comfort. Concerning the "modification of the public debt," Madison viewed the $13 million owed to foreign creditors differently than he did the rest. He explained to Hamilton that he believed "the foreign part of the debt" should be fully funded and repaid by keeping all promised terms. The most important condition for public credit was to demonstrate to the foreign money markets that the new government was trustworthy and could be lent to safely. Like Jefferson, Madison believed public credit depended almost entirely on being able to borrow at reasonable rates in the foreign money markets. Therefore, Madison viewed the domestic debt quite differently than he did the foreign debt. Writing what could only cause Hamilton concern, Madison emphasized that the "domestic part is well known to be viewed in different lights by different classes of people." Given how extensively ownership of the debt had changed over the previous decade, there was a real possibility that soldiers and suppliers of the revolution might receive no compensation for their labors. Therefore, Madison suggested that it "might be a soothing circumstance to those least favorably disposed, if by some operation the debt could be lessened by purchase made on public account; and particularly if any impression could be made on it by means of the western lands."[23]

Madison's ideas for "soothing" policies were highly troubling to Hamilton. Madison was suggesting that there should be a distinction drawn between original and current debt holders—a policy he would soon call discrimination in the funds. It was highly likely that the value of the debt would rise to par now that the national government had the power to tax and Hamilton was seeking to fund the debt. With discrimination, Madison hoped to prevent the original holders from absorbing all of the loss, and the current holders from reaping all of the gain, if the debt regained its full value.

Also of concern to Hamilton was Madison's idea of placing a great deal of publicly owned western land on the market all at once, or perhaps of distributing the land to help compensate original holders. Doing so would drive the price of land down since supply would match demand. That fit well with Madison's desire for movement across space to recreate the third stage. It also fit well with his hope for a lawful and orderly, but also rapid, westward expansion. Madison reasoned that the "appetite" for western land was endless. If the appetite was "not regularly fed, it may produce licentious settlements, by which the value of the property will not only be lost, but the authority of the laws impaired."[24] If there was no lawful way to acquire the western lands, Madison feared that people would simply take them when they could not buy at reasonable prices. If the lands were affordable, settlers could move west as lawful citizens with land titles and a clear sense of connection to the national government that had made their landed independence possible.

Hamilton already believed the western Massachusetts of Daniel Shays was barely governable. What would happen to law and order and "durable liberty" if hundreds of thousands moved even farther west beyond the reach of national governance?

But if public lands were kept off the market, their price would remain high, making them excellent collateral for future loans. In addition, the citizenry would be kept in a much more manageable area for governance.

While he was writing his "Report," Hamilton received many suggestions that rejected Madison's ideas that consideration should be shown to original as well as current holders of the debt. In October 1789, the week before Madison's letter arrived, Boston merchant Stephen Higginson told Hamilton that "everything national should assume the appearance of system and stability." Higginson urged that the national government should take over responsibility for the $25 million owed by the state governments. "System and stability" required that the national government have the sole connection to the wealthy debt holders. Higginson knew his proposal would infuriate many. He told Hamilton that people who thought as he did had to plan for the outrage that would come if the national government took over the entire debt and paid only the current holders. Because the original holders had sold their debt claims so cheaply during the deeply economically depressed 1780s, "the great loss thereby sustained have soured a vast many people; and they will think it unjust in the extreme, to pay imposts, or any other taxes, for such a purpose." Most people, Higginson acknowledged, would "not think it right for those, who have bought [the debt certificates] at 2/ to 3/ in the pound [i.e., at ten to fifteen percent of the original value] to derive so great an income from them, and eventually to receive the full sum of the principal in specie."

Higginson realized that rewarding only the current holders would infuriate most citizens because they "would consider this, when done by any sort of taxes upon the public, as stripping the poor to increase the wealth and influence of the rich." That should not stop Hamilton. "System and stability," in other words "durable liberty," mattered most. And anger toward the rich was inevitable. "Rich men are in all countries and at all times," Higginson claimed, "objects of envy with the common people." But even Higginson had some hesitations in this case, since he knew the situation of the revolutionary debt was particularly galling. Typical envy would be greatly intensified since so many citizens would think that the wealthy were the only beneficiaries of his proposal, and "that the poor are depressed to increase their wealth." Despite recommending his ideas to Hamilton, Higginson warned that everything that "tends rapidly to transfer [wealth] from the poor to the rich will naturally excite irritation, and there cannot be a case imagined, in which such a transfer would be more apprehended, and the passions of the people more highly excited."[25]

Higginson had eloquently stated the dilemma. The changed ownership of the debt offered a huge opportunity. Funding it would connect the wealthy to the national government and provide the foundation for the social order that Hamilton believed the United States desperately needed. Yet the vast majority would likely be outraged if only current holders were repaid. Higginson recommended limiting how much current owners would be rewarded. But only the current holders could be the government's concern. Before anything else, the new government had to reestablish its ability to borrow and so "[j]ustice must eventually be done to the public creditors." Due to the free decision to enter into private sale and purchase of the debt certificates, the current debt holders were the only citizens to whom the government had a contractual obligation, and "the faith of Government must be preserved, as far as possible, and the public credit restored."[26]

Yet as Higginson contemplated the certain furious reaction to his proposals, he blanched and suggested his own version of a soothing policy. He advised Hamilton to reduce the interest on the public debt to two or perhaps three percent. Higginson was suggesting a minor qualification. In general, federal debt bore an interest rate of six percent. Of course six percent of nothing was nothing. Higginson was proposing that those who had purchased debt at between ten and twenty percent of its full value, should now receive two to three percent of the full value in annual interest payments of gold and silver, and eventually be repaid the full face value in gold and silver as well. Under Higginson's proposal, the original holders would receive nothing. There was only so much he felt could be done in the way of Madison's "soothing." The price of "durable liberty" was high.

Not surprisingly, William Bingham agreed with Stephen Higginson. As early as November 1789 he had written to Hamilton that public credit depended on providing full compensation to the current holders. For Bingham public credit was the most important priority. The new government had to secure the support and confidence of the public creditors immediately, "especially, as they will constitute an essential part of the monied interest of the country to whom government will often be compelled to have recourse. . . ."[27] Bingham argued that the ownership of the debt provided an opportunity to create a lasting connection between the national government and "the monied interest," the most prominent citizens in the nation. Indeed, the way the debt had changed hands was a welcome opportunity. Since ownership of the debt was so highly concentrated, if the government funded the debt it could forge a close connection with the wealthy men who Hamilton considered the most reliable to lead the Republic.[28]

THE REPORT ON PUBLIC CREDIT

When Hamilton delivered the "Report on Public Credit" to Congress on January 9, 1790, he fully endorsed the Higginson–Bingham position. His "Report" made it clear that he rejected Madison's and Jefferson's view that public credit was primarily a matter of being able to borrow in the foreign money markets. For Hamilton, public credit was meant to connect the national government to the right sorts of citizens, and so servicing the domestic debt was at least as important as fulfilling obligations to foreign creditors. Public credit, Hamilton argued in the "Report," had to be established.[29] To do so, Hamilton insisted, the government had to honor its pledge to those who currently owned its debt; there could be no discrimination between original and current holders. He explained to Congress that public credit depended on "a punctual performance of contracts." The United States would be able to borrow only if the wealthiest citizens received the same treatment they expected in their most reliable business dealings. Because those who owned the debt were now in general wealthy and "enlightened men," in exchange for this fair dealing they would look to the nation's best interest and accept modifications of the terms of the contracts. They would agree to the changes because modifying the terms of the debt contracts would further the public good.[30] Hamilton then proposed honoring the claims of only the current debt holders while reducing the interest rate from six percent to about four percent (higher than Higginson had suggested).

Next in the "Report" Hamilton explained how funding the debt without discrimination would allow him to establish two of the three priorities—public credit and a circulating medium—that, along with a national bank, he had described for Robert Morris back in 1780. If the government honored its contracts to its debt holders and fully funded the debt without discrimination, then the debt certificates would rise in value and trade at par. Once the debt certificates reliably generated regular interest payments, they would be in such demand that people could exchange them for goods and services. Funding the debt properly, then, would attach the government to its creditors, "the most enlightened friends of good government." The confidence of these "enlightened friends," and the rising value of the debt, would provide the extensive circulating medium because "in countries in which the national debt is properly funded, and an object of established confidence, it answers most of the purposes of money. Transfers of stock or public debt are there equivalent to payments in specie. . . ."[31]

Hamilton did not spell out another outcome. The funded debt would also dominate the nation's money supply. There was very little specie, the new Constitution prohibited the state governments from issuing money, and the new national government would not be providing any paper currency (the national government did not issue its own paper currency until the Civil War). Given who owned the debt, future projects of economic development and other investment opportunities, as with the money supply, would very likely be controlled by a small group of the wealthiest citizens. But the very way in which they had access to money, by owning funded public debt, would connect them to the national government and would commit them to involvement in public issues and obligations.

Hamilton next turned to specifics for funding the debt. He agreed with Jefferson and Madison about the debt owed to foreigners. But discrimination between current and original holders would violate the security of contract, the protection of private property, and the rights of the current debt holders. Hamilton understood and even sympathized with the desire for discrimination. Discrimination's defenders could not simply be dismissed when they insisted "that it would be unreasonable to pay twenty shillings in the pound [the British pound contained twenty shillings] to one who had not given more for it than three or four." And Hamilton understood that it was painful "to aggravate the misfortune of the first owner, who, probably through necessity, parted with his property at so great a loss, by obliging him [now] to contribute to the profit of the person, who had speculated on his distress."

But discrimination was not the best policy for the nation. In fact, it was "unjust and impolitic, [and] ruinous to public credit." Discrimination "was a breach of contract; in violation of the rights of the fair purchaser." Current and original holders had freely bargained, and had agreed to purchase and sell private property. Private property was only as safe as the contracts that determined its possession and sale, Hamilton argued. Many original holders had entered into contracts they now regretted. But that was not the fault of the current holders because "[w]hatever necessity the seller may have been under, was occasioned by the government, in not making a proper provision for its debts. The buyer had no agency in it, and therefore ought not to suffer."[32] Failure to protect property and contract rights would also undermine the value of the debt and prevent it from functioning as a reliable circulating medium, wrote Hamilton. Discrimination would undermine "the stock of the nation, which is essential to its capacity for answering the purposes of money—that is the *security* of *transfer.* . . ."[33]

Hamilton's final argument against discrimination was that it violated the new Constitution, which required the new government to honor all the debts and obligations of the Articles of Confederation government. In this case the obligation was to honor the promises of repayment the Confederation Congress had made to debt holders, not to those who had chosen to sell their debt certificates to others. The Constitution and the new government would be fatally exposed as useless right at the start if Congress was unable to honor its obligations and protect the rights of property and contract. Though "the case of those, who parted with securities from necessity, is a hard one," wrote Hamilton, discrimination was immoral, illegal, unconstitutional, fatal to pubic credit, and disastrous for the future of the nation.[34]

Hamilton knew his position would infuriate many. Never one to avoid a conflict he considered necessary, he next raised an even more controversial issue. In addition to supporting funding without discrimination, Hamilton accepted the suggestion of Stephen Higginson and explained that "after mature reflection on this point, [there must be] an assumption of the debts of the particular states by the union, and a like provision for them, as for those of the union. . . ." Assumption meant that the national government would take over responsibility for the $25 million owed by the state governments, and fully fund it at face value along with the $41 million the national government owed to its domestic creditors. The debt of the states had also changed hands in much the same way as the national debt. Even more infuriating to people like Jefferson and Madison, Assumption was so unexpected that at first there had been less speculation in the state debts. Hamilton's call for Assumption led to new speculation. News of the "Report" circulated first in Philadelphia and New York, where newspapers printed some of the details. Many wealthy speculators rushed to rural communities, particularly in the south, where they bought as much state debt from the original holders as cheaply as they could, before news of Hamilton's support for Assumption had reached those areas.[35]

For Hamilton, assuming the state debts was as crucial as funding the national debt. Assumption would separate holders of state debts from the state governments and connect them much more closely to the national government. Funding with Assumption would create the stable partnership between a strong national government and the most prominent and wealthy citizens, which Hamilton believed was necessary for "durable liberty." With Assumption, all the debt holders would "receive their dues from one source." As a result, the wealthy citizens who had purchased the various public debts would develop "the same interests" and would "unite in the support of the fiscal arrangements of the government."[36]

To Hamilton Funding and Assumption without discrimination, and all that would follow from it, was the only way to lay the foundation for "durable liberty." As he closed the "Report" he hammered home the claim that his proposals alone could provide "the firm establishment of public credit." And being able to borrow was all that stood between protecting and losing independence and liberty. Resisting Madison's call for discrimination would establish "the character, security, and prosperity of the nation." Funding and Assumption would also prove the value of the Constitution and the new national government to "the enlightened class of citizens, zealously devoted to good government." Given these tremendous benefits, Hamilton hoped that his "plan . . . will experience the cheerful and prompt acquiescence of the community."[37]

* * *

By the end of January 1790 the new government had existed for only one year. Yet already Jefferson and Madison had perceived how great their disagreements were with Hamilton. Hamilton was also becoming aware of the differences, though his awareness was developing more slowly. As he sent the "Report on Public Credit" to Congress, he had no idea of just how swift and angry the response would be.

NOTES

1   *PAH* 5: 370–371.
2   *Republic of Letters* 1: 536.
3   *Republic of Letters* 1: 536.
4   *Republic of Letters* 1: 568.
5   *PJM* 12: 65.
6   *PJM* 12: 71–72.
7   *PTJ* 16: 600.
8   *PJM* 12: 100.
9   *PJM* 12: 99.
10 *PJM* 12: 110–112.
11 *PJM* 12: 112, 218.
12 *Republic of Letters* 1: 618–620, emphasis original.
13 *PJM* 12: 125–126.
14 *PJM* 12: 111, 163–164.
15 *PJM* 12: 108, 230.
16 Stanley Elkins and Eric McKitrick, *The Age of Federalism: The Early American Republic, 1788–1800* (New York: Oxford University Press, 1993), 124.
17 *PAH* 5: 483–484, emphasis original.
18 *PAH* 5: 425.
19 *PAH* 5: 488–489.
20 E. James Ferguson, *The Power of the Purse: A History of American Public Finance, 1776–1790* (Chapel Hill: University of North Carolina Press, 1961), 252–253.

21 Terry Bouton, "A Road Closed: Rural Insurgency in Post-Independence Pennsylvania," *Journal of American History* 87 (2000): 855–887, 863.
22 *PJM* 12: 435–436.
23 *PJM* 12: 450–451.
24 *PJM* 12: 450–451.
25 *PAH* 5: 466, 510.
26 *PAH* 5: 510–511.
27 *PAH* 5: 540–541.
28 *PAH* 5: 545–546.
29 Jacob E. Cooke, ed., *The Reports of Alexander Hamilton* (New York: Harper and Row, 1964), 2, emphasis original.
30 *Reports of Alexander Hamilton*, 3.
31 *Reports of Alexander Hamilton*, 4–5.
32 *Reports of Alexander Hamilton*, 7–8.
33 *Reports of Alexander Hamilton*, 10, emphasis original.
34 *Reports of Alexander Hamilton*, 9, 11.
35 Whitney K. Bates, "Northern Speculators and Southern State Debts: 1790," *William and Mary Quarterly* 19 (1962): 30–48.
36 *Reports of Alexander Hamilton*, 14.
37 *Reports of Alexander Hamilton*, 39–40.

5

CONFLICT: FUNDING, ASSUMPTION, AND THE NATIONAL CAPITAL

HAMILTON DID NOT GET "cheerful and prompt acquiescence." After reading the "Report on Public Credit," Madison decided to lead the opposition to Funding without discrimination and to Assumption under any conditions. To him the "Report" looked like a calculated scheme to enrich wealthy speculators at the expense of the poorer citizens who had sacrificed for the revolution. He explained with disgust to Jefferson that because of the proposal for Assumption "emissaries are still exploring the interior and distant parts of the union in order to take advantage of the ignorance of the holders."[1] In reacting to the report, and to Hamilton's opposition to foreign policy proposals that challenged Britain, Jefferson and Madison came to understand just how wide the gulf was between their values and Hamilton's. By the end of 1790, where this chapter concludes, the three men had a much clearer sense of the ground on which they operated, how extensively they disagreed, and just how much was at stake concerning the increasingly angry argument they were having.

THE BATTLE FOR DISCRIMINATION IN THE PUBLIC DEBT

One month after the "Report" came to Congress Madison launched his attack, first on the argument that there should be no discrimination between the original and current holders of the national debt. On February 11, 1790, Madison took to the floor of the House of Representatives. The House had been debating the "Report" for the past three days. Madison urged his fellow representatives to "consider, first, by whom the debt was contracted, and then let us consider . . . to whom it is due." Public credit was essential, but establishing it did not require forsaking the original holders or rejecting "a just and equitable decision."[2] All agreed, Madison reminded the House, that the foreign debt should be fully paid. Doing so, he insisted, would solidify the nation's credit where it truly mattered, the European money markets. But with regard to the domestic debt, there had to be discrimination among current and original holders. Madison insisted that Congress faced a great moral question. Would American citizens be paid for the goods and services they had provided the revolution? Discrimination would preserve the independence of tens of thousands of citizens now falling into poverty. Madison implored his fellow representatives to think about the plight of the original holders, and especially about "the suffering of the military part of the creditors," which should "never be forgotten, while sympathy is an American virtue."[3]

Having played on emotions, Madison next got practical and outlined his plan for discrimination between the original and current debt holders. The plan was based on his estimation that the market value of the debt had already risen by as much as fifty percent above the price at which current holders had bought. Thus current holders would make a substantial profit. Yet the value of the debt would soon rise far higher, almost certainly to par. Madison proposed that the amount the value of the debt rose above the point where it was when the debate about commercial discrimination began should go to the original holders. Madison's plan would have worked like this, using his estimate of a fifty percent rise. Say a current holder had purchased a debt certificate worth $100 at ten percent of its original value, or for $10. Now that certificate was worth $15. Madison proposed that the current holder should receive $15 and the original holder should receive the rest of the value as the certificate continued to rise toward par. If it reached par the original holder would receive $85. Thus the current holder would make a $5 profit on his investment. The original holder, who had parted with $100 of his goods and services in the first place, would ultimately end up with a $5 loss rather than the $90 loss he would have under Hamilton's plan. With this proposal, Madison explained, the "original sufferers will not be fully indemnified; but they will receive from their country, a tribute to their merits, which, if it does not entirely heal their wounds, will assuage the pain of them."[4]

Madison's break with Hamilton over how to fund the debt was now in open view. A few days later he wrote to Jefferson that the debate in the House over the "Report of Mr. Hamilton" was growing intense and that progress, if any, was slow. There was still unanimity about funding the current holders of the foreign debt, but great conflict over what to do about "the domestic." Madison was growing concerned the majority would not support his plan that "the highest market price only should be allowed to the purchasers, and the balance be applied to solace the original suffers, whose claims were not in conscience extinguished by a *forced* payment in *depreciated* certificates." Speaker after speaker was claiming it would be impossible to discover and disentangle who had bought and sold what. Madison doubted that concern was the real reason for the opposition. He informed Jefferson, "I am aware of the difficulties of the plan, but believe they might be removed by one half the exertion that will be used to collect and color them."[5]

As the extent of the opposition to his plan became clear, Madison grew angrier. Congress was planning to provide a windfall to current holders while refusing to take on the challenging task of finding justice for the original holders. Congress's values were backward, for "America ought to erect the monuments of her gratitude [to] those who saved her liberties, [not] to those who had enriched themselves in her funds." Madison pleaded with his fellow Congressmen to consider what had happened when the original holders, facing desperate circumstances, had sold their debt certificates at bargain-basement prices. In a passionate speech to the House, he reminded his colleagues that the revolution had relied on the labor, much of it death-defying, of hard-working men and women, labor worth tens of millions of dollars. Americans should have been paid immediately in gold and silver, but "a piece of paper only was substituted." Even at the time, the paper was worth a fraction of the value of the services provided. Beyond that, the original receivers of debt certificates had rarely had a choice. The government had seized their property for the sake of the revolution and offered only the certificates in return. Any fair person had to admit that the "relation of the individual to the government, and circumstances of the offer, rendered the acceptance a forced, not a free one." Indeed, Madison reminded his colleagues, there were "even cases where the consent cannot be pretended; where the property of the planter or farmer has been taken at the point of the bayonet and a certificate presented in the same manner." These were the people, who had never received fair value for the enormous service they had done, who would be ignored by Hamilton's plan. Supporting discrimination was a moral act for "the loss to the original holders has been immense. The injustice which has taken place has been enormous and flagrant, and makes redress a great national object."[6]

But it was not just a moral question. Madison argued that Hamilton's plan would concentrate too much wealth. It would reward the exploitation of the poor by the rich, behavior regrettably typical in monarchies and fatal for republics. He reminded the House that wealthy and better informed citizens had rushed to purchase depreciated debt certificates after learning earliest that they would soon rise in value. Many of those taken advantage of, Madison insisted, "were poor and uninformed." Doing justice by them would strengthen, not weaken, the United States. And it would not jeopardize public credit, as opponents of discrimination claimed. In fact, Madison countered, his plan was "perfectly consistent with the establishment of public credit."[7] And so it was, given the way Madison defined and understood public credit, as principally maintaining good relations with the foreign money markets and the investors who held the foreign portion of the debt.

In mid-February the debate grew truly bitter. Egbert Benson of New York, a close friend and longtime ally of Hamilton, asked Madison, "[S]uppose I had purchased a certificate of 100 dollars . . . of which when I go to fund, I find but half allowed me, the other 50 dollars are retained in the treasury for him." Madison did not hide his fury, even contempt, for the concern Benson showed to the current holders while appearing to feel no sympathy for the original holders. Angrily Madison responded,

"I would beg leave now, in turn to ask the gentleman a question: suppose he had been one of those who resorted to our army at the time it was disbanded, and he had found a soldier, one of that band, who had established the liberties of his country." An honorable man would have shaken the soldier's hand and offered whatever aid and comfort he could. But how should Benson think of himself, and others view him, Madison asked, if instead he

> had obtained, from the necessities of the soldier, the evidence of his claim, at a tenth of its value . . . [and] was now to have the interest with the principal, or even half the principal funded. I ask whether the delicacy of the gentleman would not be shocked at the reflection that this exorbitant accumulation of gain was made at the expense of the most meritorious part of the community, and whether his conscience would refuse a participation of it. . . .[8]

Hamilton and Jefferson said very little as the debate raged in Congress. It would not have been proper for them to take public stands. Both were members of President Washington's cabinet and he had not yet decided the position of the executive branch. But they had a dispute during the discrimination debate that helps to explain their thinking on the issue. In the spring of 1790 the national government settled accounts of back pay to soldiers in Virginia and North Carolina who had served in 1781 and 1782. The amount of money involved was tiny compared to the public debt, slightly over $40,000 owed to various officers and privates. The money was to be paid in specie. Charges quickly surfaced that some people had received advanced information of whose names were on the list and had bought up the paper promises at a fraction of their face value before the soldiers learned they would soon receive their full back pay in gold and silver. Now the current holders would receive the payments. Outraged members of Congress instructed Hamilton that in each case where full payment had not been received by "the original claimant," to make sure that the soldiers or their heirs were paid in full.[9]

Hamilton urged President Washington to refuse to support Congress's direction. He argued that the government had to place the right to be secure in private contracts above the other issues involved. If the government overturned the private sales of the payment promises, there would be no protection of the rights of property and contract. In his written opinion to Washington, Hamilton made an implicit comparison to the debate over discrimination. If the government overturned the private sales in this case, people would not have confidence that private contracts would protect them in the future. Such an action by the government was "an infraction of the rights of individuals, acquired under preexisting laws, and a contravention of public faith." Intervening would salve the consciences of many Congressmen. But if Congress overturned private contracts, then "the intercourses of business become uncertain, the security of property is lessened, the confidence in government is destroyed or weakened."[10] Hamilton's arguments in this case were precisely those being made by the opponents of discrimination.

Jefferson disagreed with Hamilton about what should happen with the soldiers' pay. At a deeper level, he disagreed about the best uses of government and public power. In responding to Hamilton, Jefferson argued that the sale of the promises of payment was not a contract but a fraud. Implicitly, Jefferson compared the sale to the methods by which many had very late in the day bought up state debt certificates. The list of which soldiers would be paid and how much, Jefferson wrote, "became known to certain persons before the soldiers themselves had information of it, and those persons, by unfair means, as is said, and for very inadequate considerations [i.e., at cheap prices] obtained assignments [the paper payment promises] from many of the soldiers." What did a republican government exist for if not to prevent just this sort of injustice, wondered Jefferson? Intervening would not be violating the rights of property and contract. Instead the government would "be doing in this case what every individual, I think, would feel himself bound to do." A republican government should "give the advantage to the party, who had suffered wrong, rather than to him who had committed it. It is not honorable to take a mere legal advantage when it happens to be contrary to justice."[11]

Jefferson won this minor skirmish. Washington decided to let stand the charge Congress had made to Hamilton. Most likely, he was swayed by the argument that the sales were fraudulent. But the issue was much too close to the ongoing argument over discrimination in the funds for Hamilton's comfort. What if Jefferson's notion that an abstract sense of justice could, at times, trump established laws began to influence views about how to fund the debt? But Hamilton quickly gave up the battle in hopes of winning the war. He chose not to dispute the claim that the case was a particular instance of fraud. He then relied on his congressional supporters to repeat the point he had made in his "Report": that the original holders of the public debt were victims of circumstance, not of fraudulent acts committed by the current holders. Yet it was clear to him how close Jefferson's ideas were to Madison's regarding discrimination in the funds.

ASSUMPTION AND THE DANGER OF A COURT

Hamilton's strategic retreat also made sense given where the debate had moved on Funding and Assumption. By the time Hamilton and Jefferson had their dispute, Madison had already lost the battle over discrimination between original and current holders of the $41 million of federal government debt owed to domestic creditors. Madison sadly reported to his father that his proposal had been voted down "less perhaps from a denial of the justice of the measure, than a supposition of its impracticability."[12] Yet Madison was still determined to defeat Assumption, or force some form of discrimination with the state debts, and Hamilton hoped to convince Jefferson to work with him to reconcile Madison to it. Hamilton backed away from his argument with Jefferson about the soldiers' claims to focus on the much bigger issue.

As the debates in Congress turned from Funding to Assumption, Madison argued that Assumption was far worse than Funding without discrimination.

Funding without discrimination would dangerously concentrate wealth in ways that were typical of monarchies and destructive of republics. But at least the relationship between the national government and its debt holders already existed. Assumption would obliterate relations between the state governments and debt holders and create an entirely new degree of much more centralized authority. The states were necessary counterweights to central authority, but Assumption would make them far too weak to fulfill that function. Because of Hamilton's proposals, Madison claimed to his fellow congressmen, those at the center of power in New York City and Philadelphia were already buying up much of the state debt "to such an amount as to make it probable that if they are provided for by us nearly the whole will follow."[13]

When expressing his concern about a concentration of financial and political power in a national capital, or any great city, what Madison feared was London, or, more specifically, what London represented. To Madison and Jefferson and those who shared their views, London was the location of all the intersecting concentrations of political, financial, social, and cultural power that allowed for rule by a few and the exploitation of the many. The institutions of monarchy produced funding systems, long-term debts, and seemingly endless warfare. But those institutions, they believed, required a culture of monarchy, an ethos of distant, aloof, arrogant, unaccountable power. Jefferson and Madison believed that this ethos, or culture, of monarchy depended on a physical location, an actual place that brought together in the same close space the small, overlapping group who possessed political authority, financial and economic power, social dominance, and cultural preeminence.

In 1790 the best example of such a place was London. Political theorists called such physical spaces that combined all these different sources of power and dominance a court. "Court" (the term came from a king's court) was both an abstract concept and a very real place where real people, who collectively possessed these different sources of power, came together to use it. Madison was becoming gravely concerned that Hamilton's policies were introducing to republican America the culture of monarchy, and that his policies were building an actual space for a very real court. The capital of the nation for now was New York City, though it would soon move to Philadelphia. Either location was dangerous. They were the two largest cities in the United States and many of the debt holders lived in them. Holders of state debt (by 1790 often many of the same people who owned the federal debt) would be drawn to the capital. The politically powerful and the economically dominant would be compressed together in a small, intimate place—rich soil in which to grow the culture of monarchy.

As the debate over Assumption continued in the spring of 1790, the fears of both Jefferson and Madison grew graver. Madison wrote to Jefferson that the House was evenly divided on Assumption even though the proposed vast "increase of the federal debt will . . . only prolong the evil. . . ." Jefferson wrote to his fellow Virginian Henry Lee, the father of Robert E. Lee, that the vote on Assumption would likely be very close. He had no doubt that the virtuous citizenry agreed with

These drawings of an impressive street in Philadelphia and the bustling Philadelphia wharf, both from the 1790s, look simple and peaceful to our modern eyes. To Thomas Jefferson they suggested a dangerous concentration of urban wealth and power that he associated with the monarchical court. The Bank of the United States Hamilton created is the impressive white-columned building to the right in the drawing.

him on the issue. He hoped that "the voice of the nation will perhaps be heard."
Yet that might not be enough given how vocal the defenders of Hamilton's plan
were. "Unluckily," he lamented to Lee, "it is one of those cases where the noise will
be all on one side, and therefore likely to induce a false opinion of the real wish of
the public."[14]

Yet by late spring Congress was so evenly divided that Hamilton began to fear he
would lose on Assumption. Losing Assumption would largely undermine his overall
plan for creating the proper relations between the "enlightened" "monied interest"
and the new national government. While the actual negotiations and agreements are
murky, since they were mostly arranged in private conversations, the evidence suggests that Hamilton and his supporters decided to offer a deal. They would give up
the location of the capital in New York City or Philadelphia, or any urban area, in
exchange for Assumption.

Jefferson and Madison had long hoped to place the nation's capital far from any
place where a court and the culture of monarchy could develop. Also, being local
boosters, they hoped to bring the national capital to Virginia. But it was not just
local pride. They reasoned that placing the capital of the Republic in an isolated, rural
setting, far from stock markets, banks, and wealthy merchants and financiers, would
prevent the confluence of political, economic, social, and cultural power that produced the culture of monarchy. They, as well as President Washington, had longed
for a location on the Potomac River that is present-day Washington, D.C. In 1790 it
was the tiny rural village Georgetown, about as far from being Philadelphia or New
York as a place could be.

Preventing the creation of a court was as important to them as defeating
Assumption. Madison had made that clear since the beginning of the first Congress.
He had opposed the motion that "a permanent residence ought to be fixed for the
general government . . . at some convenient place . . . near the center of wealth, population, and extent of territory." In response Madison moved "to strike out the word
wealth." A seat of great wealth made sense for the capital of a monarchy, especially
to those who wished to preserve it. But in a republic, insisted Madison, government
was "intended for the accommodation of the citizens at large." If anything, republican government was best located far from any concentrations of wealth. Instead, said
Madison, "the government ought rather to move towards those, who are least able to
move toward it, and who stand in need of its protection."[15]

A rural location was the only place to house a republican government with
the values necessary to preserve the agricultural third stage. It had to be the isolated spot on the Potomac. Those writing to Madison during the debates about
Assumption and the capital's location reinforced this thinking. Fellow Virginian
Walter Jones described his concern about European monarchical behavior growing in New York and Philadelphia. He despised "the ruinous adoption of European
fashions . . . and . . . those impudent upstart pretentions to European ranks, which
some men affect." A rural location was "the greatest repository of republican

This scene of Washington's 1792 Inauguration in Philadelphia shows everything Jefferson hoped to escape by moving the nation's capital to a tiny rural village. He associated the dense urban bustle depicted here with London and the fourth stage. The three men in the middle of the painting are, from left to right , President George Washington, Vice President John Adams, and Secretary of State Thomas Jefferson.

principles." And Virginia was an ideal place for the capital, Jones insisted, due to "the absence of great towns, the equality of rights in the holders of the soil, [and] the close gradation in quantity possessed by a numerous race of landholders." Henry Lee agreed, writing to Madison, "Change the seat of government to the territorial center . . . and the abolition of gambling systems of finance might and would effect a material change."

Virginia had an additional advantage, Walter Jones believed, that made republican government safer there: "the existence of slavery.... When I mention slavery... of the securities of our liberty." Jones did not elaborate on how slavery helped to secure liberty being "much in haste."[16] But his brief remark suggests that he understood the complex relationship between white men not needing to exploit each other because they could so completely exploit black men and women. The conditions that made Virginia ideal for Jones's republic were entirely entangled with slavery, something Jones understood. His remark showed how complex and compromised the understanding of liberty was as Congress debated where to place the nation's capital.

As the debates about Assumption and the capital's location proceeded simultaneously, Hamilton saw an opportunity. He was also growing desperate. On April 13th Madison reported to Edmund Pendleton, an elder statesman of Virginian politics and a revolutionary leader, that assumption had been defeated in the House 31 to 29. Though that should have been that, Madison believed; "[I]t seems however that it has yet to be abandoned." Madison explained to Pendleton that Hamilton's supporters were playing a bold but dangerous game. Though they could certainly get Funding without discrimination, but not Assumption, the "other part of the Secretary's Report has been studiously fastened to the Assumption by the friends of the latter. . . ."[17]

This tactic was, to be anachronistic, the nuclear option. Supporters of Assumption were saying there could only be Funding if there was also Assumption. Of course Madison would have been happy to see Funding without discrimination go away, but there were plenty of Congressmen who did not want to lose Funding without discrimination, but who also opposed Assumption. And the supporters of Assumption were threatening to vote down the entire "Report" if they could not get Assumption. Doing that would mean not repaying the foreign creditors. The nuclear option would threaten even the more limited conception of public credit that Jefferson and Madison wanted.

The strategy caused great anxiety for Stephen Higginson, the Boston merchant. As soon as he heard about it he wrote with concern to Hamilton that "the idea demands a very careful and cool attention before it be practiced upon." Higginson worried that the tactic could backfire and that perhaps the entire package of Funding and Assumption would be voted down. That would be disastrous he warned, for if "the whole body of public creditors remain without any provision, an irritation much more general and violent may be apprehended." Higginson could endorse the risky plan, but only if it worked. He insisted to Hamilton that the "prospect of success should be very clear, before such a measure be taken. If gent[leme]n can be assured of this, it may be well to attempt it."[18]

A DEAL FOR A CAPITAL

Higginson had written on May 20, 1790. In the next few weeks how Jefferson and Madison discussed Assumption and the capital's future location began to change dramatically. They discussed the two issues together and began to hint that they were connected. On June 1st Madison wrote to James Monroe, his fellow Virginian and, like Madison, a future President of the United States, that Assumption had been revived, though it was still unlikely to pass.[19] Two days before Madison wrote to Monroe, Jefferson sent a somewhat more revealing letter to his son-in-law, Thomas Mann Randolph Jr. Jefferson reported that a motion had narrowly failed in the Senate to move the capital to Philadelphia, and that Assumption was again being considered in both Houses. The capital location and Assumption were being discussed simultaneously and this time Assumption "with some modifications . . . may yet prevail."[20]

In June Jefferson began to give more specifics about the issue of the capital's location. In a letter to fellow Virginian and Revolutionary War hero George Mason, written in mid-month, Jefferson was confident that Philadelphia would become the temporary capital, which would then move permanently to Georgetown. He then discussed Assumption, which he still considered unlikely to pass. But it was making sense to Jefferson to discuss the two issues together, and it was becoming clearer that they would likely be linked.[21] Two weeks later, on June 27th, Jefferson revealed even more in a letter to George Gilmer, a highly respected Virginia physician. He explained that negotiations were taking place to pass Assumption and "that perhaps this might bring about so much good humor as to induce [Congress] to give the temporary seat of government to Philadelphia, and then to Georgetown permanently."[22] In that same week Madison wrote again to Edmund Pendleton, and this time spoke about Assumption with a tone that was subtlety different from his past remarks. He informed Pendleton that the "affair of the state debts has been a great source of delay and embarrassment," one that he felt should be resolved. In fact he worried that the Congressional session would end most unhappily "unless some scheme of accommodation should be devised."[23]

Meanwhile, on July 4th, Jefferson wrote to another relative, his brother-in-law Francis Eppes. He explained that two "interesting questions" had dominated Congressional debate, the future location of the capital and the fate of Assumption. He was delighted to tell Eppes that the location had been resolved. The capital would move from New York to Philadelphia until 1800, and then would relocate permanently to Georgetown! While the fate of Assumption was still undecided, Jefferson now believed that it could not "be totally rejected without preventing the funding of the public debt altogether, which would be tantamount to a dissolution of the government." One week later, in a letter to James Monroe, Jefferson made the connection even more clearly between his preferred outcome for the capital's location and the improved prospects for Assumption. With the capital relatively soon to be safely in Georgetown, he predicted that "Congress will now probably proceed in better humor to funding the public debt." Jefferson reminded Monroe that once Congress adopted the measures that had been so controversial it would "secure to us the credit we now hold at Amsterdam." Public credit was invaluable, Jefferson insisted to Monroe; "[O]ur business is to have great credit and to use it little. Whatever enables us to go to war, secures our peace."[24]

Two weeks later Madison also wrote to Monroe, and now it was clear that relocating the capital had cleared the way for the full implementation of Hamilton's financial plan. Madison reported that despite the bitter arguments of the summer, Assumption would almost certainly pass "as part of a general plan for the public debt." It was now part of the bill coming from the Senate and there was a small majority for it in the House. A few days later Madison wrote to his father that Assumption had passed both houses; Hamilton's full program would now become law.[25] Madison had not voted for Assumption, but in the final weeks of the debate he had said almost nothing to oppose it. The nuclear option appeared to have worked; he was genuinely concerned that supporters of Assumption would risk all public credit as the price for denying Assumption. But in a decade the capital would be in Virginia and a deal seems to have been struck—the change of location for Assumption—which made it much easier to give in to the nuclear option.

The strongest evidence for the bargain likely came two years later (establishing the precise date of the document is impossible) when Jefferson wrote an account of a private dinner he hosted for Hamilton and Madison in the final weeks of the capital location and Assumption debates. Hamilton and Madison left no records of the dinner, which is unfortunate. Jefferson described remembering that one day he had been on his way to visit President Washington during the weeks when it seemed certain Assumption would fail. On his way "I met Hamilton as I approached the door." Jefferson could see that Hamilton was deeply worried, his "look was somber, haggard, and dejected beyond description. Even his dress uncouth and neglected." According to Jefferson, Hamilton spoke heatedly about the importance of Assumption and "the necessity of it to the general fiscal arrangement and its indispensable necessity towards a preservation of the union." Taking pity on him, Jefferson invited Hamilton and Madison to dinner the next day for "a friendly discussion of the subject." At the dinner, Jefferson remembered, Madison agreed that Assumption should again be brought up for consideration in the House of Representatives, and "though he would not vote for it, nor entirely withdraw his opposition, yet he should not be strenuous, but leave it to its fate." During that conversation, the possibility of a bargain emerged. Jefferson recalled that it "was observed, I forget by which of them, that as the bill would be a bitter one to the southern states, something should be done to soothe them; that the removal of the seat of government to the Potomac was a just measure, and would probably be a popular one with them, and would be a proper one to follow the assumption."[26]

In the event, the capital location had been decided first. And Madison could not probably have made enough House votes switch by himself. But the promise of the capital and the fear for all public credit probably carried the day. Jefferson and Madison reasoned that even Assumption and funding without discrimination could do little harm if there was no court or an American version of London. In rural Virginia there would be a proper conception and use of public credit, "to have great credit and use it little." In the Virginia countryside statesmen would borrow infrequently and primarily from the European money markets. They would not permanently transfer tax revenue in the form of interest payments to the wealthiest Americans.

HAMILTON TRIUMPHANT?

Jefferson and Madison could look forward to their isolated, rural capital, but Hamilton now had his financial program. He moved swiftly to spell out the implications. He had very different plans than did Jefferson and Madison for public credit and the newly funded and consolidated public debt. For Hamilton one of the most crucial features of the way the nation had established public credit was that it created the close connection between the small group of wealthy debt holders and the

national government. On September 1st he issued a public address to the public creditors emphasizing how valuable their debt holdings now were. They could look forward to a long and productive partnership with the national government. Hamilton
explained that Congress was promising interest payments of four percent in gold and
silver. He could guarantee that the value of the debt would now rise to par. All debt-
holders should hold onto their certificates, which would soon become immensely
more valuable than the price they had paid for them. The same thing would happen
with the state debt certificates now that Congress had enacted Assumption.[27]

Hamilton's deep relief and joy at the outcome were obvious in his public address.
Perhaps those emotions caused him to overplay his strong hand. The address was not
so much a reassurance as a victory lap. It was probably not solely responsible for the
quick response, but it likely did not help. Five weeks later Hamilton wrote a worried
letter to his fellow New Yorker John Jay, the third collaborator, along with Madison,
on the *Federalist Papers*. He enclosed copies of two resolutions passed by the Virginia
House of Representatives. The resolution of November 3rd read:

> That so much of the act of Congress, entitled "an act making provision
> for the debt of the United States" is repugnant to the Constitution of the
> United States, as it goes to the exercise of a power not expressly granted to the
> general government.

The Virginia Legislature followed it with a second resolution of November 5th
that stated:

> That so much of the act . . . limits the right of the United Sates in their re-
> demption of the public debt, is dangerous to the rights and subservient of
> the interest of the people, and demands the marked disapprobation of the
> General Assembly.

To Hamilton, the resolutions were outrageous and confirmed what he had long
believed. Only an authoritative, consolidated, centralized authority could prevent
liberty from degenerating into licentiousness, and so provide "durable liberty." The
resolutions, he informed Jay, were "the first symptom which must either be killed or
will kill the Constitution of the United States. . . . The war is still going on."[28]

It was a war Hamilton had every intention of fighting. By the final months of 1790
he was speaking far more candidly to the English agent George Beckwith, and giving
opponents such as Madison far less benefit of the doubt. Order and "durable liberty"
in the United States were still very much in danger. His financial program was a first
step toward lessening that danger. So it was all important to keep close and affection-
ate relations with Britain. That nation was the source of most of the tax revenue for
Funding and Assumption. Only Britain offered an alternative example of stability to
revolutionary France and certain badly behaved states in America. Hamilton reas-
sured Beckwith that "between you and us there are other circumstances: originally

one people, we have a similarity of tastes, of language, and general manners." Now that his financial program was law, Britain did not have to worry about the friendship of the United States. The government had to fund its debt, and virtually all of the revenue needed to do it would come from taxes on British imports. The financial system guaranteed good relations between the United States and Britain. It also made excellent economic sense, Hamilton told Beckwith, since "you have a great commercial capital and an immense trade, we have comparatively no commercial capital, and are an agricultural people, but we are a rising country, shall be great consumers, have a preference for your manufactures, and are in the way of paying for them." All in all, Hamilton concluded, "I cannot foresee any solid grounds of national difference between us."

Yet dangerously, Hamilton explained to Beckwith, he was concerned that some might seek to provoke confrontation on unsolid grounds. Unfortunately, Hamilton lamented, though all reasonable people wanted a cooperative and friendly relationship with Britain, "[W]e have two parties with us; there are gentlemen, who think we ought to be connected with France in the most intimate terms." Hamilton was concerned that the present circumstances favored the position of the supporters of France, and that "they are zealous to improve it." He admitted to Beckwith that he believed the Republic's public affairs were now at a critical juncture. Britain had the respect and friendship of the Secretary of the Treasury, and so "the present therefore is the moment to take up the matter seriously and dispassionately, and I wish it done without loss of time."[29]

Hamilton would waste no time. Funding the debt, providing a circulating medium, and creating the close relationship between a powerful national government and the "enlightened" "monied interest" had accomplished only two of his three objectives. In the final pages of the "Report on Public Credit," though Jefferson and Madison never mentioned it, and might not have noticed it, Hamilton told them that more would soon come. He closed the report by stating the "Secretary contemplates the application of this money [the funded debt] through the medium of a national bank, for which, with the permission of the House, he will submit a plan. . . ."[30]

As Hamilton began to make use of his financial system, Jefferson and Madison concluded that getting the capital in a rural location, and at that only after ten years, would not prevent developments that terrified them. At the center of those developments was Hamilton's plan for a national bank. The best indication of Jefferson's mood, as he reacted to Hamilton's efforts in the months after the debt and the capital were settled, can be found by briefly returning to his account of his dinner with Hamilton and Madison. He closed his remembrance with bitter fury:

This is the real history of the assumption, about which many erroneous conjectures have been published. It was unjust, in itself oppressive to the states, and was acquiesced in merely from a fear of disunion, while our government was still in its most infant state. It enabled Hamilton so to strengthen himself by corrupt services to many, that he could afterwards carry his bank scheme, and every measure he proposed in defiance of all opposition, in fact it was a principal ground whereon was reared up the speculating phalanx, in and out of Congress, which has since been able to give laws and to change the political complexion of the government of the U.S.[31]

***

The conflict over Funding and Assumption profoundly divided Hamilton from Jefferson and Madison. Over the course of 1790 Hamilton had come to doubt that he could rely on the two Virginians, and they had come to believe that his plans for the Republic offered very little they could support. Over the next two years they would all conclude that the United States could survive as a republic only if the ideas they opposed were defeated and silenced forever.

NOTES

1 *PJM* 13: 4.
2 *PJM* 13: 35.
3 *PJM* 13: 37.
4 *PJM* 13: 38.
5 *Republic of Letters* 1: 653–654, emphasis original.
6 *PJM* 13: 48–52.
7 *PJM* 13: 48–52.
8 *PJM* 13: 56–57.
9 *PTJ* 16: 455–457.
10 *PAH* 6: 434–438.
11 *PTJ* 16: 468–470.
12 *PJM* 13: 66.
13 *PJM* 13: 167, 174.
14 *Republic of Letters* 1: 655; *PTJ* 16: 386.
15 *PJM* 12: 369.
16 *PJM* 12: 403–404; 13: 137.
17 *PJM* 13: 148–149.
18 *PAH* 6: 422–423.
19 *PJM* 13: 233–234.
20 *PTJ* 16: 449–450.
21 *PTJ* 16: 493.
22 *PTJ* 16: 574–575.
23 *PJM* 13: 252.
24 *PTJ* 16: 598; 17: 25.
25 *PJM* 13: 282, 284–285.
26 *PTJ* 17: 205–207.
27 *PAH* 7: 1–4.
28 *PAH* 7: 149–150.
29 *PAH* 7: 73–74.
30 *Reports of Alexander Hamilton* 43.
31 *PTJ* 17: 207.

6

A MIGHTY ARGUMENT: THE CONSTITUTION, THE BANK, AND THE STOCK MARKET CRASHES OF 1791 AND 1792

In DECEMBER 1790 HAMILTON wrote the report calling for a national bank. His bank proposal relied on the immense concentration of wealth created by Funding and Assumption. Hamilton intended the Bank of the United States to bring together the moneyed men he considered reliable and the national government in a trusting and productive partnership. Finally, with this third objective secured, the United States would have "durable liberty." In response to Hamilton, over the course of late 1790 and 1791 Jefferson and Madison made their complete opposition clear. They were furious that he would propose such a bank and outraged by the method of constitutional interpretation he used to defend it. They also blamed the bank and the financial system for the stock market crashes of 1791 and 1792, the first market collapses in the nation's history. By early 1792 Jefferson's and Madison's breach with Hamilton was beyond repair.

HAMILTON'S NATIONAL BANK

Hamilton's proposals for Funding and Assumption all along had been leading to a national bank. Over several months in 1790 Hamilton worked on what he titled "The Second Report on the Further Provision Necessary for Establishing Public Credit," the report more commonly known as the "Report on the Bank of the United States." By the end of November, it was finished. After Madison's opposition to the ideas in his first report, Hamilton gave him an advance look at this second one. On November 24th he wrote to Madison, "You will oblige me by taking the trouble to peruse the Report... and if weather permit I will call upon you some time tomorrow or next day to converse on the subject of it."[1] Neither man left a record of what would have been a fascinating conversation!

Hamilton delivered the bank report to Congress on December 13, 1790. In it he argued that the nation's finances and its ability to tax and borrow depended on the bank he was proposing. The bank "would be of the greatest utility in the operations connected with . . . public credit. . . ."[2] The bank could lend to the government "especially in sudden emergencies." In addition, a substantial bank would attract the deposits and investment of the nation's wealthiest citizens. That money could then be "collected to a point, and placed under one direction." The bank would organize and mobilize the wealth of these citizens, and bring them into a partnership with those responsible for administering policy and pursuing the public good. The bank, then, would play a central role in strengthening the nation and placing "durable liberty" on a sound footing. Those conditions and connections would provide the nation with public credit, which revealed the "intimate connection of interest between the government and the bank of a nation."[3]

Hamilton proposed that the bank issue corporate stock up to $10 million in the form of 25,000 shares of $400 each. It was a massive expansion of banking. Ten million dollars in 1790 would have the impact of about $890 billion in the U.S. economy of the twenty-first century . When Hamilton proposed the bank there were only five other chartered banks in the United States, and they had a combined capital of only $3 million.[4] The structure of the bank assured the close connection between the government, the bank, and the moneyed class. The bank owed its existence to the government because Hamilton called on Congress to pass a law granting a corporate charter allowing the bank to operate for twenty years. Though the national government would create the bank, it would be substantially a private business, and Hamilton expected "the management [to] be in the hands of private individuals." But the bank would not be entirely a private business corporation. Instead, Hamilton imagined a close and ongoing partnership between the private investors and the national government. He made it clear in the bank report that the government should "be a holder of a part of the stock of the Bank, and consequently a sharer in the profits of it."[5]

Hamilton called for the national government to become a minority investor in the bank by purchasing with gold and silver over the next ten years $2 million of the total $10 million of bank stock.[6] Government investment would lay the foundation for specie holdings to support extensive issuing of paper notes. Hamilton devised a different way for private citizens to invest in the bank, one that ensured the close connection between the private owners of the bank and the government. Hamilton proposed that each $400 share of stock available for sale to private citizens be purchased with $100 of gold and silver and $300 worth of the variety of public debt certificates that bore an interest rate of six percent.[7] This structure for private investment did not simply allow for private citizens to invest in the bank. It also reinforced the connection between the bank and the national government already created by the government's $2 million investment. Of the $10 million in stock, $8 million could be purchased by private citizens, and three-fourths of that, $6 million, would be purchased with public debt certificates. In other words, holders of public debt would transfer $6 million of public debt to the bank in exchange for $6 million of bank stock. The transfer would make the bank a public creditor receiving $360,000 per year in interest from the government paid in specie. The interest payments would solidify the backing of the government. And the bank would have a strong interest in the success of the government since it would be a significant holder of public debt.

This structure also meant that decisions about credit and finance would be overseen by the moneyed men who Hamilton was confident believed in "durable liberty." They were the major holders of the public debt, and so would purchase most of the bank's stock. The more stock they purchased; the more control they would possess over the bank. Hamilton structured the voting process for bank officers so that bigger investors would get additional votes, with the largest investors getting 30 votes each. Because so much of the investment in the bank came from stock shares purchased with public debt, Hamilton was confident that the bank would serve as the final connection between the government and those citizens most capable of providing the leadership necessary for "durable liberty." For Hamilton it was a source of relief and comfort that "the debt . . . will always be found in considerable quantity among the monied and trading people." Any who worried about "the fitness of the public debt

The Bank of the United States, with its grand columns and white marble façade, was larger and much more impressive than the buildings surrounding it on third street in Philadelphia. The bank was meant to convey power, strength, and stability. To its critics it represented all the dangers of monarchy.

for a bank fund" could stop doing so. For "the Bank of England in its first erection rested wholly on that foundation."[8]

Had he been trying, Hamilton could not have done more to arouse the worst suspicions of those who feared institutions they associated with a culture of monarchy and the fourth stage. The Bank of England reference only made it worse. Having read the advance copy Hamilton had given him, throughout the winter of 1790 and into 1791 Madison made an extensive study of banks, beginning with Renaissance Italy, and scrutinizing the Bank of England. He was seeking all the reasons to oppose the bank. He wrote to his father in late January 1791, just before the House of Representatives began to discuss the "Report" and the bank bill, "[t]he Bank is also come from the Senate, but will not go thro' if at all without opposition."[9]

MADISON, THE BANK, AND THE CONSTITUTION

On February 2, 1791, the House began debate of the bank bill, which included all of Hamilton's significant proposals. The bill had already passed in the Senate. Madison had two major arguments in opposition. The first was his bitter dislike of the particular bank Hamilton proposed, and the second was the interpretation of the Constitution Hamilton relied on to justify the national government providing the bank with a corporate charter. Concerning banks and the best way for a republic to do banking, Madison argued that Hamilton's bank was beyond dangerous because it was so big and would dominate all other sources of credit. Madison acknowledged that some of the services Hamilton's bank would provide were useful. But the United States would be far better off without such a concentration of wealth and power, and so "the most important of the advantages would be better obtained by several banks properly distributed than by a single one." Madison maintained that concentrating so much wealth within one bank would also concentrate political power in the vicinity of that bank. That might make sense to those in England wishing to preserve monarchy, but the "case in America was different from that in England [where] . . . the monarchy favored the concentration of wealth and influence at the metropolis."[10]

In his remarks Madison invoked the threat of a monarchical court and linked a large national bank to monarchy itself. Fortunately, Madison argued, the fundamental law of the United States prevented the creation of the bank. Madison now turned to his second objection, Hamilton's interpretation of the Constitution. Madison insisted that Congress did not have the authority to issue the bank a charter of incorporation because the Constitution had not granted it the power to create a banking corporation. The Constitution, argued Madison, was not a general grant of power that prevented the government from doing specific things. Rather, it was a grant of very specific and limited powers, and the national government possessed only those powers the Constitution had expressly granted.[11] This understanding of the Constitution was fundamental to popular sovereignty, insisted Madison. The people were sovereign, all powerful. For their convenience they had granted specific powers to the national government to equip it to better promote and defend their interests. All other power they had kept for themselves or given to the state governments. Where in the Constitution had the people granted the national government the power to create a bank via a corporate charter? Nowhere, insisted Madison.

Madison rejected the interpretation Hamilton relied on to claim that the Constitution allowed the national government to incorporate the bank. He insisted that Hamilton's claims about the Constitution destroyed the fundamental values that had shaped the new government's creation. In order to argue that the Constitution allowed the national government to charter the bank, said Madison, Hamilton had to squeeze power into two clauses that neither clause actually provided. Since nowhere did the Constitution say the national government could charter a banking corporation, Hamilton had to rely on the clause that granted the national government "[t]he power to lay and collect taxes to pay the debts, and provide for the common defense and general welfare" and the clause that granted "[t]he power to pass all laws necessary and proper to carry into execution those powers." Madison's and Jefferson's disagreement with Hamilton over what those phrases from the Constitution meant— "provide for the common defense and general welfare," and "power to pass all laws necessary and proper to carry into execution those powers"—lay at the heart of their bitter conflict with him. Were these phrases open-ended grants of power that provided a great degree of flexibility, a clear path to going beyond the powers the Constitution expressly enumerated (i.e., listed) as belonging to the national government?

Madison argued vehemently that they were not. Instead, he insisted, the phrase "provide for the common defense and general welfare" applied only to the specific act of laying taxes. The taxes could be used for a variety of general purposes to achieve the public's welfare. But in no way did the phrase itself grant any power beyond actually laying and collecting taxes because the general welfare clause was tightly bound to the enumerated power "to lay and collect taxes, duties, imposts, and excises." Any interpretation of the phrase that severed it from the power to tax "would give to Congress an unlimited power; would render nugatory [meaningless] the enumeration of particular powers; would supersede all the powers reserved to the state governments." Therefore, the phrase "provide for the common defense and general welfare" was not an additional freestanding grant of power, but merely clarifying language stating that the general welfare was advanced by granting the national government the power to tax.[12]

The statement that came at the end of Article One, Section Eight of the Constitution, that Congress had the power "[t]o make all laws which shall be necessary and proper for carrying into execution the forgoing powers . . ." was as limiting as the general welfare clause, Madison insisted. It was limiting because "[w]hatever meaning the clause may have, none can be admitted that would give an unlimited discretion to Congress." The clause came after the long list of enumerated powers that the sovereign people had given to the new national Congress. Therefore, insisted Madison, it was bound to and subordinate to those powers. As a result, "its meaning must, according to the natural and obvious force of the terms of the context, be limited to mean necessary to the end, and incident to the nature of the specified powers." Congress could enact additional laws that were "necessary" to make it possible to carry out the enumerated powers. But "necessary," Madison argued, meant Congress could only pass supplementary laws when it would be impossible for it to use its enumerated powers unless it passed these additional laws. Any other use of the necessary and proper clause would mean that the "essential characteristic of the government as composed of limited and enumerated powers would be destroyed."

There was no enumerated power that Congress would be unable to use if it did not have Hamilton's bank. In no way was the bank necessary, and, based on his most fundamental beliefs, Madison certainly did not think it was proper. If the power to lay taxes and borrow money could be turned into the power to also lend money, and then, by extension, to the ability to incorporate a bank, "if implications thus remote and thus multiplied, can be linked together," Madison warned, then "a chain may be formed that will reach every object of legislation, every object within the whole compass of political economy." If the power to tax could somehow lead to the power to incorporate a bank, a creative mind could imagine connections that would allow the government to do just about anything. Building on one vague and tenuous connection after another would very quickly lead to the government claiming powers no one had ever dreamed of granting it. The bank was a prime example of where misinterpreting the Constitution and claiming powers from the general welfare and necessary and proper clauses would lead. The bank, Madison concluded, was clearly unconstitutional, for "the power exercised by the bill was condemned by the silence of the Constitution, was condemned by the rule of interpretation arising out of the Constitution; was condemned by its tendency to destroy the main characteristic of the Constitution . . . and [I hope] it would receive its final condemnation by the vote of this house."[13]

JEFFERSON, THE BANK, AND THE CONSTITUTION

Madison hoped in vain. The House joined the Senate in passing the bank bill and sent it to President Washington to sign into law. Madison's attack on the bank quickly became the first part of a coordinated effort. Two weeks after Madison spoke, Jefferson wrote an opinion for Washington to consider as he deliberated whether to sign the bill. Jefferson built on Madison's arguments by invoking what would soon become the Tenth Amendment to the Constitution, that all power not given to the national government was reserved for the states or the people. Jefferson argued that the Constitution created a stronger national government that was still carefully bounded and limited to specific actions. The Constitution granted specific powers to the national government with the understanding "that all powers not delegated to the U.S. by the Constitution are reserved to the states or the people." Like Madison, Jefferson raised the specter of a dangerous national government if those in power moved beyond the grants of power specifically provided by the Constitution.

He implored Washington to veto the bank bill, insisting that the interpretation that allowed a bank also allowed the national government "to take possession of a boundless field of power, no longer susceptible of any definition." Quite simply, Jefferson concluded, the "incorporation of a bank, and other powers assumed by this bill have not . . . been delegated to the U.S. by the Constitution."[14]

Since the Constitution did not expressly grant Congress the power to incorporate a bank, the only way to claim that it could was with an interpretation that Jefferson rejected. Jefferson agreed with Madison that the power to incorporate a bank could not be found within the general welfare clause because that clause was subordinate to the power to lay and collect taxes. Promoting the general welfare resulted because Congress now had the power to tax. Like Madison, Jefferson insisted that the general welfare clause was not freestanding and did not imply additional discretionary power. Instead, it simply clarified that the powers expressly granted had been granted because doing so promoted the general welfare. The general welfare clause did not add any additional power, for "no such universal power was meant to be given." In fact, the clause "was intended to lace [Congress] up straightly with the enumerated powers, and those without which, as means, these powers could not be carried into effect."[15]

Jefferson also agreed with Madison's understanding of "the second general phrase . . . to make all laws necessary and proper for carrying into execution the enumerated powers." If there was no bank Congress could still make use of every enumerated power granted by the Constitution, Jefferson insisted to Washington. Since that was the case, the "bank therefore is not necessary, and consequently not authorized by this phrase." In his written opinion Jefferson focused on defining precisely "necessary," and on distinguishing its meaning from "convenient." He reminded Washington that in the bank report Hamilton had said the bank would be highly convenient. Yet, wrote Jefferson, even if that was true, the Constitution only allowed Congress to do things that were necessary to carry out the enumerated powers, not things that were merely convenient. If people wrongly interpreted the Constitution as allowing Congress to go beyond its expressly granted acts of power to take actions that were merely convenient, there would quickly be no limit to Congress's power. With such flexible interpretation, there would be no action "which ingenuity may not torture into a convenience, in some way or other, to some one of so long a list of enumerated powers. It would swallow up the delegated powers, and reduce the whole to one phrase. . . ."[16]

The framers chose "necessary," Jefferson insisted, because that word allowed Congress to claim additional power through a supplementary law. But Congress could claim that additional power only if something of the gravest importance could absolutely not be accomplished without this additional law. Hamilton's Bank did not measure up, for the government could collect taxes, borrow, and regulate commerce without the bank. It did not matter that it could do those things more conveniently with the bank. "Necessary" meant indispensible, impossible to do without, and "[n]othing but a necessity invincible by any other means can justify a prostration of laws which constitute the pillars of our whole system. . . ."[17]

HAMILTON RESPONDS

The day after Jefferson wrote to Washington, the president wrote to Hamilton explaining that the bill was on his desk but the "constitutionality of it is objected to. . . . I now require in like manner, yours on the validity and propriety of the . . . Act."[18] Hamilton wrote feverishly and one week later delivered a response that, at around 13,400 words, was almost seven times longer than Jefferson's opinion. Hamilton responded to the claim that the Constitution gave the national government enumerated powers with additional powers only when they were directly connected to the enumerated ones, and then only if without them the government could not make use of its enumerated powers. Hamilton rejected such a limited interpretation outright. He informed Washington that Jefferson's views would "be fatal to the just and indispensable authority of the United States." When Jefferson maintained that the national government could not charter corporations, Hamilton explained to Washington, he sought to deny it power that was "inherent in the very definition of government and essential to every step of the progress to be made by that of the United States. . . ."

According to Hamilton, Jefferson also showed dangerous ignorance about what the Constitution meant and how the power and authority functioned that it granted to the national government. The Constitution gave the national government specific powers such as to lay and collect taxes. But it was the case "that every power vested in a government is in its nature sovereign." Therefore, every power the government possessed by grant of the Constitution contained within it the power to take any actions to carry out the expressly granted power, as long as the actions taken were not expressly forbidden by the Constitution.[19] Nowhere did the Constitution forbid the national government from incorporating a bank. In effect, Hamilton turned Jefferson's and Madison's arguments upside down. They argued the Constitution did not grant the national government the power to incorporate a bank and so it could not. Hamilton countered that the Constitution did not deny the national government the power to incorporate a bank and so it could.

To strengthen his case, Hamilton provided Washington an alternative way to interpret the Constitution, and to understand the power it granted the national government. His interpretive method revived the remarks he had made in 1780, when he had argued that even the Confederation Congress possessed enormous discretionary power by virtue of its being a government with the duty to govern well. In the Constitution, Hamilton told Washington, power was not solely a limited grant tied closely to the enumerated powers, as Jefferson and Madison claimed. In fact, even they did not deny that Congress had implied powers, powers not expressly granted by the Constitution. Congress could use these implied powers to more effectively carry out its enumerated powers. Given that there were implied powers, the only question

was how they were understood and what limits there were on them. Erecting a corporation could be an implied power as easily as any other action. The only relevant question was, was erecting this particular corporation reasonably connected to actions
that everybody agreed Congress had the right to do?

It was simply not the case, Hamilton explained to Washington, that interpreting the Constitution in this way would lead to the national government claiming
unlimited power. There clearly were limits since the implied power had to be reasonably connected to an enumerated power. Thus for example, he explained, Congress
could not make use of the implied power to erect a corporation to assist it in policing
Philadelphia. There was no implied power to erect a corporation that would provide
such assistance because the Constitution did not grant Congress any power to regulate the municipal affairs of that city. But the Constitution clearly granted Congress
the power to tax. Since the power to tax was sovereign, with it came the power to
do anything that would assist in exercising that power as long as the action was not
expressly forbidden by the Constitution. The bank would obviously make collection
of taxes and payment of government obligations easier. Since a bank could be connected to more effectively carrying out the enumerated power to lay and collect taxes,
it was within the authority of the national government to incorporate it.[20]

But wasn't Hamilton simply repeating that a bank was convenient? Jefferson had
acknowledged its convenience, but had argued that the necessary and proper clause
demanded a much higher standard—that Hamilton had to show that the government
would be unable to tax at all unless it had the Bank. That was clearly an impossible
standard to meet, and Hamilton did not bother to try. Instead, he sought to demolish
Jefferson's position on the necessary and proper clause. Jefferson argued, Hamilton
wrote, that an action could be justified through implied power in the necessary and
proper clause only if the express power would be impossible to use unless the action
was taken. Hamilton dismissed Jefferson's definition of necessary as ridiculous. He
insisted "that neither the grammatical nor popular sense of the term" defined "necessary" in such a confining and limited way. In fact, wrote Hamilton, for reasonable
people "necessary often means no more than needful, requisite, incidental, useful,
or conducive to." People frequently described something as being necessary "when
nothing more is intended or understood, than that the interests of the government
or the person require, or will be promoted by the doing of this or that thing." That
was the true meaning of the necessary and proper clause, Hamilton concluded. It was
not meant to confine and limit the government. Jefferson's dubious definition had to
be rejected, for to "understand the word as the Secretary of State does, would be to
depart from its obvious and popular sense, and give it a restrictive operation; an idea
never before entertained. It would be to give it the same force as if the word absolutely
or indispensably had been prefixed to it."[21]

Quite simply, Hamilton's Constitution was not one that Jefferson and Madison
recognized. It was not a sharply limiting grant of power. Instead it was a vast provision
of power limited only by those very few things the Constitution expressly forbade the
national government from doing. How did you judge what was constitutional, asked

Hamilton? Any action was constitutional when it was reasonably and clearly taken to assist in carrying out an enumerated power and was "not forbidden by any particular provision of the Constitution."[22]

Hamilton convinced Washington, who had been as angry as Hamilton over the inability of the national government during the revolution to govern the nation and fight the war. The bonds forged from their shared frustrations caused Washington to want Hamilton to have the chance to resolve the problems he knew Hamilton had been wrestling with for over a decade. Washington signed the bank bill, and decided not to make use of the veto message that Madison had helpfully (and hopefully) drafted for him.[23] Hamilton had done it. Funding and Assumption had turned useless paper into a vast amount of wealth possessed by those he believed most capable of protecting "durable liberty." Now with such a powerful, extensive, and national bank, which was closely connected to the national government, the moneyed class and the government could work in partnership to provide internal stability and external strength for the United States. They could protect republican institutions and the citizens' liberty from the Republic's monarchical enemies, and from the licentious impulses of the citizens themselves.

STOCK MARKET MANIA, THE CRASH OF 1791

Starting up such a large bank took time, and excitement about it grew as it prepared to open for business in summer 1791. For Hamilton all the news was good. William Seton, a New York City merchant and high-ranking official of the Bank of New York, as well as a trusted friend and ally, wrote to him in late June 1791 that investors were ecstatic about the bank's possibilities. In thirty minutes New Yorkers had deposited $60,000 in Seton's bank with instructions to invest it in the stock of the Bank of the United States as soon as it went on the market. An additional $20,000 had quickly followed.[24] More good news and praise came to Hamilton from Benjamin Goodhue, a member of Congress from Massachusetts. Goodhue congratulated Hamilton for the invaluable service he had already done the nation. He had heard accounts that the news of Hamilton's achievements had spread to Europe where "the change which has been wrought in the opinion of that part of the world respecting the U. States is almost wonderful."[25]

Yet Jefferson and Madison could see nothing worth celebrating. On May 1, 1791, as they gloomily watched the opening of the Bank drawing near, Madison wrote to Jefferson describing the effect that he believed Hamilton's financial program was having on the citizens of the United States. Madison was traveling through New York City and told Jefferson about a fraud being perpetrated there. Swindlers were posing as the agents of deceased soldiers who had no next of kin in order claim outstanding debts owed to them. This "knavery" was an embarrassment to the nation and rewarded "the worst of its citizens."[26] Bank stock was not yet for sale. But the prospect of quick wealth raised by Hamilton's program was already warping sensibilities, Madison feared. Madison blamed this behavior on the climate Hamilton's policies had created. It caused citizens to hunt for any opportunity to obtain money without virtuous effort, even if it meant cheating dead soldiers. How would people behave when the far greater possibilities promised by bank stock became available?

On July 4, 1791, the market opened for national bank stock in Philadelphia, New York City, Boston, Baltimore, and Charleston. What sold on the 4th was called bank scrip. Each piece of scrip represented the right to purchase one share of the bank stock priced at $400 per share. A feverish demand for scrip quickly caused the price to skyrocket. Those who bought the scrip available on July 4th created a new market just for scrip. Scrip that sold for $25 on July 4th sold for $325 by August 10th. The frenzy of the scrip market spilled over into the market for the public debt. People reasoned that scrip was so valuable because bank stock was going to become valuable. And since bank stock was going to be so valuable, it made sense to buy as much public debt as possible since it could be converted into bank stock. At one point in the summer of 1791 public debt sold for 130 cents on the dollar. People were paying thirty percent above the face value because they were so confident they could convert the debt into even more profitable stocks. The overheated market for public debt pushed the price of scrip even higher.[27]

At the center of all this speculation, and of the bubble in the price of paper, was a New Yorker named William Duer. Duer was a close friend and ally of Hamilton, and for a time served under him as Assistant Secretary of the Treasury. Hamilton was drawn to Duer, who had a somewhat similar background and past life experiences. Duer had been born in England to a father who owned plantations in the West Indies. As a young man Duer developed extensive commercial contacts in the West Indies, and also in New York through Hamilton's future father-in-law, Philip Schuyler. Duer understood credit, commerce, and debt and was a truly charming companion. As Hamilton achieved prominence, he came to know and rely on Duer. In 1791 he looked to Duer to play a large role in supporting the new bank.

Hamilton miscalculated badly by trusting Duer. As Hamilton rolled out the new national bank, he had no idea that Duer was speculating heavily in bank scrip, bank stock, and public debt. But secrecy was crucial to how Duer operated—almost no one ever fully knew what he was up to. Duer bought as much scrip as he could, believing the price would continue to rise long enough for him to sell high. He bought scrip at between $135 and $140, began to sell at $185, and was still selling in August at $325. That a person who others assumed knew things was investing so heavily contributed to the overheating of the market.

The reaction of Jefferson and Madison to all of this buying and selling was predictable. On July 10th, less than a week after scrip went on sale, Madison wrote in disgust from New York to Jefferson that the price of bank scrip was ballooning in New York and Philadelphia. People seemed to think profits were guaranteed and the "subscriptions are consequently a mere scramble for so much public plunder, which will be engrossed by those already loaded with the spoils." Madison believed that, given the way Hamilton had structured investment, almost all of the bank stock would be held by those who owned most of the debt. The scramble for bank scrip revealed "in what proportions the public debt lies in the Country—What sort of hands hold it, and by whom the people of the U.S. are governed." Most loathsome of all, Madison claimed that members of Congress were rushing to purchase bank scrip. He also reported to Jefferson the rumor that Hamilton's father-in-law, Philip Schuyler, would likely become a bank director. Getting rich quick via the bank seemed to be all that people were thinking about. "Nothing new is talked of here," Madison complained, "stock jobbing draws every other subject. The coffee house is an eternal buzz with the gamblers."[28]

Jefferson clearly had additional sources of information. The same day Madison wrote to him, Jefferson wrote to James Monroe expressing his disgust at the scramble for scrip. He had heard that the "bank filled and overflowed in the moment it was opened. . . ." If these conditions continued, he feared that all honest work would be given up to pursue dreams of getting rich quickly, with as little effort as possible. "It is impossible to say where the appetite for gambling will stop," Jefferson lamented, "[t]he land-office, the federal town, certain schemes of manufacturing, are all likely to be converted into ailment for the rage."[29]

Throughout July and into August 1791, as the price of scrip continued to rise, it seemed to Madison that the worst sort of behavior and conditions, those he associated with monarchical Britain, had come to the United States in an instant, and all because of Hamilton. Toward the end of August he received a letter from Henry Lee describing Lee's impressions of his journey from Philadelphia back to Virginia in late July. Lee reported that his

> whole route presented to me one continued scene of stock gambling; agriculture, commerce and even the fairer sex relinquished, to make way for unremitted exertion in this favorite pursuit—thousands even at this late hour . . . participat[ing] in legal spoil. . . . [A]ll orders of people seem to reckon this appreciation of the public paper. . . .[30]

In early August, Duer began to sell his scrip at a tremendous profit. Observing the sale, Madison wrote to Jefferson from New York City that the mania for investment was producing such a demand for any kind of stock that all the prices were rising dangerously high, much higher than their real value. He was certain a collapse in price would soon follow, a crash of the stock market. On August 8th he informed Jefferson that there was a "mysterious cause for a phenomenon in the stocks." Rumors were spreading that more would be done at the next session of Congress to make an even better provision for the public debt. In the frenzied climate created by the mad rush for bank scrip, people seemed to think anything was possible. Who knew what was true? Perhaps, Madison speculated, the rumors were invented by holders of the public debt who wished to talk up the price in order to sell high. Even more worrying, Madison could not dismiss that the rumors were true and there was secretive communication between government insiders and public debt holders. He feared most a repeat of what he believed had happened with assumption of the state debts, that those farthest from the great cities, and with the least information, would be the victims. He gloomily reported to Jefferson "that packet boats and expresses are again sent from this place to the southern states, to buy up the paper of all sorts which has risen in the market here."

During the 1780s Madison, as much as anyone, had opposed the state governments printing vast amounts of paper money. He was disgusted as he watched the paper money create hyperinflation, which allowed poor debtors to pay off wealthier creditors with money worth a fraction of the value of the original loan. He believed the states, by printing paper money, were refusing to protect private property, despite their duty to do so. The Constitution was supposed to ensure the protection of private property, in part by forbidding states from printing paper money. But two years after its ratification, Madison now doubted that the system Hamilton claimed the Constitution enabled was any better, in fact likely much worse. He informed Jefferson that the impact of Hamilton's financial program raised the question "whether the system of the old paper under a bad Government, or the new under a good one, be chargeable with the greater substantial injustice." Madison had come to believe that the "true difference seems to be that by the former the few were the victims to the many; by the latter the many to the few."[31] Madison did not doubt that the Articles of Confederation was a bad government or that the Constitution provided a good one. But in his view Hamilton's outrageous interpretation of the Constitution allowed the wealthy to victimize the poor, and possibly caused worse damage than the government it had replaced. If only Washington could have understood that convenient did not mean necessary!

For Jefferson there was no doubt that the Constitution, when interpreted to the point of its abuse by Hamilton and his supporters, was worse. In late August, as he digested Madison's letter and all the other news of the rage for stocks, he wrote to the South Carolinian Edward Rutledge asking, "What do you think of this scrippomany?" Jefferson knew what he thought of the rush to invest in the bank. He believed the temptation of rapid wealth was distracting citizens from solid and useful pursuits. Because of the scramble Hamilton encouraged,

> [s]hips are lying idle at the wharfs, buildings are stopped, capitals withdrawn from commerce, manufactures, arts, and agriculture, to be employed in gambling, and the tide of public prosperity . . . is suppressed by the rage of getting rich in a day. No mortal can tell where this will stop. For the spirit of gaming, when once it has seized a subject, is incurable. . . . I imagine . . . we shall shortly hear that all the cash has quitted the extremities of the nation and accumulated here [Philadelphia].[32]

Yet by August Hamilton was also quite concerned. He had never wanted a stock mania, bubbles, or destructive crashes. He had expected that Funding, Assumption, and the Bank would judiciously place wealth in the hands of responsible moneyed men who would work in partnership with the national government to create the conditions for "durable liberty." Hamilton was naïve to think that the moneyed men around him, Duer in particular, would be guided by the same values of public service and the ideals of classical virtue and honor that mattered so much to him. The stock mania of 1791 was the opposite of what he wanted, but it followed directly from what he had done.

Hamilton was also beginning to fear that a crash was coming, and that it might destroy confidence in both the Bank stock and the public debt. Loss of confidence could potentially destroy the financial system, which, he had no doubt, offered the nation the best chance for "durable liberty." In mid-August, after peaking at $325 on August 10th, the price for scrip crashed as it became clear that the Bank stock was unlikely to be profitable enough to justify the price of scrip. Duer had already made his money, having sold at the height of the market, but those still holding scrip lost heavily. By the end of August scrip was selling for $185. The crash of scrip threatened a collapse in confidence both in Bank stock and the public debt. As people panicked that scrip which had seemed so valuable was not, they grew terrified that the same was true of all stocks. If such panic intensified, all would seek to sell at once, leading to a vast supply of stocks, little demand, and the willingness to sell at any price, causing a race to the bottom for stock prices. Hamilton was especially frightened that confidence in the public debt would collapse since the price had risen so high during the scrip mania. When the scrip market collapsed, public debt bearing six percent interest had been selling for fifteen percent above face value.[33] In a climate of panic what had been valued above its face value would likely fall far below it.

Hamilton intervened quickly to reverse the crash. In mid-August he drew money from the Sinking Fund, a fund that was set aside to buy back public debt and so reduce the amount of principal and interest the government owed. Yet Hamilton was shrewdly implementing what today we call fiscal policy. He purchased at face value between $300,000 and $400,000 of the public debt bearing six percent interest, even as people were losing confidence and private buyers were refusing to pay face value for the debt. Hamilton was hoping to create a market for the public debt at face value, to keep its value steady, and save those who had bought high and might now have to sell very low.[34]

Hamilton explained his actions to William Seton of the Bank of New York when he deputized Seton to make purchases for him in that city. Hamilton told Seton that the rush to buy scrip had produced "imprudent speculations." Frenzied and rash buying and selling was the last thing Hamilton wanted, and so it was necessary for judicious men such as Seton to keep the price of all stocks from falling too low. To that end, when Seton used treasury funds to purchase stock at above market value, he should look to buy from "gentlemen who support the funds."[35] Hamilton was instructing Seton to buy at face value rather than as cheaply as possible. Buying cheap would reduce the government debt more quickly, but it would also contribute to the collapse in confidence in the value of the debt and destroy the wealth of those invested in it. In addition, Hamilton was urging Seton to purchase debt at face value from those he believed had invested in debt to support its value and, presumably, the uses Hamilton had for it. Seton was to try to avoid purchasing from those who had jumped in to buy as the price fell, presumably to sell it quickly as soon as the price rose. He wanted sober, steady, long-term commitment to the debt, not short-term selfishness, which only increased panic and volatility in the market.

Hamilton instructed Seton on August 16th to act as his purchasing agent. The next day he wrote to the major source of the problem, his old friend Duer. By the 17th, Bank scrip was falling to about $180. Hamilton had now heard stories of Duer's role, though he did not believe the worst of them. He hoped Duer would begin to buy scrip again to limit the price collapse. Hamilton told Duer that in Philadelphia

> the conversation here was—"Bank scrip is getting so high as to become a bubble" in one breath—in another, "'tis a South Sea dream" [a reference to the South Sea Bubble of 1720, a stock market crash in Britain], in a third, "there is a combination of knowing ones at New York to raise it as high as possible by fictitious purchases...." In another "Duer...and some others are mounting the balloon as fast as possible."

Hamilton implored Duer to be better than the rumors circulating about him, urging "as to myself my friend, I think I know you too well to suppose you capable of such views...or to harbor the most distant thought that you would wander from the path either of public good or private integrity." By this point Hamilton probably did not consider Duer wholly trustworthy, but he did want his help. Hamilton estimated that the true value of bank scrip was about $190, a figure Duer had quoted to him previously as the realistic value. Now Hamilton wanted Duer to intervene to stop the fall in the price of scrip. He closed his letter, "I sincerely wish you may be able to support it at what you mention." Duer chose not to do so.[36]

Hamilton's efforts did not fully prevent a collapse, but they did help to stop a devastating stock market crash. On September 5th William Seton reported that over the past month the price of public debt bearing interest-deferred payment (one of the varieties of public debt securities) had continued to fall. And scrip was selling at only $150. Two days later Hamilton advanced Seton an additional $50,000 to purchase debt, and by the end of September the price had begun to return to par.[37] Hamilton's intervention had certainly helped, but in the end the public debt had been saved by Funding and Assumption. The guaranteed interest payment on the debt certificates was so reliable that panic about the debt's value could not last very long. Hamilton told Seton on September 7th he was confident the market value for debt would rise and that "the evil is temporary." After all, he proudly informed Seton, the "Bank is as good a thing as it ever was. The United States are as solid as they were. The provision for the debt appears every day more and more ample. In short everything promises well and the timid will soon rally." Seton was to make it clear that Hamilton was not worried and that "the Treasurer is purchasing...."[38]

By the end of September the timid had rallied, but the cost was greater than Hamilton knew. Jefferson's and Madison's deep suspicion had turned to implacable hostility. They were convinced that Hamilton was subverting republican society. They believed he was creating a court of concentrated wealth and power, and was rapidly introducing monarchical institutions and monarchical thinking into the United States. The only reason one would do so was to destroy the Republic. Hamilton viewed the events of the summer of 1791 as a temporary fall in stock prices as people learned how to make use of a very good system. Jefferson and Madison saw the same events as the beginning of the end for the Republic unless it could all be stopped from going any further. And Hamilton had another problem. Duer had done quite well in his speculations in scrip. He had made a handsome profit and was eager for more.

CONFLICT BEYOND REPAIR: DUER AND THE CRASH OF 1792

Duer's next plan, which he put into effect in January 1792, was even bolder. He set out to corner the market on the public debt itself, to buy up most of the debt so that when the government paid the interest it owed it would primarily be paying William Duer. The specifics of Duer's scheme are murky, and it is not clear that it even made sense. It was a serious gamble that he took between January and March 1792. As it began to fall apart, his actions made less and less sense. To describe Duer's scheme in the simplest terms, he started rumors of a plan to have the state of New York charter three banks, later combined into one bank, known as the million dollar bank, though it ended up selling over $11 million in stock. The bank itself was much closer to a value of zero than $11 million. Awash in cash from his stock sale, Duer bought a great deal of the stock of the highly legitimate Bank of New York, which pushed the price of that stock up as others began to follow him. As the value of his stock rose, he sold at a profit and began to use the proceeds to purchase as much public debt as he could. He began buying public debt heavily in February, figuring he could profit in one of two ways. Either the buzz of all the purchasing would further drive up the price of public debt and he could sell at a profit, or he could own most of the debt and receive a vast interest payment when the next quarterly payment from the government came due in April.

The problem was that it was a long time until April, and this time Duer became the victim of his own mania. In order to buy as much public debt as possible, he borrowed heavily from anyone he could, paying usurious interest rates, sometimes as high as ten to fifteen percent per month. He even borrowed from small shopkeepers and, in one instance, the Madam of a well-known brothel. His true mania was that he likely borrowed more than the interest on the public debt would have brought him. By early March that payoff was still a month away, people were growing alarmed as they realized how in debt Duer was, and the panic prevented the rise in the value of the public debt that Duer had counted on. Instead, those he owed demanded that he pay them back. Duer could not; he lost everything, and went to debtors' prison on March 9th. His collapse set off a panic over the value of the public debt that had the potential to be far more destructive than the relatively minor crash of 1791.[39]

Hamilton, who probably already mistrusted Duer to some extent, reacted quickly in January as soon as he heard of Duer's million dollar bank. On January 18th he wrote William Seton that he had heard the news of Duer's plan to start the new bank, a scheme he thought "in every view pernicious." Hamilton was coming to see Duer for what he was and informed Seton that such "extravagant sallies of speculation do injury to the Government and to the whole system of public credit, by disgusting all sober citizens and giving a wild air to everything."[40] As Duer put his plans for the million dollar bank in motion, Hamilton wrote again to Seton in early February hoping that the new bank would collapse before it could do any serious damage. But given the effect speculations of this sort had had on the bank scrip the previous summer, Hamilton confessed that "I fear more than I hope.... Every day unfolds the mischievous tendency of this mad scheme. The enemies to Banks and credit are in a fair way of having their utmost malignity gratified."[41]

Once Duer's scheme began to fall apart, Hamilton again intervened to try to prevent the price of public debt from plummeting. Hamilton had to try something, for public debt that had sold in Philadelphia at $127.50 in January fell to $100 in early April. The drop in New York was also steep, from $121 in January to just under $104 by the end of March.[42] Had Hamilton not intervened in the market it is likely the drop would have been far worse. As the crash began in March, Hamilton summoned the Commissioners of the Sinking Fund to have them once again authorize his purchase of public debt at above the current market price. Jefferson was one of the Commissioners, and this time was in no mood to give any more aid to Hamilton's financial system. He voted against allowing the above the market price purchases. When he lost this vote he tried to postpone the purchases for as long as possible by insisting that Commissioner John Jay, Chief Justice of the Supreme Court, who was detained in New York on court business, could not issue his vote in writing but had to travel to Philadelphia to vote in person. Jefferson failed with this effort too. But clearly he was willing to see the much larger crash destroy the market in debt and Bank securities if he could.[43]

Hamilton poured close to $400,000 into the debt securities market (which would have an impact in the U.S. economy of the twenty-first century of just under $30 billion) between late March and mid-April. He bought at above market price and so saved the market, which did not suffer the complete collapse Jefferson hoped for.[44] He did so, he explained to his New York ally Philip Livingston, hoping that after the system was saved "there should be a line of separation between honest men and knaves, between respectable stockholders and dealers in the funds, and mere unprincipled gamblers. Public infamy must restrain what the laws cannot." Hamilton had never liked mere money-making men; he had always viewed his financial program as a means to the much grander end of building republican institutions that could protect "durable liberty." Substantial and trustworthy gentlemen were supposed to use their wealth responsibly to provide the United States virtuous leadership and stable guidance. But Hamilton was coming to the dismaying conclusion that men such as Duer had nothing to offer the Republic. Going forward his system could survive only by infallibly distinguishing between the "honest men" and the "knaves." In anguished frustration, he informed Livingston that the proper "spirit must be cultivated among the friends of good government and good principles." Knaves such as Duer were discrediting "a just system." Hamilton had not conceived his brilliant system merely to enrich such men, and "contempt and neglect must attend those who manifest that they have no principle but to get money."[45]

Yet it was just these distinctions, between "respectable stockholders" and "unprincipled gamblers," between "honest men and knaves" that Jefferson and Madison did not believe could be made. By spring 1792 they had concluded that the very system Hamilton had created was the source of the danger, not mismanagement and abuse of it. It stood to reason, they decided, that a system would be rotten to the core that depended on indefensible interpretations of the Constitution. Hamilton had abused the Constitution and now his system abused the nation.

To them Duer was not an isolated, rogue knave; he was "the prince of the tribe of speculators." This tribe existed solely because of Hamilton's schemes, and it was poisoning the citizenry and destroying the independence that citizens needed. In early April, in the weeks just after Duer's imprisonment, Jefferson described his fear that behavior like Duer's was warping the values and expectations of the nation's citizens. Republics, in the end, survived only if the people were virtuous, of that he had no doubt. But how could virtue survive when citizens were endlessly tempted by elusive and unlikely wealth? This sort of gambling, this "stock jobbing speculation," Jefferson wrote, distracted citizens from sound ventures "in commerce, manufactures, buildings and agriculture." Citizens had to be protected from the sorts of policies that created opportunities for men like Duer, for "Mr. Duer . . . obtained money from great numbers of small tradesmen and farmers tempting them by usurious interest, which has made the distress very extensive." Citizens were being destroyed "by the desperate throws and plunges of gambling scoundrels." These gamblers promised "a fallacious prosperity," Jefferson wrote to Madison in mid-April. Writing to his son-in-law, Thomas Mann Randolph Jr., four days later, Jefferson reported that he had heard the total loss of wealth in New York City was figured at around $5 million. Jefferson was staggered by the sum "which is reckoned the value of all the buildings in the city: so that if the whole town had been burnt to the ground it would have been just the measure of the present calamity."[46]

* * *

The events of 1791 and the first half of 1792 horrified Jefferson and Madison. Duer might be in prison, yet the forces that allowed him to wreak such havoc appeared to be growing stronger. After their experience with the Bank of the United States, Jefferson and Madison had no doubt that Hamilton was destroying the Republic. They would only grow more convinced of that as Hamilton next turned his attentions to promoting industrial development. By 1792 the two Virginians had decided that Hamilton had to be stopped, even if that meant appealing directly to that combustible and potentially destructive force, the American people.

NOTES

1 *PJM* 13: 306.
2 Jacob E. Cooke, ed., *The Reports of Alexander Hamilton* (New York: Harper and Row, 1964), 47.
3 *Reports of Alexander Hamilton,* 50–51.
4 David J. Cowen, "The First Bank of the United States and the Securities Market Crash of 1792," *Journal of Economic History* 60 (2000): 1041–1060, 1042.
5 *The Reports of Alexander Hamilton,* 73.
6 *The Reports of Alexander Hamilton,* 77–78, 81.
7 *The Reports of Alexander Hamilton,* 74. There were three different types of public debt. The first bore an interest rate of six percent, the second bore three percent, and the third bore six percent with interest payment deferred for ten years. Most debt holders owned all three varieties, which produced a combined interest rate of about four percent. But the Bank report obligated investors to purchase stock using only the six percent debt certificates.
8 *Reports of Alexander Hamilton,* 76, 78–79.
9 *PJM* 13: 358, 364–369.
10 *PJM* 13: 373.
11 *PJM* 13: 374.
12 *PJM* 13: 374–375.
13 *PJM* 13: 376–378, 380–381.
14 *PTJ* 19: 276–277.
15 *PTJ* 19: 277.
16 *PTJ* 19: 278.
17 *PTJ* 19: 279.
18 *PAH* 8: 50.
19 *Reports of Alexander Hamilton,* 83–84.
20 *Reports of Alexander Hamilton,* 86–87.
21 *Reports of Alexander Hamilton,* 87–89.
22 *Reports of Alexander Hamilton,* 91.
23 *PJM* 13: 395.
24 *PAH* 8: 494.
25 *PAH* 8: 516.
26 *PJM* 14: 15–16.
27 Robert F. Jones, *"The King of the Alley": William Duer, Politician, Entrepreneur, and Speculator, 1768–1799* (American Philosophical Society: Philadelphia, PA: 1992), 159–178; Forest McDonald, *Alexander Hamilton: A Biography* (W.W. Norton: New York, 1979), 222–224.
28 *PJM* 14: 43.
29 *PTJ* 20: 297–298.
30 *PJM* 14: 73.
31 *PTJ* 22: 17.
32 *PTJ* 22: 74.
33 *PAH* 9: 61.
34 *PAH* 9: 67–68.
35 *PAH* 9: 71–72.
36 *PAH* 9: 74–75.
37 *PAH* 9: 176, 184.
38 *PAH* 9: 185.
39 Jones, *"King of the Alley,"* 159–178; McDonald, *Alexander Hamilton,* 244–248.
40 *PAH* 10: 525.

41 *PAH* 11: 28.
42 Cowen, "The First Bank of the United States," 1044, 1051.
43 *PAH* 11: 193, 218, 224, 272.
44 *PAH* 11: 190–191, 225, 266, 272.
45 *PAH* 11: 218–219.
46 *PJM* 14: 263, 288; *PTJ* 23: 287, 387, 436.

7

THE MIGHTY ARGUMENT GOES PUBLIC:
THE REPORT ON MANUFACTURES
AND THE ORIGINS OF PARTY POLITICS

WHEN THE BANK OF THE United States had opened for business in the summer of 1791, Hamilton was working on his last great report, the "Report on Manufactures." Connected to that report, he was also writing the prospectus for a new corporation, The Society for Establishing Useful Manufactures. The Society was the most extensive industrial enterprise to that point ever planned in North America. As with the national bank, Hamilton structured this industrial project so that it could draw upon the wealth provided by the funded debt. The bank and the factories of the Society were substantial institutions meant to connect holders of the debt to the national government that was funding it. The "Report on Manufactures" and the prospectus for the Society fully revealed the interconnected genius of Hamilton's sophisticated and complex vision. It also exposed, as far as Jefferson and Madison were concerned, the true monarchical horror that Hamilton and his supporters seemed determined to impose on the United States. Over the course of 1792 they grew determined to expose to the public what they believed Hamilton was up to. Hamilton responded with a public and spirited defense of his policies. By the end of 1792 the conflict between Hamilton and his two most powerful enemies was fully before the American people. At that point this mighty argument belonged to everybody.

CRAFTSMEN AND THE REPORT ON MANUFACTURES

Hamilton hoped that improving the nation's manufacturing output would provide the United States with the resources it needed to protect itself from its monarchical enemies, who were all too eager to wage war. In his bank report Hamilton had pointed out that Funding and Assumption created a great deal of wealth placed in the hands of those he considered the most reliable and trustworthy citizens. It was their stable, sober virtue that would make the Bank such a benefit to the nation. But to secure external strength, more needed to be done with the wealth Funding and Assumption had created.

The "Report on Manufactures" took Hamilton the longest time to write since he knew far less about manufacturing than he did about finance and banking. Over the course of 1791 he sent requests to his customs collectors to interview local craftsmen throughout the mid-Atlantic and New England states. The collectors were to report to him what the craftsmen said they needed to increase the nation's manufacturing capacity. Hamilton's employees forwarded the needs of hatters, manufacturers of woolen and cotton cloths, buttons, and many other items. There was a clear and over-whelming message delivered to Hamilton by the nation's craftsmen and manufacturers. From hat makers Hamilton learned " that foreign importations . . . very much injure the business here." Cloth makers felt that "fabrics [produced in Hartford, Connecticut] are very fine and good . . . [but] they do not command that ready market in cash that imported cloths do." Button makers believed that they could make buttons of equal quality to European buttons, but the Europeans could export so much product that the American manufacturers could not compete. In order for the nation to become independent of the British and others for this essential item, the button makers begged "that Congress would . . . take up the matter with spirit and resolution and lay such heavy duties on the article of buttons that it will amount to a prohibition of importing buttons into this country."[1]

Duties that would "amount to a prohibition" were known as protective tariffs, taxes imposed on imports that were so high they made those imports too expensive to be competitive. Such tariffs, then, protected the domestic market for domestic manufacturers. It was conventional wisdom among most of the nation's craftsmen that Britain had such an extensive industrial head start that it could produce more, and do so more quickly and cheaply. Without protective tariffs, craftsmen doubted there could ever be much manufacturing in the United States.

Cotton manufacturers agreed with button-makers about the need for protective tariffs. Moses Brown of Providence, Rhode Island, who would become a powerful textile industrialist in the nineteenth century, wrote that he hoped the national government would provide "a bounty on the raw materials . . . and on the goods manu-factured equally to be paid out of additional imposts on all cotton and cotton linen goods and cotton yarn imported into the states from abroad." A bounty was a direct grant of money made by the government to a manufacturer to assist production. Brown was suggesting that when foreign textiles were imported, the government should use the revenue from the tariffs to create bounty funds to support domestic producers competing with foreign imports. But Brown believed that bounties would not provide enough assistance by themselves. To truly encourage manufacturing, bounties needed to supplement protective tariffs, and "therefore no importation of the yarn ought to be admitted without a large impost if at all." Manufacturers could produce all the yarn the nation needed if there "was encouragement given to protect the manufacturer from . . . the sale by foreign importation. . . ."[2]

Hamilton delivered the "Report on Manufactures" to Congress on December 5, 1791. At around 40,000 words it was twice as long as the "Report on Public Credit," the second longest report. It was a gigantic labor and a testament to how seriously Hamilton took promoting manufacturing in the United States. Again he hoped for Madison's approval and sent him an advance copy two weeks before delivering it to Congress.[3] At the start of the "Report" Hamilton's general remarks could only have pleased the artisans and craftsmen of the Republic. He opened by stating the importance of "encouraging manufactures in the United States. . . ." A nation was not safe when it relied so heavily on foreign markets for sale of its primary output, in this case agriculture. The danger was even greater when the United States depended on foreign nations to supply it with the manufactures it needed to fight wars. It was vital that the United States create much more domestic demand for its agriculture. Once the United States developed its own industry, and a growing population of craftsmen and manufacturers, they would become consumers of American agriculture and could supply American farmers with the manufactured goods currently imported primarily from Britain. Sound economic policy was even sounder political policy for, Hamilton explained, to be truly independent the nation "ought to endeavor to possess within itself all the essentials of national supply. These comprise the means of subsistence, habitation, clothing, and defense."[4]

Yet how did an underdeveloped and almost entirely agricultural country develop manufactures, especially when competing against the tremendous advantages enjoyed by Britain? Hamilton pointed out that the "want of capital for the prosecution of manufactures . . . [was] the most definite of the objections. . . ." Yet, Hamilton explained, because of Funding and Assumption, all of a sudden the holders of the public debt had highly valuable stock securities. The public debt could function as capital, and could be invested in worthy projects such as manufacturing enterprises. The public debt functioned as an effective source of investment capital not only because it bore interest and the certificates traded at par, but also because a relatively small group of wealthy men owned most of the debt. In its concentrated form, investors could more easily mobilize and direct this wealth. Because the "public funds" were "held by monied men" the problem of scarce capital had been solved.[5]

Once again, the funded debt was the answer. If holders of the debt invested in manufactures, there would be no shortage of capital to fund virtually any project. Yet Hamilton's desire to make funded debt the primary source of investment in manufactures meant that his priorities were fundamentally in conflict with the needs of the hatters, button-makers, clothiers, and most of the other craftsmen who actually did the manufacturing. That conflict was not at all surprising. After all, who were the nation's craftsmen? Hamilton could look back on the events of the 1770s and 1780s and see craftsmen regularly behaving in ways he considered licentious. They were often politically radical and challenged those he considered more reliable and dependable. Back in 1788 Hamilton had insisted that craftsmen,

> [m]echanics and manufacturers will always be inclined, with few exceptions, to give their votes to merchants in preference to persons of their own professions or trades.... They know that the merchant is their natural patron and friend....

But he hadn't needed Melancton Smith to tell him that claim was wishful thinking.[6] Hamilton understood well that George Clinton had counted New York craftsmen among his supporters, and craftsmen had regularly endorsed the most radical political options in Pennsylvania as well.[7] To promote manufacturing in ways that gave craftsmen more social and economic power would strengthen dangerous citizens who had already abused their liberty. The purpose of Hamilton's financial system was to accomplish the opposite, and the protective tariffs craftsmen wanted would have weakened that system economically, politically, socially, and culturally.

Above all else, to continue to be funded, the debt required revenue. Hamilton's entire system had as its foundation maximizing the reliable and steady supply of revenue to the national government. Well over ninety percent of that revenue came from taxes (imposts) on imported goods. Such imposts were known as revenue tariffs because they generated revenue for the government every time foreign goods were imported into the nation. Since there was virtually no market for agricultural goods in the United States, the vast majority of U.S. imports were manufactured items, which was what so frustrated the nation's craftsmen. Their solution was protective tariffs. But Hamilton well understood that protective tariffs were protective because they discouraged and so diminished imports. If the volume of imported goods shrank, the revenue would shrink too, which would make it much harder to keep paying the interest and funding the debt. Loss of revenue threatened to undermine the value of the debt and projects the debt was supposed to fund, such as the Bank of the United States and the manufacturing ventures Hamilton was imagining. The financial system depended on there being few if any protective tariffs.

A careful reader of the "Report on Manufactures" could see Hamilton's preferences. When he discussed how to encourage domestic manufactures, in his 40,000-word report he gave protective tariffs 127 words. Hamilton acknowledged that protective tariffs could successfully promote manufactures and left it at that. He devoted about 2,000 words to bounties and premiums. Premiums were another type of direct government grant and functioned similarly to bounties. Hamilton praised bounties, describing them as "one of the most efficacious means of encouraging manufactures and in some views the best . . . a species of encouragement more positive and direct than any other. . . ." Unlike Moses Brown, who had discussed bounties as supplementary and complimentary to protective tariffs, Hamilton suggested that bounties should be enacted instead of them. Bounties were more desirable than protective tariffs, Hamilton argued. Protective tariffs suddenly cut off imports that had been finding a ready market, which led to very high prices as consumers had to buy domestically produced goods. Hamilton praised bounties over protective tariffs because "[b]ounties have not, like high protecting duties, a tendency to produce scarcity [which] . . . is commonly the ultimate effect of an additional duty."[8]

Hamilton rejected Brown's notion that bounties should reinforce protective tariffs. By doing so, Hamilton conceived a way to promote manufactures that directly offered very little to the actual artisans and craftsmen who owned the shops and tools and did the manufacturing. Bounties, which were "positive and direct" government grants of assistance, could go to particular manufacturing enterprises that were able to produce enough to meet the conditions for earning the bounties. But the funds for the bounties would come from revenue available primarily because foreign manufactures continued to pour into the United States. And that vast volume of foreign goods made it difficult for craftsmen to compete and so earn the bounties.

Having defended bounties against protective tariffs in his "Report," Hamilton next discussed a dangerous issue he knew he would have to face after the conflict over the Bank of the United States. Nobody disputed that protective tariffs were constitutional. The national government had the right to lay taxes and could set them as high as it liked. But did it have the right to give some of its revenue directly to selected, preferred citizens, which is what a bounty amounted to? Obviously it did, insisted Hamilton. He had already succeeded in building a bank out of the general welfare clause, so of course he could offer a bounty. In order to make that case, once again Hamilton relied on his open-ended interpretation of the general welfare clause. He reasoned that bounties were constitutional because the general welfare clause merely required that all taxes Congress imposed be uniform throughout the United States. There was no limitation on the power to tax, and the only stipulation was that the money raised provide for the common defense and the general welfare of the nation. It was the duty of Congress to determine how best to do that. The Constitution, argued Hamilton, "left to the discretion of the national legislative to pronounce upon the objects, which concern the general welfare, and for which under that description, an appropriation of money is requisite and proper." If Congress decided to promote the general welfare by using its power to tax to fund bounties to support manufacturing, then of course it could for "whatever concerns the general interests . . . are within the sphere of the national councils as far as regards an application of money."[9]

JEFFERSON, MADISON, AND THE REPORT ON MANUFACTURES

The "Report on Manufactures" aroused Jefferson's and Madison's worst fears. It relied on the same open-ended interpretation of the Constitution on which the Bank had depended. To them the "Report" sought to move the United States away from the agricultural third stage and to the fourth stage of manufacturing, finance, banking, debt, and the culture of monarchy. But the "Report" also denied to craftsmen what they believed they needed most, protective tariffs. Those tariffs would encourage all manufactures. Bounties funded by the revenue generated from imports would assist only the manufacturing enterprises that received them. With the

"Report" Hamilton was provoking a strange alliance in opposition to him: those most dubious about encouraging the growth of extensive manufactures, and those most directly interested in their encouragement.

On January 21, 1792, Madison answered a letter from Henry Lee in which Lee had denounced the "Report on Manufactures" as an example of "the principles and measures heretofore adopted and to me execrable [disgraceful]."[10] Madison agreed. He told Lee that after everything else Congress had done at Hamilton's urging, if it backed the vision contained in the report then "I shall consider the fundamental and characteristic principles of the Govt. as subverted." If after the bank, Hamilton's method for interpreting the Constitution also allowed for bounties, then the Constitution could no longer be understood as having created a government "possessing special powers taken from the General mass." Instead, in Hamilton's hands the Constitution would create a national government "possessing the gen[era]l mass with special powers reserved out of it." This interpretation subverted the Constitution, Madison had no doubt. And the subversion took "place in defiance of the true and universal construction and the sense in which the instrument is known to have been proposed, advocated, and ratified."

In Madison's view the situation could not be more alarming. He could easily fit these developments into the pattern that had destroyed all past republican experiments. It was easy for him to interpret the events of the past year as producing the dangerous concentration of power that would eventually allow a despotic government to destroy liberty. If this situation continued, Madison informed Lee, the only question that would remain was whether "the people of this country will submit to a constitution not established by themselves, but imposed on them by their rulers." In the past, in England in particular, Madison believed despotic power had destroyed liberty because the people had been so confused and unaware that they had not even noticed as tyranny descended on them. That could not be allowed to happen in the United States. And so, Madison concluded in his letter, regarding the citizens of the United States it "must unquestionably be the wish of all who are friendly to their rights, that their situation should be understood by them, and that they should have as fair an opportunity as possible of judging for themselves."[11]

By January 1792, indeed several months before that, Madison had decided that the argument he and Jefferson were having with Hamilton could not remain contained to the halls of Congress and the dueling opinion memos of the President's cabinet. But now with the "Report on Manufactures" he felt the case was strong enough that the people would listen. If all went well, his conflict with Hamilton would spread to the streets and his would become the people's cause.

Jefferson agreed. In February 1792 he sketched a memo titled "Notes on the Constitutionality of Bounties to Encourage Manufacturing." Hamilton had anticipated precisely this constitutional objection when he tried to preempt it in the "Report." Clearly Jefferson was unconvinced. Like Madison, Jefferson argued that the sovereign people granted specific powers to the national government, and it could not stray beyond them. With manufacturing, then, the question was "How to encourage?" To start, insisted Jefferson, people had to understand that Hamilton's interpretation of the Constitution was dangerously wrong. The Constitution was a precise document intended to enlarge the scope and power of the national government, but in specific and clearly stated ways. When it came to encouraging manufacturing, the national government could not move beyond the powers granted to it by the Constitution, in this case the power to tax. The only constitutional way to encourage was therefore crystal clear: the "means in the hands of the general government for encouraging our own manufactures is to ensure a preference and encourage a demand for them by overcharging the prices of foreign by heavy duties." Jefferson did not support protective tariffs in principle, though he acknowledged that they were constitutional. But bounties clearly were not, for "the general government has no powers but what are given by the Constitution; as the levying of money on the people to give out in [bounties] is not among the powers in that instrument, nor necessary to carry out any of the enumerated powers. . . . [I am] unable to say that the General Government can avail itself of this incentive to improvement."[12]

WILLIAM DUER AND THE SOCIETY FOR ESTABLISHING USEFUL MANUFACTURES

Since 1790 Hamilton had become well used to proceeding without the support of Jefferson and Madison. Now, by making use of public debt, he had conceived how to promote manufacturing without protective tariffs. But to understand the full impact William Duer had on Hamilton's grand vision, it is necessary briefly to return to the second half of 1791 to see how Duer became entangled with Hamilton's plans for the nation's industrial development. When Duer's stock schemes had finally collapsed in March 1792, he did not only damage thousands of lives and shake confidence in the nation's public credit. He also inflicted a fatal blow to Hamilton's hopes to use the funded debt and the credit structure the Bank provided to promote industrial development in the United States. Hamilton believed that to give life to the ideas in his "Report on Manufactures," he needed the support of those moneyed men he felt he could trust. In the spring of 1791, to his later unending regret, he saw no reason not to trust his longtime friend William Duer. Hamilton approached Duer with his plan for manufacturing in April 1791, three months before the bank scrip went on sale, and nine months before the million dollar bank scheme, the stock gamble that finally revealed Duer's true character to Hamilton. Hamilton's timing could not have been worse. Had he waited to set his plans in motion until the fall of 1791, it is inconceivable that he would have entrusted them to Duer as he did that spring.

On April 20, 1791, Hamilton sent Duer his plan for the Society for Establishing Useful Manufactures, the grand industrial project that would put into practice the ideas he was working into the "Report on Manufactures."[13] The Society brought together all of the ideas Hamilton had conceived in the early 1780s and implemented in 1790–1791. It was intended to encourage economic growth and diversification. It would also strengthen the reliable moneyed men by reinforcing the social relations of hierarchy and deference. If the Society succeeded as Hamilton hoped, industrial development would encourage free, republican citizens to use their liberty responsibly without degenerating into licentiousness. Hamilton's decision to support bounties and rely on the public debt, while rejecting protective tariffs, fit perfectly with this vision of political economy and the proper social and cultural order for the United States.

In the prospectus for the Society for Establishing Useful Manufactures, Hamilton wrote that capital to support manufacturing would come from "a proper application of the public debt, [and be] an enhancement of the value of the debt; by giving it a new and additional employment and utility." Hamilton then proposed that the Society be granted a charter of incorporation, this time by New Jersey. He did not feel like fighting the issue of the national government and corporate charters so soon after the bank bill. He planned the Society to manufacture on a grand scale, possibly employing over a thousand laborers and producing paper and cloth goods as well as linens, cottons, shoes, pottery, hats, and brass and iron ware.

The Society would be capitalized at $1 million, meaning it would be authorized to sell $1 million worth of stock in $100 shares. The crucial feature was how the stock would be purchased: "one half in the funded six percent stock, or three percent of two dollars for one, and the other half in deferred stock."[14] In other words, the entire stock of the Society would be purchased with public debt from the three varieties of public debt. Over all, the three varieties together paid an interest rate of about four percent, and we can estimate that four percent is what the Society would receive. If the plan worked, the Society would sell $1 million of its stock and receive $1 million in public debt. The Society would become a public creditor earning about $40,000 per year in interest payments paid by the national government in gold and silver. The interest payment amounted to a massive annual government subsidy; an amount that would have the impact of about $3.25 billion in the U.S. economy of the twenty first century. Since there would be no protective tariffs, that was just the sort of assistance a manufacturing enterprise needed in order to compete with foreign manufactures.

Adding insult to injury for smaller craftsmen, the revenue that paid the Society its interest came from the taxes on the very imports that were doing the craftsmen such harm. Yet because of the subsidy, the Society would be able to produce goods competitive with those imports, and so would be in a position to earn the bounties that Hamilton planned as a secondary form of assistance. This plan was very much a top-down model for promoting manufacturing that fit well with Hamilton's sense of the social and cultural relations the United States needed. Debt holders, the moneyed men, would own the manufacturing enterprises. Actual craftsmen would need to behave with respect and deference, and be supervised and mentored by those more capable of shouldering the responsibilities of liberty. Revolutionary political culture meant that craftsmen had stopped looking on moneyed men as "their natural patrons and friends." Hamilton's industrial policy would now give them little choice but to do so. Hamilton expected his methods for promoting manufacturing to provide the Republic the economic development it needed, while also promoting "durable liberty" and discouraging craftsmen from the exuberant liberty that led to licentiousness.

To direct the Society, Hamilton chose William Duer. Over the next several months, Duer's spectacular failure led to the eventual collapse of the Society. Desperately trying to avoid bankruptcy, Duer raided the Society's capital reserves in early March 1792, just a few days before being hauled off to debtor's prison. Many of the Society's investors, closely connected to Duer, were also destroyed by his fall.[15] The Society never really recovered. Unlike the public debt, which continued to bear interest and so could rebound, or the Bank, which was better capitalized and not controlled by Duer's speculating circle, the Society was far too tied up with Duer's schemes.

But the reason for the Society's failure, indeed for the failure of this top-down model for industrial development in the first half of the nineteenth century, was as much cultural and social as it was financial. Hamilton promoted manufacturing while offering little to the aspirations for freedom, autonomy, and self-improvement of actual craftsmen. It took a skilled craftsman to explain his fellow laborers to Hamilton. In October 1791, Thomas Marshall wrote to Hamilton. Marshall was an English artisan Hamilton had hired to oversee the Society's cotton mill.[16] As he looked over the plan for the Society, Marshall worried that the enterprise was too big to be manageable. It was also structured in a way that alienated rather than encouraged and valued the craftsmen whose skills and knowhow were essential for the project to succeed.

In his letter Marshall warned Hamilton, the "more I think on this affair, I am persuaded that there is a great risk in pursuing it in the manner in which it is proposed." Marshall knew how proud, skilled craftsmen thought. He was especially worried that they would resist being under the authority of others, especially those who did not share their knowledge and love of their crafts. He explained to Hamilton that though large industrial enterprises had at times succeeded in Europe, they were most likely to do so when the craftsmen "were all employed for their own profit, and not as hirelings." The Society for Establishing Useful Manufactures appeared to him to provide the worst possible organization and the least likelihood of success. Given all the different varieties of manufacture, it would need a director for each branch that the craftsmen would respect, and managers below the directors "each capable of following the branch entrusted to him with the eye of a real and intelligent manufacturer." It was unlikely that the gentlemen who owned most of the debt, and who would therefore own and control the Society for Establishing Useful Manufactures, possessed these qualifications. And so the Society would end up having "to depend absolutely on the head Work-men," the proud skilled craftsmen whose political behavior had so concerned Hamilton in the first place. Yet, Marshall implored Hamilton, even the most honest craftsmen would find the situation intolerable, for they could "never be stimulated by the interest which animates those who work for themselves." Ultimately, Marshall warned, "unless God should send us saints for workmen and angels to conduct them, there is the greatest reason to fear for the success of the plan."[17]

Duer was no angel. By late spring 1792 his betrayal was clear. Duer's behavior did not only threaten to discredit the financial system; he had also all but ensured the destruction of the Society for Establishing Useful Manufactures. Distraught, Hamilton wrote to the Connecticut banker and merchant Nehemiah Hubbard that he now understood it was "far from easy to find a choice of proper characters" who met the expectations he had for the nation's most prominent and powerful citizens. Concerning the Society in particular, Hamilton could only promise that "[t]hose characters in the Direction [of the Society] who were too much enveloped in speculation to pay proper attention to the trust will henceforth be out of the question. . . ."[18]

But Marshall had pointed to an even deeper problem than the personal failings of men such as Duer. Even moneyed men who acted honestly would oversee "hirelings," not those "who work for themselves." And "hirelings" was not what proud, independent, craftsmen inspired by revolutionary politics wanted to be. Their dream for advancing manufacturing drew on bottom-up ideas of support. Craftsmen wanted protective tariffs, the chance to develop their own crafts, and to be independent of the economic power and social authority of others. Hamilton's top-down method appeared to craftsmen to threaten their aspirations. That meant that if Madison made the direct appeals to the people he had mentioned to Henry Lee, craftsmen might very well side with a Virginia planter devoted to the agricultural third stage against the author of the "Report on Manufactures."

DECIDING TO MOBILIZE THE PEOPLE

After the "Report on Manufactures" appeared in December 1791 and the second stock market crash struck in March 1792, Jefferson and Madison were determined to provoke as loud and angry a public conflict as they could. They had tried through normal political channels to get a commercial policy that aligned the United States with revolutionary France and against monarchical Britain. They had tried to stop Funding and Assumption and the Bank. Instead, Jefferson concluded in his notes of a private conversation he had with Washington in March 1792, Hamilton had amassed so much power and influence that he had essentially taken over the executive branch. He now used this power to warp the sensibilities of the citizenry and to undermine the integrity of the Republic's institutions. Hamilton was "deluging the states with paper money [and] withdrawing our citizens from the pursuits of commerce, manufactures, buildings, and other branches of useful industry, to occupy themselves and their capitals in a species of gambling, destructive of morality, and which had introduced its poison into the government itself." Jefferson accused "particular members of the legislative" of voting for Hamilton's programs so they could "feather their nests." How could he hope to convince those whose corrupt gains depended on their not being convinced? The only recourse, he decided, was a direct appeal to the people.[19]

That Jefferson and Madison had decided to mobilize the people requires consideration. They were as committed as was Hamilton to the idea of a natural aristocracy. Jefferson and Madison agreed that the people had acted licentiously during the 1780s, and had posed the greatest threat to liberty during that decade. Madison had convinced Jefferson of the need for a much stronger national government by arguing that the people themselves had far too much power, and that the tyranny of the majority would destroy liberty. How could Madison decide to appeal directly to and seek to mobilize the people? He had argued in 1788 that the people were the most likely source of tyranny and oppression. He had told Jefferson that the "real power lies in the majority of the community and the invasion of private rights is *chiefly* to be apprehended, not from the acts of government contrary to the sense of its constituents, but from the acts in which the government is the mere instrument of the major number of the constituents."[20]

In 1788 Madison had considered it extremely unlikely that "a succession of artful and ambitious rulers, may by gradual and well-timed advances, finally erect an independent government on the subversion of liberty." He was so convinced that the real problem was the tyranny of the majority, and not the ambitions of a dangerous minority, that he had informed Jefferson, "I must own that I see no tendency in our government to danger on that side." What a difference four years had made. What Madison had thought highly unlikely in 1788, even in the distant future, he now believed had already happened, and not after a long succession of artful rulers, but during the first president's first term. Yes, the majority could act tyrannically and indulge in dangerous licentiousness. Direct appeals to the majority were highly risky. But Madison had grown convinced that the alternative was the total certainty of the rise of the oppressive culture of monarchy, brought about by the poison of Hamilton's system and the gambling of his corrupt followers.

Jefferson was also prepared to provoke a public debate. Almost from the start of his tenure as Secretary of State, as he tried to bring the United States closer to revolutionary France, he had been prevented by Hamilton's commitment to Britain.[21] Only a monarchist, he decided, would oppose the spread of republican revolution. To support a republic rising in the heart of monarchical Europe was clearly the only policy for the United States. Jefferson wrote to his Virginia ally George Mason that if republican government arose in France then "it will spread sooner or later all over Europe." Yet if it failed in France Europe would remain a stronghold of monarchy and a dangerous, perpetual enemy to the United States. The future of the American Republic depended on the French Revolution, which revealed how truly sinister Hamilton's actions were. He denied the French Republic support while seeking to restore British institutions in the United States. Who could deny, Jefferson told Mason, "that we have among us a sect who believes ... [the British constitution] to contain whatever is perfect in human institutions; that the members of this sect have ... names and offices which stand high in the estimation of our countrymen." Like Madison, he had no choice but to gamble that "the great mass of our community is untainted with these heresies. . . . On this I build my hope that we have not labored in vain, and that our experiment will still

THOMAS JEFFERSON.

Jefferson as he looked during the time of his mighty argument with Hamilton.

prove that men can be governed by reason." It had become necessary to speak directly to that "great mass" for "more attention should be paid to the general opinion."[22]

By July 1792 Jefferson had so perfected his denunciation of Hamilton that he could reduce it to a brief memo. The memo, titled "Note of Agenda to Reduce the Government to True Principles," called for creating the "Committee to Count Money in the Treasury." This Committee would "divide the treasury department...abolish the bank...[and] condemn report on MANUFACTURES."[23]

DISSENTING FROM FEDERALIST 10, MADISON'S ESSAYS IN THE *NATIONAL GAZETTE*

Yet how did you excite, but also guide and educate, the great mass? That was the task Jefferson and Madison set for themselves. The first step was to intervene in public debate and discussion, which both Jefferson and Madison believed Hamilton had been dominating. A primary reason for that, they thought, was that most of the influential newspapers, particularly John Fenno's Philadelphia *Gazette of the United States*, supported Hamilton's policies. Jefferson wrote to Madison in late July 1791 that people were not being told the truth about Hamilton's system due to "Fenno's being the only weekly or half weekly paper, and under general condemnation for its Toryism."[24]

The solution was to support a newspaper that would rouse the "great mass," but that could also refine and educate it. The people could then zealously protect their liberty by defeating Hamilton and destroying his system. But instruction from true natural aristocrats would also teach the people to carefully respect fundamental natural rights. The people would then not act tyrannically as they exercised their considerable power. In the summer of 1791, as the Bank of the United States prepared to open for business, Jefferson and Madison had reached out to an old friend and college classmate of Madison's, the poet and newspaper writer Philip Freneau. Over the summer they negotiated with him and eventually brought him to Philadelphia. Jefferson sweetened the deal by employing Freneau as a part-time translator in the office of the Secretary of State.[25] Freneau's real job was to start a newspaper to challenge Fenno's *Gazette of the United States*. On October 31, 1791, Freneau published the first issue of the *National Gazette* in Philadelphia, and for the next two years it provided unceasing criticism of Hamilton. The situation was surely bizarre. The Secretary of State was subsidizing regular denunciations of the Secretary of the Treasury. The conflict Hamilton had with Jefferson and Madison had finally gone public.

The most significant articles Freneau published were unsigned but written by Madison between December 1791 and September 1792. These were the months that saw the release of the "Report on Manufactures," Duer's direction of the Society for Establishing Useful Manufactures, and the second stock market crash that ruined so many, including Duer. In these essays Madison sought to explain what he thought a true republic should look like. He described the central role a majority of the people played in forcing their leaders to build that republic. The essays were Madison's effort to educate "the great mass" about its responsibility to force the government to obey the majority, while not violating the rights of minorities. It was a very tall order. The essays reflected the full maturation of Madison's political thought, and the clearest description of the sort of republic he and Jefferson wanted. His important essays for the *Federalist Papers* had speculated about how the Constitution would function. His *National Gazette* essays came after the experience of living under the Constitution he had done so much to create.

The first essay, titled "Consolidation," warned readers to fear "a consolidation of the states into one government," which Madison was convinced was happening. The danger was that the leader of such a government would receive "an accumulation of powers in the hands of that officer, as might by degrees transform him into a monarch." To prevent consolidation, the state governments had to keep a great deal of power and authority over their own affairs. But having many powerful states raised the problem of too little coordinated action, and possibly even states seeking to injure each other. The solution was to increase "the mutual confidence and affection of all parts of the union." With greater affection for each other, states would "concur amicably, or differ with moderation . . . and by such examples . . . guard and adorn the vital principle of our republican institutions."

In "Consolidation" Madison argued that state governments were closer and more accountable to the people than the national government. If states remained powerful, and if mutual affection among the people could be encouraged, then different and divisive interests would be less likely to develop among American citizens. Madison reasoned that if people's experiences and living conditions remained relatively similar, "the less supposed difference of interests, and the greater concord and confidence throughout the great body of the people, the more readily must they sympathize with each other." People living in similar conditions, who could, therefore, more readily sympathize with each other, would feel "a common manifestation of their sentiment." And such a republican citizenry, unified by its common concerns and experiences, was much more likely to "take the alarm at usurpation and oppression, and the more effectually will they consolidate their defense of the public liberty."[26]

Dissenting from his previous arguments in "Federalist 10," Madison now sought to unleash the power of the majority. Madison still feared the tyranny of the majority. But the tyranny of Hamilton's minority was the far greater danger. And so he would now have to overcome the obstacles to organizing the majority, obstacles that he had done more than anyone to put in place with the structure of the Constitution and support for the growing size of the nation. To organize and unleash the majority safely, Madison now argued, those who did so had to foster mutual affection among the citizens who would comprise that majority. The United States had somehow to create in the majority circumstances and conditions of life that greatly lessened the differences and the variety of interests among the people. A majority that thought and lived the right way could use its great power to protect liberty. If most people lived in similar conditions and sympathized with each other, there would be very few people who would not benefit from what benefitted the majority.

This sort of majority was the only force that could preserve liberty. No government could long resist the majority, nor would it be just if it regularly sought do so. Government could not resist the majority for very long because "[p]ublic opinion sets bounds to every government, and is the real sovereign in every free one." Yet confusion could undermine that sovereign. Confusion came from ignorance or division of interests, from concentrations of great wealth and corresponding extensive poverty. If a small group of the self-interested seeking power wished to undermine sovereign majority public opinion, that group would pass laws and pursue policies that would encourage such divisions and confusion. Madison explained to the *National Gazette* readers that "there are cases where not being fixed [public opinion] may be influenced by the government." That danger was especially significant in the United States because "the larger a country, the less easy for its real opinion to be ascertained, and the less difficult to be counterfeited. . . . This is favorable to the authority of government." In 1788 in "Federalist 10" Madison had praised the Constitution and the extended sphere of the nation's size because they limited the majority's capacity to unite and act forcefully. In 1792 he now believed the structure and the size were enabling Hamilton's faction to fracture majority will and impose the tyranny of the minority.

Public opinion—majority will—was the only just sovereign. Justice came only by knowing what majority will was. Just as important, majority will had to be educated and enlightened so that its views were always very close to the public good of the protection of all fundamental, natural rights. Madison, still very much the eighteenth-century political thinker, was not saying that what the majority wanted was automatically just. But he believed Hamilton's system was gravely injuring the majority. Only the majority's determined effort could stop the triumph of the culture of monarchy.

Rousing the majority was the only option. So it was essential to do everything possible to ensure that the majority once roused knew what justice was, and shared the mutual affection and common interests that would prevent it from abusing its power. For there to be justice, the majority had to act justly. The majority least likely to abuse its power was one made up of citizens who felt common sentiments due to their similar living conditions and experiences. Therefore it was vital to support "[w]hatever facilitates a general intercourse of sentiments, as good roads, domestic commerce, a free press, and particularly a circulation of newspapers, through the entire body of the people, and Representatives going from and returning among every part of them...."[27]

Majority public opinion, shaped by commercial and social interactions, and by shared ideas provided by virtuous, enlightened writers in a free press, would be committed to "defending liberty against power, and power against licentiousness: and in keeping every portion of power within its proper limits." Ultimately, the only protection against licentiousness and anarchy was the majority's virtue and its decision to behave well, for nothing could limit the actions of the majority once roused except its own decision not to behave badly. As Madison explained to the readers of the *National Gazette*, every government, even absolute monarchies, ultimately rested on the people's good opinion. If the vast majority denied any government allegiance, that government would soon crumble. The people's opinion—public opinion—was truly all powerful, and the responsibility for the sort of government people had really rested with them. Therefore Madison informed his readers, "[a]ll power has been traced up to opinion. The stability of all governments and security of all rights may be traced to the same source." It was essential "that the public opinion of the United States should be enlightened; that it should attach itself to their governments ... derived ... from the legislative authority of the people."[28]

The only way, Madison argued in an essay of late January 1792, to rouse an enlightened majority was by organizing it into a political party. It seemed a shocking thing for Madison to say. He had equated parties with factions in "Federalist 10." In that essay he had argued that there was a single tangible public good, and had concluded that parties competing with each other were seeking their own interests rather than trying to secure it. But it was now clear, as far as Madison was concerned, that one of these selfish parties, the very powerful unified faction of moneyed men, had seized control of government. The solution was not permanent political parties or an institutionalized party system. Instead, the citizens of the United States needed to build one great political party. In his essay Madison called it a "natural" party, as opposed to the "artificial" parties that behaved as factions by pursuing their own interests distinct from the public good. Madison's "natural" party was the vast majority. It would be held together by mutual affection, shared conditions and expectations of life, a zeal for liberty, and the enlightened education received from a free press and the writings of true natural aristocrats capable of explaining the public good. The way to prevent factions (i.e., "artificial" parties) and competition among selfish interests was to shape society so it could produce the one great "natural" party of the virtuous majority.

Such a society would develop only if all of its citizens lived in political equality. But the right to vote and equal protection under the law were only the start. A republic seeking to produce a proper majority also had to prevent all "*unnecessary* opportunities for a few to increase the inequality of property, by an immoderate, and especially an unmerited accumulation of riches." Political equality was possible only with a great deal of economic and social equality. If the majority used its political power wisely it would, through "the silent operation of laws," protect the rights of property. But the majority would also "reduce extremes of wealth towards a state of mediocrity [i.e., closer to the average] and raise extreme indigence towards a state of comfort." Clearly policies such as bounties had no place in a proper republic. The majority had to prevent all "measures which operate differently on different interests, and particularly such as favor one interest at the expense of another." Few readers would miss the references to Hamilton's proposals, or that the emphasized word "unnecessary" invoked his interpretation of the Constitution. Madison was arguing that the natural order of things in the United States would prevent extremes in wealth and poverty, and just laws could assist that natural order. But Hamilton's system, he claimed, unnaturally and artificially increased distinctions, to fracture the people, divide public opinion, and create the conditions for unaccountable government and the tyranny of the few. People who supported such polices, Madison concluded, thought "[l]et us then increase . . . natural distinctions by favoring an inequality of property; and let us add to them artificial distinctions by establishing kings, and nobles. . . ."[29]

Between February and September 1792 Madison wrote additional essays that addressed the specific conditions of the United States, and that denounced the policies of Hamilton. On February 4th he explained to readers what he thought the government of the United States was supposed to look like, and how it could be preserved in the way the Constitution intended. American citizens understood "by universal experience," wrote Madison, that "[p]ower . . . [was] liable to abuses. . . ." They had therefore divided power. They had created a separation of powers by creating the executive, legislative, and judicial branches of government.

But they had not simply divided power within the national government. They had also divided it between the national government and the state governments. Now the people had to make sure that those in power at the national level continued to respect the authority the Constitution had always intended the states to have. Making the national government respect the authority of the states was difficult. Those who came together in the nation's capital were jealous to keep as much power as possible. And with Hamilton's financial program, the temptation grew even stronger to imitate a court culture. The enlightened majority had to force the national government to respect the proper constitutional division of power. It was true that under the weak Articles of Confederation the states had been far too powerful and had threatened to tear the nation apart. But now men such as Hamilton used the threat of division, of schism among the states, as a pretext to consolidate power and move the national government beyond the control of the people. No condition was more fatal to liberty or the Republic than such consolidation of power, Madison informed his readers.

A true republican balance had to be struck between the national government and the states, and those who "pronounce it impossible offer no alternative to their country but schism or consolidation; both of them bad but the latter worst, since it is the high road to monarchy. . . ."[30]

The implication was clear. The structural system of a separation of powers and a federal division of authority between the nation and the states would protect liberty. A key way federalism protected liberty was by limiting the national government so that it could not do things like incorporate the Bank of the United States or provide bounties to the Society for Establishing Useful Manufactures. But the experience of the last two years had also convinced Madison that liberty could not be protected by structure alone. After all, the Constitution had established the proper structure. Yet Hamilton was about to impose the culture of monarchy. The ultimate source of safety, Madison told his readers, was them. They had to organize themselves immediately as a zealous, angry, righteous, enlightened, and rational great majority party. Of course, wrote Madison, "partitions and internal checks of power" were essential. But they were not the primary source "nor the chief palladium of constitutional liberty." No structure, no matter how thoughtfully conceived and carefully defined, mattered without a virtuous, enlightened majority able to use its absolute power of public opinion to demand the public good. The Constitution could only do so much; the "people who are the authors of this blessing, must also be its guardians." Only the majority could truly preserve liberty and their "eyes must be ever ready to mark, their voice to pronounce, and their arm to repel or repair aggressions on the authority of their constitutions; the highest authority next to their own because the immediate work of their own. . . ."[31]

Madison had come to believe that a properly educated and enlightened majority had a perpetual constitutional role to play in overseeing, but also administering, republican government. The majority needed unceasingly to measure the conduct of its government against the Constitution. Citizens had to elect only those statesmen who would respond to and try to reflect well-reasoned and judicious public opinion. And if public opinion had been cultivated properly, it would always end up very close to the public good.

Citizens could only form this proper majority if they felt "a common manifestation of their sentiments," if they "sympathized with each other." In his *National Gazette* essays, then, Madison also discussed the material conditions citizens needed, where and how they should live. Only the right material conditions would allow for the "common manifestation of sentiments" in a virtuous and substantial majority. The citizens who comprised this majority had to be widely distributed across the nation, and should have the occupations that allowed for a mostly equal population without great wealth or poverty. Madison argued that "[t]he best distribution is that which most favor health, virtue, intelligence, and competency in the greatest number of citizens." Competency was a term all readers of the *National Gazette* understood. In the eighteenth century it meant owning the resources, usually land, which could sustain a family and keep it from depending on resources owned by others. Madison had no doubt that a nation primarily of farmers would best maintain these conditions. For, he argued, "Competency is more universally the lot of those who dwell in the country, when liberty is at the same time their lot. It follows, that the greater the proportion of this class to the whole society, the more free, the more independent, and the more happy must be the society itself."

Yet Madison did not reject all manufacturing, just the conditions that produced those whom Thomas Marshall had called "hirelings." Skilled, intelligent craftsmen, who Marshall had described as "stimulated by that interest which animates those who work for themselves," could also make a useful contribution to the Republic. The United States had to prevent for as long as possible the large cities of Europe and the extremes of poverty found there, particularly among those who labored in industrial drudgery. But skilled, independent craftsmen were another thing entirely. And so, Madison explained, when "appreciating the regular branches of manufacturing and mechanical industry . . . whatever is least favorable to vigor of body, to the faculties of mind, or to the virtues of the utilities of life, instead of being forced or fostered by the public authority ought to be seen with regret. . . ."[32] That message was far more attractive to most craftsmen than was Hamilton's.

Madison explained the distinctions he was making between desirable and undesirable manufacturing occupations by discussing the plight of a group of English shoe buckle makers. In an essay titled "Fashion," which appeared on March 20, 1792, just two weeks after the second stock market crash caused by Duer, Madison discussed a "humble address . . . presented to the Prince of Wales by the buckle manufacturers of Birmingham." Twenty thousand buckle makers had suddenly lost their jobs and could find no work because the fashion had changed from buckles to shoe strings and slippers. Here was a lesson for republican citizens regarding what should concern them about the policies driving the nation to the fourth stage and the culture of monarchy. Madison warned that "[t]he most precarious of all occupations are those depending on mere fashion." Fashion and luxury were possible only with great wealth, and great wealth went hand in hand with inequality and poverty, conditions fatal to republics and the formation of a proper and enlightened majority. Manufactures of luxuries, Madison warned, "[O]f all the occupations . . . are the least desirable in a free state, which produce the most servile dependence of one class of citizens on another class. This dependence must increase as the *mutuality* of wants is diminished." Destitute as they now were, the buckle makers had sunk "to the lowest point of servility.[33]

The deplorable state of the buckle makers was the culture of monarchy and the fourth stage reduced to its essence. In considering the buckle makers' tragedy, Madison invited comparison of their plight, and of those ruined by Duer's schemes, with the conditions of farmers and independent craftsmen who produced necessities. "What a contrast" the buckle makers were "to the independent situation and manly sentiments of American citizens who lived on their own soil, or whose labor is necessary to its cultivation, or who were occupied in supplying the wants, which being founded in solid utility . . . produce a reciprocity of dependence, at once ensuring subsistence, and inspiring a dignified sense of social rights." Madison contrasted monarchical Britain where "the mutuality of wants is diminished" with the republican United States, which enjoyed "a reciprocity of dependence." With these phrases Madison meant that in Britain the wealthy and powerful lived so differently from those like the buckle makers that they no longer had the same wants and needs. There were no sources of mutual affection. Far preferable was a society where the vast majority enjoyed a competency, but rarely more, and supplied agricultural goods, or owned their own tools and shops and produced manufactures "founded in solid utility" that would never go out of fashion. That society had the "reciprocity of dependence," where all needed each other, and where none could suddenly be reduced to begging.

Madison as he looked around the time he was writing his essays for the *National Gazette*.

Madison denounced what he viewed as Hamilton's vision for the Republic. The culture of monarchy, of credit, debt, stock markets, crashes, and hirelings, came from a "government operating by corrupt influence; substituting the motive of private interest in place of public duty; converting its pecuniary dispensations into bounties to favorites or bribes to opponents." Hamilton was "enlisting an army of interested partisans [all to] support a real domination of the few, under an apparent liberty of the many."[34] While such a government was not yet fully established in the United States, readers of the *National Gazette* had to consider the Republic and "who are its real friends?" They were not, Madison thundered,

those who favor measures which by pampering the spirit of speculation within and without government, disgust the best friends of union. Not those who promote unnecessary accumulations of the debt. . . . Not those who study, by arbitrary interpretations and invidious precedents, to pervert the limited government . . . into a government of unlimited discretion. . . . Not those who avow . . . principles of monarchy and aristocracy, in opposition to the republican principles . . . and the republican spirit of the people; or who espouse a system of measures more accommodated to the depraved examples of those hereditary forms, than the true genius of our own.[35]

Madison's final essay, on December 20, 1792, simply listed the values of a "Republican" and an "Anti-Republican." That was Hamilton, Madison concluded: the principal anti-republican, the chief agent of the culture of monarchy.

HAMILTON'S FURIOUS RESPONSE

Madison had committed an all-out assault. And it had had the desired effect. From friends and allies Hamilton heard of rising opposition in Pennsylvania, New Jersey, and New York. Most infuriating of all was the news he received that on a visit to New York Jefferson and Madison had formed a political alliance with George Clinton![36] A concerned President Washington wrote to Hamilton from Virginia in late July 1792, in the midst of Madison's series of essays. Since arriving at Mount Vernon he had sought the views of numerous "sensible and moderate men—known friends to the government." Washington assured Hamilton that all had praised the job he was doing as Secretary of the Treasury. Nevertheless, the President sadly recounted, "they seem to be alarmed at that system of policy, and those interpretations of the Constitution which have taken place. . . ."[37]

Hamilton was hurt and enraged by the onslaught. This was the context in which he wrote to Edward Carrington the letter mentioned in the introduction. It was a remarkable letter, close to 7,000 words. In it Hamilton vented his rage and began to conceive his public counterattack. Hamilton wrote Carrington that he felt the need "to unbosom myself to you on the present state of political parties and views." His pain and surprise were obvious, as was his profound sense of betrayal. Hamilton told Carrington that he had once viewed Madison as a friend and trusted ally. In fact, he had "accepted the office I now hold . . . under a full persuasion, that from a similarity of thinking, conspiring with personal good will, I should have the firm support of Mr. Madison." That assumption had mattered tremendously to Hamilton, who explained to Carrington that due to "the intrinsic difficulty of the situation and of the powers of Mr. Madison, I do not believe I should have accepted under a different supposition."[38]

Hamilton described how shocked he had been when Madison opposed Funding and Assumption. It had seemed to Hamilton a complete reversal of the positions Madison had taken when they had worked together on the *Federalist Papers*. Still, given the high regard he had for Madison and his "previous impressions of the fairness of Mr. Madison's character and my reliance on his good will towards me," at first Hamilton had believed that Madison was misguided but honest. But that was two years ago, and now Hamilton believed Madison no longer deserved his friendship or trust. He angrily informed Carrington that he had become "unequivocally convinced of the following truth—that Mr. Madison cooperating with Mr. Jefferson is at the head of a faction decidedly hostile to me and my administration, and actuated by views in my judgment subversive of the principles of good government and dangerous to the union, peace, and happiness of the country [and causing] a *serious alarm* in my mind for the public welfare. . . ."

How could he think otherwise, Hamilton wrote, as he recounted for Carrington the numerous times Jefferson in particular had tried to subvert the funding system? Jefferson had taken every opportunity to "throw censure on my principles . . . [and] even whispered suspicions of the rectitude of my motives and conduct." Though all men of sense and good will acknowledged the value of the national bank, Jefferson had "not only delivered an opinion against its constitutionality and expediency; but he did it in a style and manner which I felt as partaking of asperity and ill humor towards me." And he had behaved even worse during the times of greatest crisis. With frustration and anger, Hamilton informed Carrington that when the property of so many citizens had been endangered by the bursting of the stock bubble, "[a]s one of the trustees of the sinking fund, I have experienced in almost every leading question opposition from him." No matter the situation, "[w]hen any turn of things . . . has threatened either odium or embarrassment to me, he has not been able to suppress the satisfaction which it gave him."[39]

And now, Hamilton believed, Jefferson was a traitor. The Secretary of State was seeking to destroy the government. He had arranged for the publication of Philip Freneau's scandalous newspaper, and it was "notorious that contemporarily with the commencement of his paper, he was a clerk in the department of State." Supporting Freneau, and especially doing so with public funds, was treason as far as Hamilton was concerned, for "the present printer of the National Gazette . . . was a known anti-federalist." Freneau and Jefferson were "devoted to the subversion of me and the measures in which I have an agency . . . it is a paper of a tendency generally unfriendly to the Government of the U. States."[40] Madison had been thoroughly captured by Jefferson. As a result, he had behaved just as badly, if not worse. Madison had implied in congressional debate "that the public money under my particular direction had been unfaithfully applied to put undue advantages in the pockets of speculators and to support the debt at an artificial price for their benefit." Mere differences of perspective and disagreements over policy could not explain Madison's unjust cruelty. His behavior "left no doubt in anyone's mind that Mr. Madison was actuated by *personal* and political animosity." Hamilton recounted that he had even learned it was Madison who had introduced Freneau to Jefferson.[41]

Hamilton was convinced that by seeking to block his policies, Jefferson and Madison were encouraging the return of licentiousness, which would eventually destroy "durable liberty." But, incredibly, they were also seeking to speed up the process by leading a dangerous faction and inflaming the public. Hamilton told Carrington that Jefferson, Madison, and their followers were spreading their simplistic and sensationalist nonsense as widely as they could "in the legislature and the publications in the party news-papers." All their efforts were aimed at discrediting "the *principle* of a funded debt and represent[ing] it in the most odious light as a perfect Pandora's box." How could they wish to dismantle the funding system, Hamilton wondered, which was now a solemn promise made by the national

government and connected to its full faith and credit? What values did such
people have? Since the United States had committed to funding the debt, "what
would become of the Government should it be reversed?" Pouring his heart out
to Carrington, Hamilton was clearly shocked by what he believed Jefferson and
Madison had done. For the moment he was reduced to asking his friend a series of
ever more desperate questions:

> What of the national reputation? Upon what system of morality can so atro-
> cious a doctrine be maintained? In me, I confess it excites *indignation and
> horror*! . . . What are to become of the legal rights of property, of all char-
> ters of corporations, nay of all grants to a man and his heirs and assigns for-
> ever? . . . What is the term for which a government is in capacity to *contract*?
> Questions might be multiplied without end to demonstrate the pernicious ab-
> surdity of such a doctrine.[42]

Hamilton had no doubt that Jefferson's and Madison's ideas were reckless. They
would return the United States to the terrifying conditions that existed before the
Constitution had been ratified. He lamented, "In almost all questions great and
small Mr. Jefferson and Mr. Madison have been found among those who were disposed to narrow the Federal authority. The question of the Bank is one example." In
addition, in Congress Madison had "leaned to abridging the exercise of federal authority, and leaving as much as possible to the states, and he has lost no opportunity
of *sounding the alarm* . . . and of holding up the bugbear of a faction in the government having designs unfriendly to liberty." Madison's stance proved he was faithless,
indeed a liar. He had always presented himself to Hamilton as a reasonable man, as a
patriotic nationalist. Hamilton told Carrington that he knew "for a certainty it was
a primary article in his creed that the real danger in our system was the subversion of
the national authority by the preponderance of the state governments." Yet now "his
measures have proceeded on an opposite supposition."[43]

Even more inexcusably, Jefferson and Madison were seeking to subvert national
authority by linking the United States to the increasingly anarchic and dangerously
revolutionary French. France, Hamilton had no doubt, had fully degenerated into
licentiousness. Only the most thoughtless and irresponsible people, or those who
cared nothing for natural rights and "durable liberty," would want to have anything
to do with that violent nation. Yet when it came to foreign policy, "the views of these
Gentlemen are . . . equally unsound and dangerous." With as much contempt as it was
possible for him to express, Hamilton dismissed Jefferson's and Madison's view of the
European situation. They had, he informed Carrington, *"a womanish attachment to
France and a womanish resentment against Britain."* Jefferson was nothing more than
an irresponsible, dangerous, French radical. While in France he had drunk "deeply
of the French philosophy, in religion, in science, in politics." Now, "electrified plus
with attachment to France," he would even endanger his own government to advance
"the project of knitting together the two countries in the closest political bonds."

Jefferson's French revolutionary mania explained the "systematic opposition to me on the part of those gentlemen. My subversion, I am now satisfied, having been an object with them."[44]

Jefferson and Madison claimed "the existence of a monarchical party meditating the destruction of state and republican government." Yet it was Jefferson and Madison, not he, Hamilton told Carrington, who were bringing the nation closer to monarchy. They were subverting national authority and inflaming the people, who would act with violent rage and unreason. Jefferson and Madison were aiding the process that turned liberty into licentiousness. Licentiousness would then degenerate into anarchy, to be followed by the general horror that would compel the people to beg for a tyrant to impose order and save them from themselves. Outraged, Hamilton wrote that if he wanted to make a king in America, he would not promote his own policies, but instead would join Jefferson and Madison in their irresponsible incitement of the people. Had he wanted "to promote monarchy and overthrow the state governments" he would have acted precisely as Jefferson and Madison were doing now. He would seek to discredit and undermine stable, legitimate authority. He would "mount my hobby horse of popularity—I would cry out usurpation—danger to liberty etc.—I would endeavor to prostrate the national government—raise a ferment—and then ride in the whirlwind and direct the storm." Most likely the hysterical and "womanish" Jefferson and Madison did not understand what they were doing. But they were fools and dupes, for "there are men acting with Jefferson and Madison who have this in view I verily believe."[45]

Writing the long letter had obviously broken the dam holding back Hamilton's fury. After the May 26 letter he was fully prepared to go as public as Madison had gone. From the summer of 1792 on, he would confront Jefferson and Madison and participate in taking their great conflict to the people. He wrote an astonishing number of essays for the newspapers sounding the themes he had discussed in his letter to Carrington. In Fenno's *Gazette of the United States* he charged that Jefferson was subversive, really an Anti-Federalist.[46] Freneau was his creature and agent, and the end result would be licentiousness, then anarchy, and finally monarchy. If Jefferson and Madison urged the people to angrily rise up so they could lead them, Hamilton urged the people to quietly sit down so he could guide them.[47]

In late September Hamilton laid it all out for everybody to see in the *Gazette of the United States*. Many people revered Jefferson, he wrote, as they would any crafty demagogue riding the "hobby horse of popularity," but masquerading as the thoughtful friend of liberty. Indeed, "Mr. Jefferson has hitherto been distinguished as the quiet[,] modest, retiring philosopher—as the plain simple unambitious republican." In reality, Jefferson was "an intriguing incendiary—the aspiring turbulent competitor." Hamilton allowed that Jefferson was not necessarily consciously "the patron and promoter of national disunion, national insignificance, public disorder, and discredit." But the effect of his actions was what mattered, and the "political tenets of that gentleman tend to those points." Jefferson had a toxic influence on the United States. People had to see him for what he was, for "he wished to render odious, and

ALEXANDER HAMILTON.

Hamilton as he looked during the time of his mighty argument with Jefferson and Madison.

of course to subvert . . . all those deliberate and solemn acts of the legislature, which had become the pillars of public credit. . . ."

Hamilton asked his readers to consider what would happen if Jefferson succeeded. He would bring about disaster, and "[d]isunion would not long lag behind." Jefferson's careless and destructive ideas would alienate all solid and worthy citizens. Indeed, "[s]ober minded and virtuous men in every state would lose all confidence in, and all respect for, [the] government." How could such men respect a government organized on Jefferson's principles, a government that showed "so profligate a disregard to the *rights of property*, and to the obligations of good faith. Their support would of course be so far withdrawn or relaxed, as to leave in any easy prey to its enemies." Those who followed Jefferson, who would take advantage of the anarchy that came through his efforts, were a collection of the most irresponsible and dangerous figures. They were men like George Clinton who had endangered "durable liberty" since the revolution had begun. They were

the never to be satiated lovers of innovation and change—the tribe of pretended philosophers . . . who leading the dance to the tune of liberty withdraw law, endeavor to intoxicate the people with delicious but poisonous draughts to render them the easier victims of their rapacious ambition; the vicious and the fanatical of every class who are ever found the willing or the deluded followers of those seducing and treacherous leaders.

The road Jefferson would have the nation take led to only one place: "[W]here would all this end," Hamilton asked, "but in disunion and anarchy? In national disgrace and humiliation?"[48]

* * *

Both sides of this great argument were fully public now. A conflict that had begun in the private rooms and private writings of three men at one time friendly with each other, even at times close friends, now belonged to everyone. And as Madison had explained in the *National Gazette*, the people would decide.

NOTES

1 *PAH* 9: 339, 347–348, 354, 361.
2 *PAH* 9: 438.
3 *PAH* 9: 528.
4 *Reports of Alexander Hamilton*, 115–116, 161.
5 *Reports of Alexander Hamilton*, 146, 149.
6 Clinton Rossiter, ed., *The Federalist Papers* (New York: Mentor, 1961), 214.
7 Andrew Shankman, *Crucible of American Democracy: The Struggle to Fuse Egalitarianism and Capitalism in Jeffersonian Pennsylvania* (Lawrence, KS: University of Kansas Press, 2004), chapter 1.
8 *Reports of Alexander Hamilton*, 167–169.
9 *Reports of Alexander Hamilton*, 171–172.
10 *PJM* 14: 184.
11 *PJM* 14: 193–194.
12 *PTJ* 23: 172–173.
13 *PAH* 8: 300.
14 *PAH* 9: 145–148.
15 *PAH* 11: 186, 246–247, 259, 280–281, 348–349.
16 *PAH* 9: 73–74.
17 *PAH* 9: 251.
18 *PAH* 11: 355.
19 *PTJ* 23: 184, 186.
20 *Republic of Letters* 1: 564–565, emphasis original.
21 *PAH* 7: 408; *PTJ* 18: 562–564.
22 *PTJ* 19: 241.
23 *PTJ* 24: 215.
24 *PTJ* 20: 657.
25 For the discussions with Freneau, see *PJM* 14: 49–50, 52–53, 56–57; *PTJ* 19: 351, 416; *PTJ* 20: 667–668, 754, 756.
26 *PJM* 14: 137–139.
27 *PJM* 14: 170. Colleen Sheehan, *James Madison and the Spirit of Republican Government* (New York: Cambridge University Press, 2009).
28 *PJM* 14: 192.
29 *PJM* 14: 197–198, emphasis original.
30 *PJM* 14: 217–218.
31 *PJM* 14: 218.
32 *PJM* 14: 245–246.
33 *PJM* 14: 257–258, emphasis original.
34 *PJM* 14: 233–234.
35 *PJM* 14: 274.
36 *PAH* 8: 478–479; *PAH* 12: 369–370, 387; *PTJ* 24: 105, 134–135, 235–237.
37 *PAH* 12: 129.
38 *PAH* 11: 426–427.
39 *PAH* 11: 428–430, throughout the Carrington letter, emphasis original.
40 *PAH* 11: 430–43,1 emphasis original.
41 *PAH* 11: 434–435.

42 *PAH* 11: 437, emphasis original.

43 *PAH* 11: 437–438, emphasis original.

44 *PAH* 11: 439–440, emphasis original.

45 *PAH* 11: 443–444, .

46 Like Madison, Hamilton used pseudonyms. Also like Madison, most people figured out who the author was.

47 Examples of Hamilton's statements in newspapers are, *PAH* 12: 107, 157–164, 188–193, 393–401.

48 *PAH* 12: 498–501, 504, emphasis original.

CONCLUSION

Who won this mighty argument? Ultimately, this conclusion will suggest that in the long term Hamilton, Jefferson, and Madison all lost. In the short term the victors were clearly Jefferson and Madison. Over the next seven years after 1792 they led the Democratic-Republican Party as it grew into a national movement that dominated politics in most southern states, and also in Pennsylvania, New York, and New Jersey. They won in the middle Atlantic by attracting both farmers and craftsmen. Jefferson defeated Washington's former Vice President, President John Adams, in the election of 1800. He served as president for eight years and Madison followed him for an additional eight. After Madison came Jefferson's and Madison's friend, and fellow Virginian, James Monroe, president for two terms from 1817 to 1824. John Quincy Adams, the son of John Adams, followed Monroe for one term. But Quincy Adams had seen the clear direction of the future, and the process of his defection to the party of Jefferson had begun back in 1804, the same year that Jefferson's Vice President Aaron Burr killed Hamilton in a duel. Hamilton did not live to see Jefferson replace Burr with none other than George Clinton!

During Hamilton's tenure as Secretary of the Treasury the public debt rose from $79 million to around $85 million. It was still over $80 million when Jefferson took office in 1801. Between 1801 and 1811 Presidents Jefferson and Madison reduced the debt to $45 million. They managed this reduction even though Jefferson borrowed $15 million to acquire the vast territory of the Louisiana Purchase, which he was confident would allow movement across space and secure the third stage for centuries. The War of 1812 forced President Madison to borrow heavily. The debt rose by 1814 to about $125 million.[1] But it was borrowing based on Jefferson's and Madison's conception of public credit. Madison borrowed at a time of great need for a specific purpose. As soon as that purpose was achieved with peace in 1815, the national government renewed its commitment to paying off the debt. The debt was reduced to zero by the 1830s, during the presidency of Andrew Jackson. Over the course of the nineteenth century the national debt was not used to create a connection between the national government and a particular group of citizens. And it was not used as the most critical source of investment in the domestic economy for the purpose of creating a meticulously planned and particular social and cultural outcome. Instead, the national government limited itself to borrowing as needed for specific and extraordinary purposes, most obviously to fight wars, and then eradicated or greatly reduced the public debt as quickly as possible. This attitude towards public finance was Jefferson's and Madison's conception of public credit, not Hamilton's.

When the twenty year charter of the Bank of the United States expired in 1811, the Democratic-Republican Congress and President Madison did not renew it. Under Madison they created a new national bank in 1816. But the new bank operated in a world created by the last sixteen years of Democratic-Republican rule. There were now hundreds of banks at the state level. There was far more power and economic energy and policymaking in state governments than in the national government.[2] The new national bank was not Hamilton's bank. It could never hope to dominate the nation's credit structures or link the national government to a nationally unified group of private citizens who controlled much of the nation's wealth. The nation was too big, the wealth too spread out, for such a group to exist

In addition, the second Bank of the United States reflected much more Madison's view of the perpetual role public opinion played in interpreting the Constitution than it did Hamilton's argument about the nature of implied powers. In order to understand how Madison viewed the Bank and its relation to the Constitution, we must briefly examine how the bank fit with broader policy issues of economic development after the War of 1812. At the war's end, in 1816, younger supporters of Jefferson and Madison, such as Speaker of the House Henry Clay and soon to be Secretary of War John C. Calhoun, supported a broad-based system of economic development that Clay called the American System. The ideas and values of the American System were closest to those of the manufacturers who had joined the Democratic-Republican Party during the 1790s, and who had long supported Jefferson and Madison. The American System called for a new National Bank, a protective tariff, and internal improvements such as roads and canals to expand the domestic market and increase demand inside the nation for domestically manufactured goods. In addition, supporters of the American System sought to expand banking at the local level with state chartered banks to democratize access to credit for small property owners.

In this context, men such as Clay and Calhoun thought that a national bank could be useful. It would not dominate the nation's credit structures as Hamilton's bank had done. There would be far more banking capital in the hundreds of local banks than in the national bank. But the new national bank could bring some order to a very strange and confusing system of multiple paper currencies. The Constitution forbade the states from printing paper money, and the national government did not print its own until the Civil War. Instead, the hundreds of local banks issued their own separate paper bank notes. The farther from the bank of origin these notes circulated the more suspiciously they were usually viewed. People farther away often did not know whether the issuing bank was reliable. Most people, therefore, practiced "discounting," which meant demanding more notes from distant banks for goods and services than the amount required in notes from closer banks.

Supporters of the new national bank hoped to bring stability to the complex currencies and to lessen the likelihood of discounting. They reasoned that over the course of a year notes from the local banks would travel to the new national bank and its branches as Americans paid taxes, purchased public lands, or simply exchanged local bank notes for national bank notes. Once the national bank held a meaningful amount of the notes of the local banks, it could take a portion of those notes to the local bank and require specie repayment, the exchange at face value of those notes for gold and silver. Any note-holder had the right to demand that exchange. Since the local banks would know that the national bank would eventually come with this demand, they would have to issue their paper notes responsibly. If they issued too many notes, an amount dangerously beyond their actual specie holdings, so many of their notes would be in circulation, and would flow to the national bank, that it might hold more notes than the total value of specie in a bank's vaults. In order to meet the specie demands of the national bank, local banks would have to issue their notes carefully and keep reasonably close to their actual specie holdings. That meant each year, as local banks met the specie repayment demands of the national bank, they would prove their reliability. Banks that could remain in business under these conditions issued notes that did not have to be discounted, not matter how far they travelled.

But was the new national bank constitutional? Did Congress have the authority in 1816 to grant it a corporate charter? The bank bill passed the House and Senate, but the final decision lay with President Madison. In one of his last acts as President, Madison signed the bank bill into law. He drew on his constitutional sense regarding the relationship between the Constitution and the sovereign people's public opinion. In deeming the bank constitutional, Madison concluded that the necessary, thoughtful national conversation regarding the public good had taken place with regards to the national bank. Indeed, he had helped to start that conversation back in 1791. Over the next twenty five years the sovereign people had carefully deliberated and had judiciously come to accept the sort of national bank his younger supporters were seeking. That process of the sovereign people slowly and carefully coming to accept the bank had conferred upon it a constitutionality that it had not possessed in 1791, when no such conversation had yet taken place. Only the sovereign people could imbue an action or an institution with constitutionality if the Constitution itself was silent or ambiguous on the subject. And the people could do so only if their deliberations met the scrupulous standards of thoughtful care that were to be expected from any sovereign authority. By 1816 Madison believed the people had met those standards.

Clay and Calhoun were ecstatic. But Madison quickly shocked them. Though he signed the bank bill into law, he vetoed a large national internal improvements bill. The veto dumbfounded Clay and Calhoun. To them a national bank and internal improvements were equally important parts of the American System. They went together, and those who could see the value of one surely understood the value of the other. But Madison explained that there had been no protracted, thoughtful national deliberation regarding the constitutionality of federally sponsored internal improvements. The people had not yet made clear what public opinion was on this matter, and so they had not imbued the action with constitutionality. Madison felt the national government should build internal improvements, but his were merely the views of one citizen. As he vetoed the bill, Madison urged its supporters to propose a constitutional amendment allowing the national government to build internal improvements.[3] The amendment process would start the thoughtful national conversation that would allow a judicious public opinion to form. Creating a second Bank of the United States, then, in no way offered an open-ended authority through the necessary and proper and general welfare clauses, or via the doctrine of implied powers. The Constitution, for Madison, remained a limited grant of power to the national government. It remained his Constitution and Jefferson's, not Hamilton's.

Despite his constitutional disputes with Clay and Calhoun, Madison understood how different their American System was from Hamilton's ideas about what the Republic needed. Indeed, it is likely that Madison was able to reconcile his constitutional vision with the second Bank of the United States in part because that bank functioned so differently than had Hamilton's bank. In the American System, the second Bank of the United States was intended to enable an accessible, inclusive, and expansive system of credit and paper currency. Democratized access to credit would allow small property holders to take advantage of the roads and canals linking them together, and of the protective tariff that encouraged the production of independent craftsmen, and the exchange of their wares with those of the nation's farmers. The American System included a national bank and a vision for promoting manufacturing. But the social order its supporters hoped to establish, and the specific policies they used to promote that social order, constituted a complete rejection of Hamilton's vision for the United States.

Supporters of the American System expected that credit-worthiness would largely be determined by local banks in local communities serving local customers. Protective tariffs would directly assist actual craftsmen in precisely the ways they had been hoping for since Hamilton had first asked for their views back in 1791. The American System was very much a bottom-up conception of economic development, indeed a profound democratization of American economic policy. Its supporters believed they would build a much more equal social order by placing resources directly in the hands of small property-owning productive citizens—the nation's farmers and craftsmen—who were, as Thomas Marshall had once told Hamilton, "stimulated by that interest which animates those who work for themselves."

This democratization of social and economic policy also demanded the continued commitment to expansion across space. American System supporters wanted rapid and diverse economic development while not creating a social order that looked European. The only way to accomplish that was to continually acquire enough land and other resources, and allow the policies and institutions of the American System to distribute those resources widely among the nation's producer-citizens. But westward expansion continued to mean also expanding west all of the practices that Jefferson's and Madison's victory had allowed to flourish in the United States. As Americans spread west during the first half of the nineteenth century, they spread slavery with them and continued to brutally assault and destroy the native peoples they encountered. Those actions were bound up with Jefferson's and Madison's victory and, to a great extent, Jefferson's and Madison's connection of land with citizenship and equality depended on those actions being taken.[4]

Hamilton would likely have agreed that the American system sought a vastly different outcome than he had planned with his financial and industrial program. He would also likely have concluded that Madison's constitutional reasoning did not grant him the means to provide what he believed the Republic needed. Hamilton had sought to create a self-conscious ruling class that would combine political, economic, social, and cultural power, and that would use this power to protect republican institutions and "durable liberty" from the dangerously democratic excesses of the people. Without firm leadership and guidance the people would act licentiously. Though he spent a great deal of time thinking about finance, banking, and economic development, they were not Hamilton's true passions, and he never viewed them as ends in themselves. All of his efforts were to protect republican institutions in the only way he thought they could be protected. He designed his system to give the great men of the Republic the opportunity to exhibit their best versions of themselves by embracing public responsibility, by revealing their true virtue, their honor, and their devotion to protecting the ordinary citizens who needed them. Hamilton's dream was an eighteenth-century dream, inspired by the glory and honor of a neo-classical age, and it died with him.

But though Hamilton's dream died, it did not follow, even with their complete victory in the short term, that the dream of Jefferson and Madison lived. Their vision was no less elitist than Hamilton's. Above all else, they believed the United States needed a natural aristocracy. The sovereign majority was the only force powerful enough to defeat the faction promoting the culture of monarchy. But without the guidance of the natural aristocracy, the majority would abuse its power, degenerate into licentiousness, and produce the tyranny of the majority. Jefferson and Madison never believed in majority rule in the way that modern democrats do. At its core, modern democracy theorizes that each citizen is as capable as any other of determining what course of policy makes the best sense for her or him. A majority is an inherently legitimate force because it is comprised of a greater number of these equal and equally capable citizens than are all other groups. To have the majority is, by definition, to be credible.

Jefferson and Madison believed that to have a majority was to possess a force that was ultimately irresistible. But there was a tangible, comprehensible singular public good, a best course, and it did not change whether or not the majority supported it. The majority needed to distinguish between natural aristocrats and selfish monarchists, place natural aristocrats in power, and then carefully watch them to make sure they continued to seek the public good. Jefferson and Madison did not seek modern political parties or democratic politics. They would build a party of all, a party to end all parties. Their party would make itself unnecessary in the very act of its victory, which would place the natural aristocrats in power.

The dream of Jefferson and Madison grew less and less relevant to the citizens of the nineteenth-century United States. They did not elect self-proclaimed natural aristocrats. Instead presidential hopefuls had to present themselves as rough and tumble Indian fighters, as log cabin dwellers, as rail splitters, if they hoped to be elected by the people. But Jefferson and Madison had great advantages over Hamilton when it came to their original intents. Significant elements of their dream went with the grain of the Republic's revolution-inspired politics and culture, while much of Hamilton's dream ran against it. Jefferson's and Madison's dream relied on a great deal of power residing with the states at a time when a great deal of power did reside with them. Jefferson's and Madison's dream called for a nation of farmers when over ninety percent of the nation worked the land. Jefferson and Madison praised manufacturing done by craftsmen who owned their own tools and shops when that was what most craftsmen were or wanted to be. Without intending to, Jefferson and Madison did a great deal to make democracy legitimate. Yet during the nineteenth century, democracy came to mean laboring white male citizens defining their own needs and interests and pursuing them as best they could, often at the direct expense of their fellow citizens and the women, blacks, and Indians to whom they denied citizenship in whole or in part. This world increasingly had no use for the natural aristocrats Jefferson and Madison sought to be. In fact, the white male citizens of the nineteenth-century United States rapidly created an economy and society with very little "common manifestation of sentiments." Rarely did they "sympathize with each other."

It was not the case that the nation's citizens somehow failed Jefferson and Madison. Rather, it turned out that the nation was far more complex, and its public affairs far less predictable, than Jefferson and Madison had allowed. They had identified Hamilton's system as the principal, really the only, source of inequality and the concentration of wealth and power. In victory, Jefferson and Madison had transformed the nation's governing structure, the nation's size, and the relationship the national government had with the states and the citizenry. They made it impossible to rebuild Hamilton's system. But the small property holders unleashed by the Democratic-Republicans quickly took advantage of the growing and much more readily available sources of credit. They seized the resources of a continent, and created a dizzyingly-paced, rapidly developing economy of great opportunity, but also of great risk and danger. Over the course of the nineteenth century boom and bust became the order of the day. Through their experiences with the American economy and society they were building, ordinary citizens separated themselves from each other and produced far more wealth, and far greater concentrations of wealth, than Hamilton, Jefferson, or Madison could ever have imagined. The unpredictability and uncertainty of this social and economic order produced wild, tempestuous swings and frequent tumultuous disorders.

This wild and often scary new world, which in the 1820s John Quincy-Adams described as "perpetual motion—perpetual change—a boundless ocean without a shore," shattered the belief that a unified citizenry would articulate one all-encompassing public good that would allow the vast majority to be "stimulated by that interest which animates those who work for themselves."[5] Instead, as citizens experienced this nineteenth-century society and economy, they grew more divided and more unequal. They increasingly expressed their grievances and divisions from within formal, organized, competitive political parties, and they made constant political, social, cultural and economic conflict the stuff of everyday American life. Nineteenth-Century America moved very far from the stability, predictability, and ordered and durable liberty that Hamilton had felt was essential for any republican society. And yet this American economy and society looked nothing like the bucolic world of Georgetown village and the idealized and rather naïve expectations of Jefferson and Madison.

In triumphing over Hamilton, Jefferson and Madison had not eradicated inequality. Instead they had democratized it. In many ways, Jefferson's and Madison's defeat in the mighty argument could be viewed as even more bitter and devastating than Hamilton's. He lost outright. They had the subtler and more complex experience of gaining the power and authority to govern precisely as they wished, and then lived long enough to see their victory lead to outcomes that moved ever further from their original intents. Those outcomes brought the nation very far from Jefferson's and Madison's intentions, while moving the nation no closer to Hamilton's. The sum total of the desires, needs, fears, and experiences of the nation's citizenry ended up determining the ultimate outcome of the mighty argument far more than did the actions of Hamilton, Jefferson, and Madison.

Are there any usable lessons we can learn from the great conflict of Hamilton, Jefferson, and Madison? There are; in what their conflict does, but also does not, provide us. Their battle to impose their original intents provides for us no legacy of singular constitutional original intent. We should not trust any figure of the twenty first century who claims that the Constitution had one meaning for its framers that we can decipher. We should not take seriously the insistence that we can use this alleged original intent to determine what the founders would think about contemporary issues, and so what we should think about them. Three of the most important founders could not even agree about how to define the word necessary! The ideas of Hamilton, Jefferson, and Madison do not provide a blueprint for how we should live today or how to resolve our many problems. Hamilton, Jefferson, and Madison were thoroughly of the eighteenth century. They began with eighteenth-century assumptions, passed eighteenth-century judgments, and drew eighteenth-century conclusions.

Yet their conflict does provide a rich inspiration that we can draw upon. Hamilton, Jefferson, and Madison were arguing about how best to be of public service, about what role wealth and power should play in a free and just society. Hamilton, Jefferson, and Madison were arguing about what the relationship should be between governors and governed, and what the connections were between political and economic equality and liberty. The answers of none of them can be our answers. But many of their questions can, and should, be our questions. And as Madison would remind us, it is truly up to us.

NOTES

1 John R. Nelson, *Liberty and Property: Political Economy and Policymaking in the New Nation, 1789–1812* (Baltimore, MD: Johns Hopkins University Press, 1987) 177–178.

2 Andrew Shankman, "'A New Thing on Earth': Alexander Hamilton, Pro-Manufacturing Republicans and the Democratization of American Political Economy," *Journal of the Early Republic* 23 (2003) 323–352; Andrew Shankman, "John Quincy Adams and National Republicanism," in David Waldstreicher ed., *A Companion to John Adams and John Quincy Adams* (Malden, MA: Wiley-Blackwell Publishing, 2013) 263–280; John Joseph Wallace, "The Other Foundings: Federalism and the Constitutional Structure of American Government," in Douglas A. Irwin and Richard Sylla eds., *Founding Choices: American Economic Policy in the 1790s* (Chicago, University of Chicago Press, 2011) 177–213.

3 The veto message can be found in, Lance Banning ed., *Liberty and Order: The First American Party Struggle* (Indianapolis, IN: Liberty Fund, 2004) 350–351.

4 Andrew Shankman, "How Should We Think About the Election of 1800?," *Journal of the Early Republic* (33) 2013 753–761.

5 Andrew Shankman, *Crucible of American Democracy: The Struggle to Fuse Egalitarianism and Capitalism in Jeffersonian Pennsylvania* (Lawrence, KS: University Press of Kansas, 2004) 224.

A GUIDE TO FURTHER READING

Scholarship is a collective, collaborative, and community effort. The argument and insights of *Original Intents* are possible only because of the tremendous work done by other historians. But scholarship is animated as much by productive and engaged disagreement as it is by agreement. Accordingly, this guide introduces readers to further relevant reading, and to issues and debates in which *Original Intents* intervenes. Debates among professional historians can seem overly technical to those who do not study and write about the past for a living. Interested readers will find in what follows a level of professional conversation that supplements many of the discussions in the book, particularly when it comes to disagreements it has with other scholars. At all points *Original Intents*, like all books, is better because of previous scholarship, both that with which it agrees and with which it disagrees.

Many of the issues discussed in *Original Intents* are interconnected. In this guide I mention a book for the first and usually only time the first time I discuss an issue where the book is relevant. That does not mean it is irrelevant to other issues discussed in later chapters, as those who read the books discussed will quickly discover.

CHAPTER ONE

Chapter one explores classical and early modern ideas of republicanism and political thought. There is a rich and extensive literature on these subjects. For those interested in reading further about republicanism some of the strongest works are J. G. A. Pocock, *The Machiavellian Moment: Florentine Political Thought and the Atlantic Republican Tradition*; Paul Rahe's three-volume study *Republics Ancient and Modern*; two books by Bernard Bailyn, *The Origins of American Politics* and

The Ideological Origins of the American Revolution; Lance Banning, *The Jeffersonian Persuasion: Evolution of a Party Ideology*; and John M. Murrin, "The Great Inversion, or Court Versus Country: A Comparison of the Revolution Settlements in England (1688–1721) and America (1776–1816)," in J. G. A. Pocked, ed., *Three British Revolutions: 1641, 1688, 1776*. For early modern ideas of politics and government in the English-speaking world more generally, excellent scholarship incudes J. P. Sommerville, *Royalists and Patriots: Politics and Ideology in England, 1603–1640*; J. H. Plumb, *The Growth of Political Stability in England, 1675–1725*; Steve Pincus, *1688: The First Modern Revolution*; James T. Kloppenberg, *Toward Democracy: The Struggle for Self-Rule in European and American Political Thought*; Isaac Kramnick, *Bolinbroke and His Circle: The Politics of Nostalgia in the Age of Walpole*; and Richard Beeman, *The Varieties of Political Experience in Eighteenth-Century America*.

Chapter one also discusses the 1780s as a critical period of conflict and discord. Far and away the very best discussion of the ideological world of the American Revolutionary era, the 1780s, and the origins of the United States Constitution is Gordon S. Wood, *The Creation of the American Republic, 1776–1787*. However, Wood's masterpiece is best read as a collective intellectual biography of elite founders who ended up supporting the Constitution, the gentlemen who understood the 1780s as Hamilton, Jefferson, and Madison did. Essential supplements to Wood are Terry Bouton, *Taming Democracy: The People, the Founders, and the Troubled Ending of the American Revolution*; and Woody Holton, *Unruly Americans and the Origins of the Constitution*. For further reading on Hamilton's New York during the American Revolution and in the 1780s, see Alfred F. Young, *The Democratic Republicans of New York: The Origins, 1763–1797*; Edward Countryman, *A People in Revolution: The American Revolution and Political Society in New York, 1760–1790*; Thomas Humphrey, *Land and Liberty: Hudson Valley Riots in the Age of Revolution*; and Brian Phillips Murphy, *Building the Empire State: Political Economy in the Early Republic*.

CHAPTER TWO

Chapter two introduces a number of issues and developments that were crucial to shaping the seventeenth and eighteenth centuries, and ultimately our modern world. One development considered in chapter two is the rise of what historians have called taxing and fiscal states and the financial revolution. Scholars of the history of state formation and state finance describe a long process from the fourteenth through the seventeenth and eighteenth centuries in which domain states gave way to taxing states, and then in rare cases to fiscal states. A domain state, as the name suggests, was one where the monarch, virtually always the largest and wealthiest landowner, was expected to pay the costs of governance from his private estates, to live of his own. The shift from domain states to taxing states was quite possibly one of the most crucial developments leading to our modern world. The shift involved monarchs being able to distinguish between their personal estates and expenses and public or state expenses. Once monarchs could articulate and impose that distinction, they began to lay claim to a portion of the wealth of their subjects' estates in the name of funding public policies that it was not reasonable for the monarch to pay for out of his own pocket. Much of the politics and conflict of the early modern period was over how, whether, and when wealth would be transferred from subjects to the monarch in the form of taxes.

Virtually all European states had become taxing states by the seventeenth century. But only two, the Dutch Republic and Britain, became what scholars identify as fiscal states, and only Britain was able to turn that achievement into true supremacy in the eighteenth century. The difference between taxing states and fiscal states was that in fiscal states the authority to tax was separate from the personal will of the monarch. The Dutch Republic and, after the Glorious Revolution of 1688, the English\British limited constitutional monarchy had elected legislatures that possessed the sole authority to tax. That was a crucial difference from their competitor nations France and Spain. Representative legislatures such as the British House of Commons could be held to account in a way an absolute monarch such as Louis XIV of France could not be. The men who sat in the House of Commons and assessed and oversaw collection of taxes were drawn from the ranks of the property-owning tax payers, and were also their friends and relatives. This connectedness and accountability gave a measure of genuine representation and protection to taxpayers that could never be equaled in absolute monarchies.

Taxation connected to representation made for much more efficient taxation with less conflict. The capacity to tax was closely connected to the ability to borrow, which meant that the Dutch and the British could borrow more heavily, but at much lower and cheaper rates of interest, than their rivals. Lenders trusted representative assemblies far more than they did absolute monarchs. In effect the difference between a taxing state and a fiscal state was that the financial policy of taxing states remained enmeshed with the personal financial priorities of a single and unaccountable person, the monarch. What made a fiscal state a fiscal state was that it created a legislature with genuine authority over its taxing and financial policies, and so clearly moved its financial policy into a public political realm where property-owning taxpayers were represented and could shape the policies that affected them.

Readers interested in exploring this fascinating history can see Richard Bonney, ed., *The Rise of the Fiscal State in Europe, c. 1200–1815*; Richard Bonney, ed., *Economic Systems and State Finance*: Mark Ormrod, Margaret Bonney, and Richard Bonney, eds., *Crises, Revolutions, and Self-Sustained Growth: Essays in European Fiscal History, 1130–1830*; Philip T. Hoffman and Kathryn Norberg, eds., *Fiscal Crises and Representative Government, 1450–1789*; P. G. M. Dickson, *The Financial Revolution in England: A Study in the Development of Public Credit, 1688–1756*; John Brewer, *The Sinews of Power: War, Money, and the English State, 1688–1783*; Patrick O'Brien, "The Political Economy of British Taxation, 1660–1815" an essay published in the *Economic History Review*; Patrick O'Brien, "Inseparable Connections: Trade, Economy, Fiscal State, and the Expansion of Empire, 1688–1815" in P. J. Marshall, ed., *The Oxford History of the British Empire: The Eighteenth Century*; Lawrence Stone, ed., *An Imperial State at War: Britain from 1689 to 1815*; Carl Wennerlind, *Casualties of Credit: The English Financial Revolution, 1620–1720*; and Michael Kwass, *Privilege and the Politics of Taxation in Eighteenth-Century France*. For a discussion that looks beyond Europe, see Bartolome Yun-Casalilla and Patrick O'Brien, eds., *The Rise of Fiscal States: A Global History, 1500–1914*.

For the origins of capitalist thought and practice, see Albert O. Hirshman, *The Passions and the Interests: Political Arguments for Capitalism before Its Triumph*; Jerry Z. Muller, *The Mind and the Market: Capitalism in Western Thought*; Jacob Soll, *The Reckoning: Financial Accountability and the Rise and Fall of Nations*; Sven Beckert, *Empire of Cotton: A Global History*; and Neil McKendrick, John Brewer, and J. H. Plumb, eds., *The Birth of a Consumer Society: The Commercialization of Eighteenth Century England*. For the political economy and culture of Jefferson and Madison and the four-stage theory, see T. H. Breen, *Tobacco Culture: The Mentality of the Great Tidewater Planters on the Eve of Revolution*, Drew R. McCoy, *The Elusive Republic: Political Economy in Jeffersonian America*; Joyce Appleby, *Capitalism and a New Social Order: The Republican Vision of the 1790s*; J. C. A. Stagg, *Borderlines in Borderlands: James Madison and the Spanish-American Frontier, 1776–1821*; and Peter J. Kastor, *The Nation's Crucible: The Louisiana Purchase and the Creation of America*.

Westward expansion inevitably meant conflict with native peoples and the strong likelihood of the growth of slavery. Chapter two also introduces the concept the "American Paradox" to suggest the connections between liberty and equality for white men and the commitment to racial inequality and hierarchy and slavery. For relations with native peoples in the eighteenth and early nineteenth centuries, see two books by Gregory Evans Dowd, *A Spirited Resistance: The North American Indian Struggle for Unity, 1745–1815* and *War Under Heaven: Pontiac, The Indian Nations and the British Empire*; Daniel K. Richter, *Facing East from Indian Country: A Native History of North America*; Collin Calloway, *The American Revolution in Indian Country: Crisis and Diversity in Native American Communities*; Peter Silver, *Our Savage Neighbors: How Indian War Transformed Early America*; Patrick Griffin, *American Leviathan: Empire, Nation, and Revolutionary Frontier;* and an essay by James Merrell, "Declarations of Independence: Indian–White Relations in the New Nation," in Jack P. Greene, ed., *The American Revolution: Its Character and Limits*. For the relations between slavery and freedom and the expansion of slavery, see Edmund S. Morgan, *American Slavery, American Freedom: The Ordeal of Colonial Virginia*; John Craig Hammond, *Slavery Freedom and Expansion in the Early American West*; Adam Rothman, *Slave Country: American Expansion and the Origins of the Deep South*; and Annette Gordon-Reed and Peter S. Onuf, *"Most Blessed of Patriarchs": Thomas Jefferson and the Empire of the Imagination*.

CHAPTER THREE

Chapter three explores issues involving the arguments and conflicts surrounding the Constitutional Convention and the process of ratification. For the role of rebellion and uprising in eighteenth-century society and politics generally, see the classic article by E. P. Thompson, "The Moral Economy of the English Crowd in the Eighteenth Century," which appeared in the journal *Past and Present*; Gary Nash, *The Urban Crucible: The Northern Seaports and the Origins of the American Revolution*; Pauline Maier, *From Resistance to Revolution: Colonial Radicals and the Development of Opposition to Britain, 1765–1776*; two books by Benjamin Carp, *Rebels Rising: Cities and the American Revolution* and *Defiance of the Patriots: The Boston Tea Party and the Making of the American Revolution*; Barbara Clark Smith, *The Freedoms We Lost: Consent and Resistance in Revolutionary America*; and T. H. Breen, *American Insurgents, American Patriots: The Revolution of the People*. For Shays's Rebellion, see Leonard L. Richards, *Shays's Rebellion: The American Revolution's Final Battle*; and the collection of essays edited by Robert A. Gross, *In Debt to Shays: The Bicentennial of an Agrarian Rebellion*.

For the intellectual ideas of the Constitution and the debates concerning ratification, see in addition to Gordon S. Wood's *The Creation of the American Republic*, the essays in Richard Beeman, Stephen Botein, and Edward Carter, II, eds., *Beyond Confederation: Origins of the Constitution and American National Identity*; Richard Beeman, *Plain, Honest Men: The Making of the American Constitution*; Jack N. Rakove, *Original Meanings: Politics and Ideas in the Making of the Constitution*; Michael Lienesch, *New Order of the Ages: Time, the Constitution, and the Making of Modern American Political Thought*; David J. Siemers, *Ratifying the Republic: Antifederalists and Federalists in Constitutional Time*; Saul Cornell, *The Other Founders: Antifederalism and the Dissenting Tradition in America, 1788–1828*; David Waldstreicher, *Slavery's Constitution: From Revolution to Ratification*; and Pauline Maier, *Ratification: The People Debate the Constitution, 1787–1788*. Fine treatments of the constitutional thought of Madison are Lance Banning, *The Sacred Fire of Liberty: James Madison and the Founding of the Federal Republic*; and two books by Colleen Sheehan, *James Madison and the Spirit of Republican Self Government* and *The Mind of James Madison: The Legacy of Classical Republicanism*. A brilliant study discussing how Madison substantially revised his notes from the Constitutional Convention over time prior to making them public in 1831 is Mary Sarah Bilder, *Madison's Hand: Revising the Constitutional Convention*.

CHAPTER FOUR

Chapter four explores the political conflicts of the early 1790s and debates about commercial policy, the French Revolution, and the Report on Public Credit. For political conflict in the decade, see Gordon S. Wood, *Empire of Liberty: A History of the Early Republic, 1789–1815*; Stanley Elkins and Eric McKitrick, *The Age of Federalism: The Early American Republic, 1788–1800*; James Roger Sharp, *American Politics in the Early Republic: The New Nation in Crisis*, which is especially good on the French Revolution; an essay by Gary Nash, "The American Clergy and the French Revolution," which appeared in *The William and Mary Quarterly*; and a classic book still worth reading, Joseph Charles, *The Origins of the American Party System*. For foreign trade, free trade, and foreign policy see two books by John E. Crowley, *This Sheba Self: The Conceptualization of Economic Life in Eighteenth-Century America* and *The Privileges of Independence: Neomercantilism and the American Revolution*; David Hendrickson, *Peace Pact: The Lost World of the American Founding*; Francis Cogliano, *Emperor of Liberty: Thomas Jefferson's Foreign Policy*; Robert Tucker and David Hendrickson, *Empire of Liberty: The Statecraft of Thomas Jefferson*; Felix Gilbert, *To the Farewell Address*; and Todd Estes, *The Jay Treaty Debate: Public Opinion and the Evolution of American Political Culture*.

Hamilton's financial program and fiscal policy have been the subject of much study by Max Edling. Edling has provided careful and valuable scholarship and deserves much credit for insisting that scholars must understand the complex issues of eighteenth-century finance. His 2003 book, *A Revolution in Favor of Government: Origins of the U.S. Constitution and the Making of the American State*, is a valuable discussion of eighteenth-century finance, though Edling unfortunately divorced his discussion from the larger political, political economy, and social and cultural questions that eighteenth-century thinkers saw as connected to financial questions. However, Edling's work is flawed, and the arguments about Hamilton in *Original Intents* seriously disagree with Edling's assumptions and conclusions. Edling argues that there was little difference in matters of finance and attitudes toward borrowing and public debt between Hamilton and the Federalist Party on the one hand, and Jefferson, Madison, and the Democratic-Republican Party on the other. In his 2014 book, *A Hercules in the Cradle: War, Money, and the American State, 1783–1867*, Edling argues that Hamilton built a system of public finance that remained intact through the Civil War. Implicitly he claims that we need not take seriously the critique of Jefferson and Madison. Edling maintains that once in power they adopted Hamilton's system, embraced public borrowing, and acted scarcely differently than he would have acted.

Edling errs because he discusses issues of finance and debt in a vacuum, without context. In fact, for eighteenth-century thinkers, matters of finance and debt were part of a larger, interconnected conversation that brought together views on finance and debt with all other aspects of economic thought and with political ideas, social values, and cultural aspirations. Edling mistakenly insists that Hamilton had little interest in creating a powerful national government. Edling believes Hamilton funded the debt solely to promote economic development, not to create a strong national government. He argues that there is no evidence in Hamilton's writings that he was interested in seeking "to forge a link between public creditors and the new federal government for political ends" (*Hercules in the Cradle*, 84). For a similar statement see Edling's remarks in a 2007 article published in *The William and Mary Quarterly* titled "'So Immense a Power in the Affairs of War': Alexander Hamilton and the Restoration of Public Credit," 294).

Original Intents quotes Hamilton at length over a period of several years precisely on the issue of the deep interconnection between political (and social and cultural) policy and economic and financial policy, with the purpose of erecting a powerful national government. *Original Intents* shows that Hamilton viewed financial policy as part of a much larger vision that he hoped would restore "durable liberty" and political and social stability. A carefully thought-out financial system and economic program were structured as they were, and supported in the ways they were, precisely to build the proper republican nation-state and government and repair deeply damaged social and cultural relations. Social and political relations were in such disarray, Hamilton believed, because of the ultimate political act—revolution. The distinction between economic ideas and ideals and political, social, and cultural ideas and ideals that Edling relies on to advance his arguments is one that would have made no sense to Hamilton, and is not sustainable through an investigation of his writings.

Edling's initial error leads him to conclusions that differ greatly from those found in *Original Intents*. Edling points out that the United States continued to borrow, and often went deeply into debt, during the several decades of Democratic-Republican rule. But he makes a crucial error, one made by many scholars who study and come to admire Hamilton. Edling assumes that if Hamilton supported something, in this case establishing public credit, it was a "Hamiltonian" issue. Scholars make a similar mistake when discussing manufacturing and comparing the first and second Banks of the United States. Others who might also have cared about establishing public credit (or supporting some sort of banking and manufacturing) are then said to be committed to something that is in its essence "Hamiltonian." As a result, scholars conclude that there is much less difference between Hamilton and these others than was first thought, and likely much less difference in general.

This assumption discourages scholars from looking much more closely at the nuts and bolts, the nitty gritty, the complexities of the very different ways in which people thought about public credit and debt—or manufacturing and banking. After all, the absolutist French monarchy sought public credit and borrowed, as did the limited constitutional monarchy of Britain and the Dutch Republic. We have no difficulty distinguishing between these quite different governments, and so we should also be able to distinguish between the very different political, economic, and financial ideals of the Federalist Party and Hamilton and the Democratic-Republican Party and Jefferson and Madison.

As *Original Intents* shows, Jefferson and Madison endorsed public credit independently of Hamilton and discussed its tremendous importance prior to Hamilton making any public statements on the matter. But they viewed the most desirable sources and purposes of public credit very differently from the way he did. Jefferson and Madison wanted loans to come primarily from foreign creditors, and they wanted public debt to have very little impact on domestic social and cultural relations. They wanted public borrowing to be episodic—borrowing only as needed with the public debt retired as quickly as possible. Hamilton, precisely because he did see a successful economy as an essential part of bolstering a stable and hierarchical national government and society, wanted public debt to be perpetual and to create a lasting relationship between the national government and the wealthiest and most powerful private citizens.

Edling does not emphasize these obvious differences in ideas about the sources and purposes of public credit that did exist between Hamilton and the two Virginians. He does not emphasize them because he mistakenly sees debt reduction and opposition to a permanent debt as a significant part of Hamilton's plans. In fact, neither was central to Hamilton or to the Federalist Party. To support his claim that they were, Edling focuses on a report Hamilton wrote in 1795, just before he left the Treasury, titled "Report on a Plan for the Further Support of Public Credit." In this "Report," for the first time, Hamilton proposed gradually reducing and ultimately fully discharging the public debt. Edling believes that by 1795 attitudes toward public debt had changed, though he ascribes no reason for these changes, and that "Hamilton sounded like a convert to Jeffersonianism." (The quotation can be found in "So Immense a Power," page 316). Because Edling does not sufficiently consider that financial matters were as much political, social, and cultural policies and statements as they were economic ones, that in the 1790s people who thought about these issues did not distinguish between and separate them as Edling does, Edling can only explain Hamilton's apparent change with a vague statement in the passive voice about the terms of debate shifting.

In fact, what had happened was the mighty argument, discussed in chapters six and seven of *Original Intents*. The mighty argument had raged in public since Madison's essays in the *National Gazette*. Hamilton's efforts to expand the tax base in 1794 to better service a debt that he had made no plan to ever pay off or reduce, and that he hoped would be perpetual, had provoked armed rebellion. In addition, the Democratic-Republican Party led by Jefferson and Madison was mounting an increasingly effective challenge, and it appeared that Jefferson might be elected president in 1796. He ended up coming in second in that election, and so became the vice president of his bitter rival in the election, John Adams. The 1796 contest left him poised for the presidential victory he did achieve four years later.

Thus Hamilton's last "Report" came at a time of profound political desperation. The accurate claim by his opponents that the Federalists had no plan to reduce a debt that was in fact growing in size was a most explosive and effective charge. It was helping to bring Hamilton's party to the brink of defeat. The mighty argument had produced a political conflict that, in a desperate hope of keeping power, gave Hamilton and his party little choice but to abandon their original intents.

Between 1795 and 1800 the Federalists did put the debt reduction plan into effect. But significantly, the reduction plan dealt only with the original debt from the Revolutionary War. While the principal of that debt shrank, in that five-year period the Federalists borrowed a great deal of new debt, so that the overall debt reached its highest point in 1796–1797, two years into the debt reduction plan. When the Federalists were ousted from power in 1801 the debt was higher than it had been ten years earlier. As discussed in the conclusion of *Original Intents*, the Jefferson and Madison administrations then reduced the entire federal debt by about forty-five percent over the next decade. Edling credits Hamilton and the Federalists for this debt reduction, arguing that the Democratic-Republicans were merely following a plan proposed by their enemies.

Ultimately readers have to choose which argument to believe. Yet when Hamilton first conceived funding and assumption in 1790, he did not imagine a successful opposition or threat to his continued power in the form in which it quickly came. In 1790 he was free to propose precisely what he wished, free from the terrible fears that the mighty argument would soon provoke. In 1790 he provided no plan to reduce the debt and put no time limit on the period of time in which principal that went unrepaid would bear interest. He created perpetual, interest-bearing debt. He then proposed policies, the Bank of the United States and the Society for Establishing Useful Manufactures, which would only fulfill his expectations if they continued to be sustained by perpetual debt. Hamilton only at the very end of his career at Treasury gestured at debt reduction. He did so when demand for debt reduction was the most crucial part of a highly effective political opposition, an opposition whose prospect of acquiring power truly terrified him and was becoming very real. Edling gives credit to Hamilton when his political enemies proceeded to treat debt precisely as they had always said they would from the very beginning should they ever get the chance.

Historians must go beyond merely looking at the fact of borrowing, or, for that matter, the fact of support for manufacturing and banking. Historians must examine the particulars of how those policies were pursued, how often very different methods for pursuing financial and economic policies were connected to very different social, cultural, and political aspirations and outcomes. Public debt, manufacturing, and banking were not by definition things Hamiltonian. Hamilton wanted them and pursued them in specific ways. Jefferson and Madison and their supporters also wanted them and supported them in very different ways for very different reasons. Those different reasons mattered a great deal, just as it mattered whether a tax-payer lived in eighteenth-century Britain or Absolutist France.

A perceptive review of *A Hercules in the Cradle* has reminded us of the vast difference between Hamilton's original intents and the way public debt was structured and managed after the Democratic-Republicans took power. In the nineteenth century the United States continued to fund its wars by borrowing. But after each war the U.S. government paid down the debt dramatically, and then borrowed again as needed when new circumstances arose. Indeed, the shift to a truly permanent public debt only occurred in the mid-twentieth century. By that point, the long and relentless historical process had imposed itself to an enormous extent. Those seeking to understand the shift would do best to study the mid-twentieth century rather than imagine a nonexistent continuity with any values or ideals that Hamilton would have recognized, admired, or endorsed. Readers can find the review, written by Samuel Watson, at the website H-net: https://www.h-net.org/reviews/showrev.php?id=43940. A very good examination of Hamilton's financial system is a classic study by Donald Swanson, *The Origins of Hamilton's Fiscal Policies*.

CHAPTER FIVE

The primary issues introduced for the first time in chapter five involve the idea of a court culture and the court vs. country dichotomy, as well as issues of luxury, refinement, and what people in the eighteenth century called the culture of "politeness." To be "polite" in the eighteenth-century sense was to be genteel, refined, respectful of authority, deferential to those who merited it, virtuous in matters of interest to the public community, in other words to be a sober and respectable subject or citizen. There is much good scholarship on these subjects. For the rise of "politeness" and genteel culture in Britain and North America, see Paul Langford, *A Polite and Commercial People: England, 1727–1783*; John Brewer, *The Pleasures of the Imagination: English Culture in the Eighteenth Century*; Margaret Hunt, *The Middling Sort: Commerce, Gender, and the Family in England, 1680–1780*; Richard Bushman, *The Refinement of America: Persons, Houses, Cities*; Richard Bushman, "American High-Style and Vernacular Cultures," in Jack P. Greene and J. R. Pole, eds., *Colonial British America: Essays in the New History of Early Modern Era*; John Fea, *The Way of Improvement Leads Home: Philip Vickers Fithian and the Rural Enlightenment in Early America*; and Sarah Knott, *Sensibility and the American Revolution*. In 2015 the *Journal of the Early Republic* devoted the entire issue of volume 35, number 2 to the issue of court culture in the early Republic.

CHAPTER SIX

Issues that arise for the first time in chapter six involve stock market crashes and bubbles. Those interested in reading further in early modern finance beyond the fascinating story of the rise of taxing and fiscal states should see John Carswell, *The South Sea Bubble*, and Richard Dale, *The First Crash: Lessons from the South Sea Bubble*.

CHAPTER SEVEN

Issues that arise for the first time in chapter seven involve craftsmen and their ideas, ideals, and aspirations, and the rise of popular politics and the role newspapers played in promoting that politics. Popular politics happens when public issues regularly become matters of public consumption and conversation, and people believe that they should understand and involve themselves in the course of public policy and events. Popular politics grew in frequency in the seventeenth and eighteenth centuries due to the rise of what scholars have termed the public sphere. The rise of the public sphere was connected to the capacity of states to tax, borrow, and mobilize wealth and power. In essence, the public sphere was the space that subjects or citizens of western European monarchies and the Dutch Republic produced during the sixteenth through the eighteenth centuries. This public space allowed them to carry on their own conversations about issues ranging from commerce to scandal to politics. The public sphere was a space distinct from the government, though many government actions encouraged its development and growth. Governments certainly sought to intervene in, shape, and even regulate the public sphere, but they could not do so completely. Over the course of the seventeenth and eighteenth centuries, the public sphere grew more autonomous.

The public sphere resulted from the dramatic and dynamic economic, social, and cultural developments of the early modern period that historians have called the financial and commercial revolutions, and that are discussed in the early chapters of *Original Intents*. Governments in the seventeenth and eighteenth centuries began to tax more effectively, borrow much more heavily, and spend much more lavishly. These actions contributed to a great deal of global economic development. Europeans and their empires became much wealthier. Large numbers of subjects and citizens found opportunities to buy, sell, consume, invest, rise and fall, succeed and fail. This burst of activity created newer and larger markets that brought people together, and new forms of commercial and financial exchange that connected people to each other. The locations where all of this activity took place—market towns, coffee houses—where so much trade and talk occurred—the proliferating newspapers and pamphlets that carried advertisements, commercial news, accounts of prices, and commentary on issues of general interest—all of that added up to what historians call the public sphere.

The public sphere was not just a place to trade and gossip. It also became a place to critique, to argue, to speculate, to foment. The rise of the public sphere made governance more challenging because it created far more opportunity for conversation and provided far greater and more widely spread access to that conversation. No matter the government, by the end of the seventeenth century all were seeking to influence and shape viewpoints and news within the public sphere. And all governments had come to understand that public opinion was a vital and mercurial force. Governance was difficult at best, and impossible at worst, if public opinion grew hostile to government.

The public sphere was intimately connected to the commercial and financial revolutions that produced the markets and interactions and the critical masses of engagement of private subjects and citizens that brought the public sphere into being. The public sphere, then, can be taken as an indication of the onset of modernity. An irony some historians have pondered is the continued relevance to eighteenth-century "moderns" of the ideals and categories of the "ancients." Hamilton, Jefferson, and Madison were preoccupied with honor, with classical conceptions of virtue, and with the broad set of political assumptions, ideas, and ideals that historians have called classical republicanism. Historians have wondered why and how there could be such a seemingly incompatible juxtaposition of material circumstances and mental worlds.

What role did classical republican political thought play in the thinking of eighteenth-century thinkers? Broadly, they used the ancients in two phases: first in the critique or opposition stage. Second, they used them in the building stage, when those who had managed to overthrow absolutist monarchy sought to replace it with something they considered more virtuous and better equipped to seek the public good. The ancients were more helpful in the critique stage because the continued relevance of classical republicanism was intimately connected to the achievements of the seventeenth and eighteenth centuries, particularly the creation of successful fiscal states. If ever there were practices likely to rouse anxieties that could be expressed most effectively with the language of classical republicanism, it was the practices of eighteenth-century fiscal states. Concerns about concentrated power, luxury, corruption, the indulgence of private interests through manipulation of the elected legislature, the pursuit of private rewards at the expense of public good, all of those fears appeared reasonable to many people contemplating the new forms of wealth and power that were becoming prominent in fiscal states such as Britain. The concerns of the ancients seemed most relevant for those states that claimed to be superior to absolute monarchies. The British limited constitutional monarchy raised expectations and then appeared to stealthily destroy them by slowly corrupting and eroding all that was republican in its politics.

But there was an irony concerning the continued relevance of classical republicanism. In the eighteenth century the dissemination and growth in popularity of the wisdom of the ancients depended on such things as coffeehouses, newspapers, and a robust pamphlet culture. In other words, classical ideas could flourish primarily because of the rise of the public sphere that has been so skillfully associated by scholars with the rise of consumer society and the freedom to pursue private interests. The same sources of wealth and comfort that gave rise to what classically inspired critics opposed, also provided those critics the institutional means to articulate their critiques, and the opportunity to be heard by people with the means to frequent the spaces and consume the materials in which those critiques appeared.

The ways in which classical republicanism became available to a broadening public, and so remained relevant in the eighteenth century, also pointed to the gaping gulf that existed between the ancients and the moderns. One can't view too many Vermeer interiors, or read the eighteenth-century British writers Joseph Addison and Richard Steele on the pleasures of the coffeehouse, or hear accounts of the pride so many middling households took in their newly mass-produced, good-quality Wedgwood pottery, without realizing how much these eighteenth-century people valued the world of the private. In the eighteenth century, societies earned the praise of the enlightened when their subjects or citizens could define their own pursuits of happiness, take advantage of commerce, and seek the new forms of wealth. Members of such societies were able, obviously within limits, to live meaningful and productive private lives. Beyond that, increasingly they measured a large part of what made each of them valuable to their nations and their nations valuable to them by their ability to consume commodities ranging from cloths and pottery to paintings, plays, and poetry.

It was the sum total of these private lives that created public spheres, and all of it amounted to a place to discuss anything from private business affairs, to the latest scandals, to affairs of state. Yet these private and privately created public spaces were just that—private and privately created—meaning they were decidedly not the world of the ancients, where meaningful expression was much more limited to public service and participation in public and political life—what the ancient Greeks termed devotion to the polis. The gaping gulf between the ancients and the moderns was that, regardless of how much like ancient Sparta some moderns might think they wanted their world to be, much of the meaning and pleasure that most people around them derived from their lives came from sources that did not center on the polis. Valuing the private did not encourage people to subordinate themselves to a public process of divining a collective public good whose pursuit was an end in itself that was larger and more edifying than their own private lives. Even modern critics inspired by the ancients depended on institutions and spaces produced most vigorously by the societies that most valued private life. This dependence underscored how gaping the gulf between the ancients and the moderns truly was.

So what happened in those places where the critique stage actually produced a building stage? How useful was classical republicanism then? It was not un-useful; but it was less useful. The gaping gulf was very real. No matter how much a revolutionary had relied on the ancients, post-revolutionary society would still need to protect the private and value the commerce and comfort that came with the private lives so many wished to lead. The most pressing question for eighteenth-century revolutionaries inspired by classical republicanism was how to properly balance public good and private interest. Modern republics had to protect at all times the citizens' liberty and property, while also directing citizens to enjoy their liberty and property in ways consistent with a tangible and pursuable singular public good in which all citizens could benefit and in which they would all equally and mutually share.

This public good was not merely the sum total of each citizen pursuing his private interest as he defined it. But at the same time, public good was wounded, possibly mortally, each time the polis prevented a citizen from pursing his private interest. Eighteenth-century republicans believed that building a viable modern republic required an essential respect for the values of classical forbears. But this respect needed to be judiciously tempered and limited given the equal respect it was necessary to have for modern private life distinct from the polis. Building the modern republic that could do all that was a very tall order. The very different solutions to this modern problem, so deeply informed by classical values and thought, produced Hamilton's, Jefferson's, and Madison's mighty argument.

Those interested in reading further in this rich subject should see, in addition to relevant works already mentioned, Peter Lake and Steve Pincus, eds., *The Politics of the Public Sphere in Early Modern England*; Tim Harris, *London Crowds in the Reign of Charles II: Propaganda and Politics from the Restoration to the Exclusion Crisis*; Arthur Cash, *John Wilkes: The Scandalous Father of Civil Liberty*; Jessica Chopin Ronney, *Governed by A Spirit of Opposition: The Origins of American Political Practice in Colonial Philadelphia*; Douglas Bradburn, *The Citizenship Revolution: Politics and the Creation of the American Union, 1774–1804*; Jeffrey Pasley, *The Tyranny of Printers: Newspaper Politics in the Early American Republic*; David Waldstreicher, *In the Midst of Perpetual Fetes: The Making of American Nationalism, 1776–1820*; Joanne Freeman, *Affairs of Honor: National Politics in the New Republic*; Albrecht Koschnik,

Let a Common Interest Bind Us Together: Associations, Partisanship and Culture in Philadelphia, 1775–1840; Johann Neem, *Creating a Nation of Joiners: Democracy and Civil Society in Early National Massachusetts*; and Marcus Daniel, *Scandal and Civility: Journalism and the Birth of American Democracy*.

For further reading on the ideas and actions of craftsmen in the early republic, see Howard Rock, *Artisans of the New Republic: Tradesmen of New York in the Age of Jefferson*; two books by Bruce Laurie, *Working People of Philadelphia, 1800 to 1850* and *Artisans into Workers: Labor in Nineteenth-Century America*; Sean Wilentz, *Chants Democratic: New York City and the Rise of the American Working Class, 1788–1850*; and Ronald Schultz, *The Republic of Labor: Philadelphia Artisans and the Politics of Class, 1720–1830*.

CONCLUSION

The conclusion to *Original Intents* touches upon wide-ranging issues of central significance to the U.S. nineteenth century and the nation's subsequent history. Even a brief list of books for every topic would be far too long. Fortunately, the period is very well treated by five excellent synthetic scholarly works that provide a wonderful place to start reading more about these subjects. Those interested should see Gordon S. Wood, *Empire of Liberty: A History of the Early Republic, 1789–1815*; Daniel Walker Howe, *What Hath God Wrought: The Transformation of America, 1815–1848*; Charles Sellers, *The Market Revolution: Jacksonian America, 1815–1846*; Harry L. Watson, *Liberty and Power: The Politics of Jacksonian America*; and Sean Wilentz, *The Rise of American Democracy: Jefferson to Lincoln*.

ART CREDITS

INDEX

Printed in the USA/Agawam, MA
May 20, 2021

775066.009